FOOD, HEALTH AND THE CONSUMER

A report on Technological Change in Agriculture and the Food Industry, and Public Policy in Relation to Food Production, Nutrition and Consumer Safety, prepared for the Commission of the European Communities, Directorate-General for Science, Research and Development, as part of the FAST Programme (Forecasting and Assessment in the Field of Science and Technology).

FOOD, HEALTH AND THE CONSUMER

T. R. GORMLEY, G. DOWNEY

and

D. O'BEIRNE

*An Foras Talúntais, Kinsealy Research Centre, Malahide Road,
Dublin 17, Ireland*

ELSEVIER APPLIED SCIENCE
LONDON and NEW YORK

ELSEVIER APPLIED SCIENCE PUBLISHERS LTD
Crown House, Linton Road, Barking, Essex IG11 8JU, England

Sole Distributor in the USA and Canada
ELSEVIER SCIENCE PUBLISHING CO., INC.
52 Vanderbilt Avenue, New York, NY 10017, USA

WITH 31 TABLES AND 5 ILLUSTRATIONS

British Library Cataloguing in Publication Data

Gormley, T. R.
   Food, health and the consumer.
   1. Food consumption—European Economic
   Community countries   2. Food industry and
   trade—European Economic Community countries
   I. Title   II. Downey, G.   III. O'Beirne, D.
   339.4′86413   HD9015

ISBN 1-85166-108-5

Library of Congress CIP data applied for

Publication arrangements by Commission of the European Communities, Directorate-
General Telecommunications, Information Industries and Innovation, Luxembourg

EUR 11020 EN

LEGAL NOTICE
Neither the Commission of the European Communities nor any person acting on behalf of
the Commission is responsible for the use which might be made of the following information.

Printed in Great Britain by Page Bros. (Norwich) Limited

v

FOREWORD

The FAST Programme's (Forecasting and Assessment in Science and Technology) mandate, as defined by the Council of Ministers, involves the analysis of scientific and technological changes in order to highlight their long-term implications and to propose timely policy options and new long term orientations for Community action, particularly in the field of science and technology.

This report is one of three cooperative studies undertaken for FAST's food subprogramme on the theme of Food and Health*. It was financed 50% by European Community funds and 50% by An Foras Talúntais.

The relationship between food consumption and health has of course always been important, but in recent years in the developed world attention has turned from the traditional concern regarding undernourishment to worries about the diseases of affluence, related to over and/or unbalanced food consumption patterns. Consumers have also become concerned that as food technology becomes more complex through the introduction of new production techniques (extrusion, irradiation, controlled and modified atmosphere packing, fractionation and recombination of food constituents etc) it likewise becomes more difficult to control the quality and safety of food products. Similar concern is expressed over

* The other two are: H. Grimme, R. Altenburger, M. Faust, K. Prietzel "Towards an Ecotrophobiosis - developing a strategy in relation to food and health from a life science point of view" FOP 106, August 1986 and J.V. Wheelock, J.D. Frank, A. Freckleton, L. Hansen "Food consumption patterns and nutritional labelling in selected developed countries". FOP Jan 1987 (forthcoming).

intensive agricultural production methods (growth hormones, antibiotics, high fertiliser applications, pesticide residues etc). Such developments raise important long-term issues for European consumers, farmers and food processors and bring into question whether we should be thinking of a reorientation of research priorities to give greater weight to these new concerns. Similarly, the question arises of whether existing policies which impinge upon the food system, of which the Common Agricultural Policy is of course the most important, can adapt to the new health concerns or whether Europe should be moving towards a common food and/or nutrition policy.

Before suggesting major reorientations in existing policies it is important to have a very clear view of the current state of knowledge, what new developments show most promise and what alternative actions for Europe really exist. Shedding light on these issues is the ambitious objective of this report, which is the end result of an extensive literature review (over 600 articles), a series of interviews and a Workshop held in Dublin in March 1986 involving leading scientists, consumer, agricultural and food industry interests.

Different Chapters of the report assess relationships between nutrition and disease; agricultural and food processing practices and food quality and safety; and food and nutritional policies in a large number of developed countries.

The report concludes with a number of recommendations for action by the European Commission. In this context, it must of course be recognised that these recommendations reflect the views of the authors and must in no way be interpreted as an authoritative statement of the views of the Commission.

Bruce Traill
Coordinator Food Subprogramme

CONTENTS

Page

SUMMARY

The purpose of this project was to study technological change in agriculture and the food industry, and also public policy in relation to food production, nutrition and consumer safety. In real terms this means a study of food, health and consumer issues and how these integrate into, and in some cases interact with, the food system. The study was carried out as part of the FAST (Forecasting and Assessment in Science and Technology) programme of the Commission of the European Communities. The data in this report are in effect a series of critical reviews based on the scientific, trade and popular literature together with the distilled views of many experts in a number of countries who were contacted during the study or who took part in an EEC FAST workshop in Dublin to review the draft findings.

CHAPTER 1 is a critical review and assessment of key nutritional issues and of the criteria currently applied for determining the effects of food of plant, animal and marine origin on human health. Food and nutrition policies are reviewed and assessed in CHAPTER 2 while agricultural production and food processing technologies are examined with respect to their possible impact on human health and in relation to consumer attitudes in CHAPTER 3. A list of 45 conclusions and recommendations is given in CHAPTER 4. It should be noted that the authors recognise microbiological food poisoning to be a major public health problem in most developed countries; however, it is outside the ambit of this report and should be the subject of a separate study.

Food, health and consumer issues will continue to be a major challenge to all involved in European food production, processing and policy-making into the next century. The consumer lobby in relation to food and health will continue to grow and an integrated European policy concerned with the quality and safety of the food supply in human nutrition terms is required to balance and complement the production oriented Common Agriculture Policy. Some of these issues could be broached initially by the formation of an elite committee spanning Directorates General in the CEC with responsibility for food, health and consumer issues.

It is important to stress that diet is often singled out unfairly as the major cause of many health problems; however, it is only part of a much larger spectrum including lifestyle and environment etc, and it is suggested that genetic factors may be of considerable importance in predisposing humans to disease and should be the subject of increased attention and research. There is still controversy and confusion among experts concerning some of the key nutrition issues of today including recommended daily allowances, cholesterol, fat and salt issues, the role of trace elements and dietary fibre, and the effects of mild overweight. An increased interdisciplinary effort is needed to resolve uncertainties in these and other areas together with structured and informed public debate (encouraged by the CEC) between scientists, industrialists, food producers and the general public using all available communications media.

While research procedures used in human nutrition are usually well founded, some are a cause for concern. These include extrapolation of results from animal experiments to humans, and also from 'at risk' groups to whole populations. Research is sometimes funded by vested interests and there is also a tendency to 'overuse' epidemiology and to carry out nutrition and health studies with insufficient numbers of human subjects. The practice of expert groups issuing major consensus statements and/or recommendations based on a 1-2 day meeting should be discontinued; such

XV

recommendations should be based on a number of meetings over a period of time where there is opportunity for continuing dialogue.

Extensive and continuing research is needed on some of the 'newer' roles being identified for certain 'nutrients'. These include the antithrombotic effect of fish oils and the effects of certain vegetables on platelet function, the role of vitamins C and E as free radical scavengers and the synergism between sodium and calcium in relation to hypertension. Mechanisms of energy use/disposal in man warrant further investigation as do rapid non-invasive techniques for measuring the regression of atherosclerosis.

The merits of promoting a European consensus on dietary recommendations should be explored by the CEC. In the absence of this, existing recommendations of expert groups in a number of countries could define nutrition policy in most member states. These recommendations include advice to avoid obesity, reduce fat, sugar and salt intake and increase dietary fibre consumption. This report does not contain specific target figures for these dietary components; instead the idea of moderation in eating and a balanced diet is advocated. A modest shift towards a greater consumption of fruits, vegetables, cereals and marine foods and a modest reduction in intake of foods of animal origin is desirable in the more Northern European countries. This advice is compromised to some extent by the lack of published information on dietary patterns in most member states; this points to the requirement for national food intake surveys. However, advocating certain dietary regimes for whole populations may be unnecessary, e.g. restriction of cholesterol and salt intake. Instead, the introduction of comprehensive screening programmes to identify those most at risk may be a better approach.

Economic and other incentives to dietary change must also be encouraged; these could include EEC support for leaner meat production and reduced-fat products, more EEC funded advertising for low fat dairy products and less for full fat products, the removal of certain statutory compositional standards thereby facilitating the marketing of low sugar and low fat products, predicting the response of consumers to differential pricing in closely related products, and the possible introduction of consumer subsidies to stimulate poultry, fish and cereal food consumption in most member states.

Improved consumer nutrition education is both a prerequisite to and a continuing need for dietary change and more comprehensive programmes need to be introduced by the EEC via health ministeries in member states. These programmes would embrace greater understanding between scientists and media personnel, the reduction of the major differences between operating budgets of national health education organisations and the advertising expenditure of food companies, and the increased use of retail outlets as purveyors of unbiased nutritional information. More responsibility must also be taken by the EEC for the provision of impartial information to the consumer on the relative importance of potential hazards in foods, and bodies representing both agriculture and the food industry should be involved in the informing process.

In the area of agricultural production, agro-chemicals appear to pose few risks for consumers in the EEC when they are used as directed, though state-of-the-art testing should be routinely applied to key existing products. However, more harmonisation of regulations, more surveillance and monitoring, more education on agro-chemical usage, and more opportunities for reduced use of agro-chemicals need to be explored and identified. In addition, the possible long-term effects of agro-chemicals per se and of interactions between agro-chemicals and other chemicals foreign to the body should be addressed. Changes in breeds/cultivars used, and in husbandry practices are also desirable, e.g. the production of animals and animal products containing less fat should be encouraged through pricing policy, and fundamental strategic research should be encouraged by the CEC on the biochemistry of the deposition of selected nutrients in key plant and animal species. The significance of the risk to human health of the chronic ingestion of natural toxicants in foods of plant origin is substantially underrated and more research and regulatory attention needs to be focused on this area; the regulation of all chemicals in foods (natural, added, contaminating, formed) should be dealt with on an equal basis.

The effects of processing on the wholesomeness and nutritive value of foods is also of major concern to many consumers; however, overall, food processing and storage do not give rise to toxicological or nutritional problems for the majority of consumers. It is recommended that only the most up-to-date toxicological, nutritional and analytical methodology should be used for assessing the safety, nutrient retention and bioavailability of nutrients in foods resulting from novel processes and that special attention, in this regard, be focused on processed foods intended for infants, geriatrics and those with special dietary requirements. The CEC should encourage industry (via support for specific R and D) to develop more 'health' formulations with lower levels of refined ingredients and also to explore possibilities for imitating the functional properties of key ingredients such as fat, sugar and salt in formulated foods through the use of other ingredients considered to constitute less nutritional hazard.

xviii

The risks to health from food additives appear to be exaggerated by consumers and some press comment. However, more attention should be given to the status of the limited number of food additives which cause allergic reactions or possible acute effects such as hyperactivity in children. Secondly, the possible long-term effects of additive intake _per se_ or from possible interactions between additives and other chemicals foreign to the body have not been adequately addressed and further research is needed in this area.

1

GENERAL INTRODUCTION

The European food system is complex and diverse and embraces many dimensions. The core of the system is the food chain, which stretches from the field to the consumer's table. Along the way there are many factors which interact with the food chain and this gives rise to the complex matrix that is the food system. The interactory aspects include environmental, economic, marketing, political, sociological, nutritional, technological, food safety, toxicological, and consumer factors and the many policy issues surrounding them. In the EEC the prominent position of the CAP has resulted in a major policy input at production agriculture level; however, corresponding policies in relation to some of the 'interactory' aspects above have not been applied downstream to the same extent and this represents a major deficiency in the European food system in relation to its future direction and planning. The project reported here addresses food, health and consumer issues, and the interaction between them, with emphasis on policy and its future ramifications. This is done, were possible, in line with the spirit of FAST ALIM 2: Food and Health, i.e. in the context of new perceptions, problems and opportunities, with the express purpose of making policy recommendations to the EEC on food, health and consumer issues.

CHAPTER 1 is a critical review and assessment of key nutritional issues and of the criteria currently applied for determining the effects of food of plant, animal and marine origin on human health. Food and nutrition policies are reviewed and assessed in CHAPTER 2 while agricultural production and food processing technologies are assessed with respect to their impact on human health and in relation to consumer attitudes (to them) in CHAPTER 3. The material in CHAPTERS 1-3 was presented as three issue papers to an EEC FAST workshop in Dublin on March 11, 1986. Experts attended from a number of EEC countries including Ireland, and this afforded the opportunity for a critical assessment of the data and the preparation of CHAPTER 4 which provides details of the overall findings together with conclusions and recommendations for possible future EEC policy in the food/health/consumer areas. This project is only one of three in the FAST ALIM 2 Food and Health programme and complements work of a team at the University of Bradford (UK) working on consumer information and education in relation to nutritional labelling, and a group at the University of Bremen (FRG) who are developing new strategies in relation to food and health from a life science point of view.

It is important at this stage to put diet in context in relation to health as many people are increasingly thinking of diet as the main factor influencing health. This may not be so and the 'circle' below shows health being influenced by lifestyle, genetic, and environmental factors. These three have been given equal segments in the circle as it is difficult to assess the relative effect of each on health. Diet, is included mostly as a lifestyle factor but also as an environmental one as well but its segment size in Fig. A is conjectural.

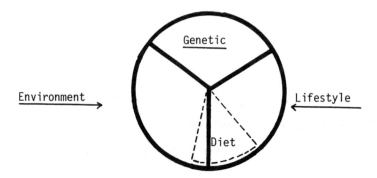

Figure A : The Health Circle

3

The enormous cost of health care in most developed countries also enters the equation and is causing concern for government ministers and local health authorities alike. In view of this a dynamic European programme of preventive medicine is a must and obviously a prudent diet and linking diets with diseases together with nutrition education are major components of such a programme.

It is also necessary to stress that the subject of microbiological food poisoning is not addressed in this report for reasons of space. This is not a reflection of its importance and it is fully recognised by the authors that food poisoning is a major health hazard in most, if not all, European countries at the present time.

4

CHAPTER 1 — T. R. Gormley

REVIEW AND ASSESSMENT OF KEY NUTRITIONAL ISSUES AND OF THE
CRITERIA CURRENTLY APPLIED FOR DETERMINING THE EFFECTS OF
FOOD OF PLANT, ANIMAL AND MARINE ORIGIN ON HUMAN HEALTH

CHAPTER 1 is a review and assessment of key nutritional issues and of the criteria currently applied for determining the effects of food of plant, animal and marine origin on human health

> - and refers to fruits, vegetables, cereals, oil crops, meat, marine foods, dairy foods and some of their related products and their role as suppliers of protein, carbohydrate (refined + complex), fat (saturated and unsaturated), dietary fibre, vitamins and minerals. The data have been assessed both in terms of individual items but also in a total dietary context. Attention has been focused on key areas such as the fat issue, complex carbohydrate, trace element nutrition and dietary fibre, and on some of the concentrates such as fat-spreads, sugar, salt and alcohol. Factors which influence current human nutrition thinking have also been assessed.
>
> The information for CHAPTER 1 has been obtained from the scientific and trade literature, from learned reports and from personal communications. Emphasis is on the areas of conflict, knowing that the specialised literature has already been subjected to critical evaluation by a large number of different independent groups.

1.1   INTRODUCTION

One may well ask of European consumers today do we 'eat to live' or do we 'live to eat'. The answer is both in that foods are eaten to supply the necessary nutrients for good health, growth and well-being, but also because eating the foods we like is a pleasurable experience. Consumers throughout the world share certain basic expectations about food. First and foremost they expect an adequate supply of safe wholesome food at a price they can afford. Of course for European consumers of today, unlike many others throughout the world, 'adequate supply' does not present a problem (1); in many cases the problem is over-nutrition (2) or excess food intake. There is sufficient food for all and there can be little doubt but that it is generally safe and wholesome. However, the question arises more and more as to whether the food is adequate in terms of current thinking on nutrition and health, and consumers now expect to be given sufficient information to enable them to know exactly what they are buying.

Much of the current interest/concern in food/health issues in developed countries stems from the publicity given to the so-called diseases of affluence (3) coupled with recent dietary advice in reports such as the US dietary goals (4), NACNE (5) and COMA (6) and others (see CHAPTER 2). The current interest is also linked to changing needs and life-styles in developed countries (7), i.e. more wives working outside the home, more eating out, falling birth rate etc, and also to the requirement for fitness (8-10), vitality and slimness. For example a recent survey showed that nearly 90% of Americans think they weigh too much and about 30% of US women and 16% of men were on diets in 1984 (11).

Coupled with these factors is the very large issue of health care and its enormous cost in most countries. While many diseases have multiple causes (12) many also have a dietary component (13). Laing (14) has calculated the annual cost of diet-related diseases to the National Health Service in the UK at about £180 million based on 1979/80 prices; this indicates the need for preventive nutrition in society.

The main aim of this part of the project is to review key nutritional issues and the criteria currently applied for determining the effect of food of plant, animal and marine origin on human health. Treatment is largely restricted to intrinsic factors, i.e. the main components of nutritional significance occurring naturally in the food as distinct from extrinsic factors such as agrochemicals, additives and toxicological aspects; some of these are discussed in CHAPTER 3.

TABLE 1: Relative priorities given to food hazards

Actual*	FDA regulatory	Press	Food industry	Fringe hysteria
M	FA	PR	M	FA
N	PR	EC	N	PR
EC	M	FA	FA	EC
NT	EC	N	PR	N
PR	N	M	EC	M
FA	NT	NT	NT	NT

M - Microbiological N - Nutritional EC - Environmental contaminant
NT - Natural toxicant   PR - Pesticide residue FA - Food additive
After Hall, 1971 (16)
* based on scientific evidence

As mentioned in the general introduction, food poisoning aspects are not discussed. However, a number of authors (15,16) list microbiological and food poisoning aspects as top of the order of priority of actual food hazards (Table 1); the data (Table 1) were published in 1971 but Gray (12) suggests that the priorities have not changed much to the present day. Miller (17) cites data showing 81 million or more cases of diarrhoea disease of food-borne origin in the US each year while Hawthorn (18) (Univ. of Strathclyde), in a personal communication, cites microbiological food poisoning as the major health hazard in our present European society. The economic loss from outbreaks of food-borne disease can be considerable (19,20). However, despite these opinions it is issues such as dieting, fibre, fat, carbohydrate, vitamins, minerals, salt, cancer, heart disease, additives, etc that arouse most public concern and media attention and result in huge amounts of money being spent on research world-wide. Despite this vast expenditure, considerable confusion exists in some of these areas at all levels, i.e. medical and scientific opinion, and among nutritionists, the agricultural and food industries, and especially among consumers. Obviously this also has major ramifications for policy-makers as it is extremely difficult to decide on what policies should be pursued.

Factors which influence current human nutrition thinking are also addressed in this chapter. A critical assessment is made of the current status of the main food components of nutritional significance and of the key issues, controversies and novel aspects surrounding them. The status of these components is then related to foods of plant, animal and marine origin and to the 'food concentrates' (fat spreads, sugar, salt, alcohol) and the concept of the prudent/balanced diet is developed recognising the food and nutrition policy measures in CHAPTER 2 and also the impact of agriculture and the food industry on the food system as discussed in CHAPTER 3.

1.2   HUMAN NUTRITION THINKING

A number of major reports on dietary intakes/guidelines/goals have been issued in recent times in a number of countries (see CHAPTER 2). Some of the broad key nutritional issues in relation to EC countries are as follows: energy intakes too high, fat consumption too high, ratio of polyunsaturated to saturated fat in the diet too low, intake of complex carbohydrate and dietary fibre too low, protein intake more than adequate, salt intake too high, some vitamins and minerals may be deficient, e.g. folic acid and iron. However, these are generalisations and may vary both on a country and on a regional basis within countries; also in every country there are likely to be sub-groups within the population who are over or under-nourished. There are many other more specific key issues including the role of trace elements, the possible link between free radical production and heart disease, the effects of alcohol on health, the health role/effect (if any) of hydrocolloids in food systems, the role of vitamin A in cancer prevention, and others.

However, the following major question must be addressed: who says that the above are key issues and who formulates current human nutrition thinking (CHNT). A distinction must also be made between CHNT and nutrition education although there is some overlap between them. The former largely refers to formulating the message to be preached in the latter. There is little doubt that CHNT on many topics is confused with experts often polarised in their opinions. This is a serious matter as it leads to considerable confusion among those formulating policy and also among consumers (see CHAPTER 3) on nutritional matters as the message coming down is often different depending on the slant put on it by the disseminator. There have also been some major 'about turns' in CHNT; for example high protein low carbohydrate/calorie diets were in vogue in the 1960s (5, 21) whereas the message now in developed countries is eat more fibre and complex carbohydrate. For example, one conclusion in a recent report of the Expert Advisory Committee on Dietary Fibre in Canada (22) is that the increased consumption of starchy foods with which fibre is associated may be of the greatest health benefit. Can we see therefore, perhaps in 10-15 years time, a reversal in CHNT on reduced fat intakes?

The formulation of CHNT is a complex interactive matrix and an attempt to show the various interrelationships is made in Figure 1. The left hand side of the diagram (boxes A-D) represents the primary producers of information; these are the people most likely to influence CHNT. However, CHNT is also influenced by those on the right hand side of the diagram, i.e. industry and promotion agencies. The top of the diagram relates to government and other agencies who would be expected to formulate nutrition policy and/or guidelines while the bottom of the diagram represents the media, consumer and market place dimensions. The interaction between

Fig. 1:   Who determines current human nutrition thinking?

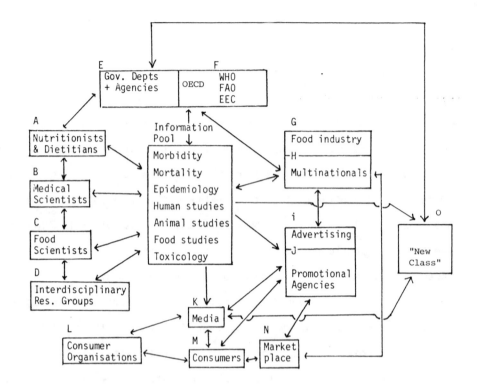

'left, right, top, bottom' is difficult to assess; for example is 'the bottom' more influenced by 'the right' than by 'the left'.

1.2.1   The primary producers of information

These are represented largely by boxes A-D in Figure 1 although boxes G, E and F also contribute.   Scientific information on human nutrition is exchanged through scientific and other publications, through conferences, workshops, meetings of expert groups and through person to person contact. Scientific and other publications present data and a formal discussion. However, they are not nearly as good, in an interactive sense, as conferences, meetings, workshops;   these allow opportunities for dialogue and consensus.

A congress such as the XlIIth International Nutrition meeting held in Brighton in August 1985 is a good example of a major opportunity for dialogue.   In addition to the plenary sessions, about 280 papers were presented orally;   there were about 1300 poster presentations and about 48 workshops.   Such a meeting obviously has a major bearing on CHNT.

While most of the research being carried out by the 'primary producers' is well-founded and of a high standard, there are, however, some aspects of research procedures which are a cause for concern:

   a) extrapolation of results of animal experiments to humans

   b) extrapolation of results from 'at risk' groups to whole
       populations

   c) use of small numbers of human subjects in human nutrition studies

   d) research often funded by vested interests

   e) 'overuse'/abuse of epidemiology

These are discussed in the order above; for example some scientists are very quick to extrapolate results of <u>animal experiments</u> to humans. While it is recognised that in many cases it is quite justified to do so, nevertheless caution must be exercised as the mechanisms involved in animals may not be the same as in humans (23). In animal studies a much greater degree of control can be exerted over the subjects and 'interactions' which could occur in humans in a 'real life' situation may not occur or may be lost. This topic was the subject of a workshop (No. 25) at the 1985 Brighton Nutrition Congress (24).

Extrapolation of results from <u>'at risk' groups</u> to whole populations may also be a 'weak spot' in many studies. It is understandable that many nutritional research projects are carried out on human subjects who are already 'sick' or at risk; presumably these people are in, or are attending, hospitals and so are readily available, and their treatment in itself may be able to be 'plugged in' as a component in a research programme. However, scientists should become more aware of the danger of extrapolating results of such trials to healthy individuals in a whole population. This in turn leads to the third issue of concern, i.e. it is difficult and costly to have <u>large numbers of healthy volunteers</u> in human nutrition experiments and there may also be ethical problems. Many such studies therefore, on which major statements/claims are often made are carried out using less than 10 healthy volunteers. In most cases this is inadequate and the results may be open to considerable doubt.

In some cases scientists may have to 'soft pedal' results when the research is funded by <u>vested interests</u>. For example, an individual food industry or a group of industries forming a segment may fund nutritional/medical research at Universities or Institutes; the fact that a scientist accepts such funds may make it difficult for him to report an 'adverse' result (as far as the supporting industry is concerned) in the same strong terms that he would have done if the funds came from a 'neutral' source. Therefore, when reading published research results it is always useful to see who commissioned/funded the particular study.

While national food surveys are a useful epidemiological resource (25) some scientists tend to overuse or abuse epidemiological data and do not seem to fully realise the implications. There are two basic types of epidemiologic investigation: correlational studies, where groups of persons exhibiting specific disease rates are compared, and case-control investigations, where individual persons with the disease (cases) are compared with suitably matched persons without the disease under study (controls). Both types of investigation are difficult and have limitations. In correlational investigations (where groups of people are studied) it is extraordinarily difficult to determine whether those in whom the disease (a specific type of cancer) develops are 'average' or at the 'fringe' of dietary practice for their particular group (26). Moreover the populations under study may differ genetically, they may have varying degrees of risk from other environmental and lifestyle factors affecting the probability of developing the cancer, and may be characterised by different patterns of disease detection, diagnosis and classification. Finally, it must be recognised that any difference between the groups will correlate with any other difference so it is essential to use care in assigning possible cause-effect relationships. For example, as societies develop, markets for consumer goods such as cigarettes and toilet paper increase. Because of this, there is a correlation between death from lung cancer and per capita toilet paper use, although few would seriously propose a cause-effect link.

14

1.2.2   Expert groups/Advisory groups

Most   major   statements   on   human   nutrition   issues   emanate   from
expert/advisory   groups.   The terms 'expert/advisory and   group/committee'
are used inter-changeably in this document.   The number of expert groups on
human   nutrition   worldwide is very large as the bibliography in any   paper
(27) on the development of dietary guidelines will show.   There is   little
doubt   that the expert group is one of the main,   if not the main,   'whirlpool'   which   formulates   and   advises   on   CHNT.   However,   the
outcome/recommendation   from the whirlpool is not always infallible.   This
may be due to a number of reasons:

a)   there may not be sufficient information available as an input to
allow a comprehensive output

b)   an expert group may be influenced excessively by one or more of its
members who have strong views and imposing personalities

c)   an expert group may be the organ of, or may be unduly influenced
by, a vested interest

d)   an   expert group may not meet a sufficient number of times and
may not contain the correct or necessary expertise to do justice
to its task.

Some   of these points are exemplified by two consensus public meetings held
in 1984 as reported by Oliver (28) in the Lancet:

"One   was   organised in the United Kingdom by   the   King's
Fund   and was on the advisability and need for   increasing
coronary artery bypass surgery here.   The other was   held
in the United States by the National Heart, Lung and Blood
Institute   and   was   on the practicability   and   value   of
lowering   blood   cholesterol   in   the   general   population.
Both were called consensus development   conferences.   The

purpose of a conference designed to develop and reach a consensus view in an area where there are numerous and disparate opinions is quite different from that of a conference which is a learned debate about whether it is possible to reach any consensus on how an unresolved subject might be developed further. The former is a contrived situation, and unlikely to be achieved with much solidarity within the short time set aside for such a meeting. But a conference established to try to achieve consensus as to how complex scientific, professional, ethical, social, and economic issues might be developed is, surely, a much weightier venture and the preferred aim - but one unlikely to be achieved through a public meeting.

Clearly, the aims of both the consensus development conferences were to try to develop a consensus view and, not surprisingly, the final statements prepared at the end of each 2-day meeting were biased. How could they have been otherwise? Those who initiated the idea were either naive or determined to use the forum for special pleading, or both. The panel of jurists for each of the conferences was selected to include experts who would, predictably, say that there should be more coronary artery bypass surgery in the UK or, alternatively, that all levels of blood cholesterol in the United States are too high and should be lowered. And, of course, this is exactly what was said. The conclusions reached by these consensus development conferences are potentially so far-reaching

that it might pay to pause for a moment and examine how
they were derived-for there are several weaknesses of such
conferences."

Ahrens, a US researcher says (29) of the same US conference:

"I am dismayed by the imbalance between the importance of
the issues at stake, on the one hand, and, on the other,
the manner in which the consensus development conference
considered these issues."

"I would have been content with the consensus statement if
it had confined itself to what we do know and what we do
not. It promises benefits without giving the evidence to
back up that promise. By failing to emphasise what we do
not know, the statement sweeps these weaknesses in our
evidence under the rug, as if they were trivial. I have
disagreed with that position."

and he concludes that -

"I believe that as scientists we are expected by the
public to render scientifically sound advice. Policy-
makers must come to their own conclusions, and will do so
for a complex of reasons - political, social, and
economic. That is their affair; ours is to be sound, as
sound as current evidence permits, stating clearly where
the gaps in knowledge exist."

It is easy to understand the reservations of these scientists in view
of the fact that the expert committee (panel) recommended that plasma

cholesterol levels in the USA be reduced towards those in countries where CHD is not a major health problem, and that dietary changes aimed at producing these reductions be undertaken by everyone over 2 years of age.

Several dissenting opinions were voiced by invited speakers and by commentators from the floor. The main questions were whether the USA public can be promised a reduced incidence of CHD if the prudent diet is widely adopted; whether the prudent diet is safe and effective for everyone over the age of 2 years; and whether the diet recommended is the best choice of several known to reduce plasma cholesterol levels. It is disconcerting that a recommendation of this magnitude was made on the basis of a 2-day meeting rather than on a series of meetings where experts have a chance to 'reflect and digest' the tabled information.

In contrast other dietary reports have been the result of much longer dialogue. For example, the panel of experts producing the recent COMA report (6) was appointed in 1981, met 10 times including a two-day residential meeting, and published the report in 1984; committees advising ministers of health (in many countries) on food and nutrition policies and other important health issues usually meet on a fairly frequent basis (30). The expert committee who drew up the WHO report on the 'Prevention of Coronary Heart Disease' (31) met in Geneva, Switzerland from 30 November to 8 December 1981. The following details are given in the Executive Summary of the report on Diet, Nutrition and Cancer (32) by the Committee on Diet, Nutrition, and Cancer (Assembly of Life Sciences, National Research Council, USA):

"A 13 member committee and one advisor were appointed to conduct the study. The diverse expertise represented on the committee includes such disciplines as biochemistry, microbiology, embryology, epidemiology, experimental oncology, internal medicine, microbial genetics, molecular biology, molecular genetics, nutrition, nutrition education, public health, and toxicology. This multidisciplinary composition has served to ensure comprehensive coverage of the scientific literature and to provide a broad perspective to the committee's conclusions. The work of the committee has been aided by extensive consultation with scientific colleagues, by specially arranged technical conferences on specific subjects, and by a public meeting to receive such additional information and advice as scientists and others wished to provide."

The above shows the considerable multidisciplinary nature of the approach and consultation procedure used in preparing this particular report.

These examples show some of the advantages and disadvantages of advisory expert groups. Obviously it is imperative that such groups be multidisciplinary and be composed not only of academics but also industrialists and those in national agencies; ideally they should meet and correspond on a number of occasions over a period of time thus allowing maximum time for comprehension, interaction, dialogue, consultation, re-orientation where necessary, and finally for agreement and publication of findings and recommendations. This subject is also considered in CHAPTER 2.

1.2.3   Food industry/multinationals/promotional agencies

These are contained in boxes G, I, J in Figure 1. The food industry/multinationals contribute to the formulation of CHNT in at least three ways

a)   carrying out in-house nutrition-based research

b)   funding nutritional research in outside institutes, hospitals, agencies

c)   hosting workshops, conferences, meetings

In many cases the research carried out, or the workshop/meeting hosted, is linked in a subtle, or perhaps not so subtle, way with product sales. If the product in question already has a 'healthy' image then the research tends to be 'offensive' in that it tends to further emphasise existing health/nutrition benefits of the food product in question and to search for new ones. This is the case in the high fibre breakfast cereal market; dietary fibre is an 'in' concept at this point in time. The third Kellogg Nutrition Symposium on "Dietary fibre: current developments of importance to health" (33) held in London in 1977 is a good example of a major international scientific meeting held under the auspices of industry to discuss the most recent findings on dietary fibre; obviously such a gathering considerably influences the formulation of CHNT. The ground-swell from this type of meeting carries on down the line and may become consumer information/education on a range of food packs and especially on packets containing breakfast cereals.

If on the other hand the food product in question has a less favourable health image currently, e.g. fat spreads; the research and approach may be more defensive. There are some examples of this in the butter versus margarine 'battleground'. Crawford (34) from the edible oils industry shows that the 60% of total fats, other than refined oils, consumed in the UK is mainly of animal origin, and stresses the importance of the edible oil industry in any move to reduce the saturated fat content and increase the polyunsaturated fat content of the diet. Hornstra (35) from Unilever research in Holland suggested that linoleic acid is the most promising dietary component for the primary prevention of coronary artery disease.

In contrast, those promoting butter interpret the information in a different way. For example a book on 'Facts on Fats' (36) published by the Butter Information Council in the UK stresses the formation of undesirable trans fatty acids during the hydrogenation of oils and shows that some processed fish and vegetable oils can end up with a higher saturated fat equivalent than butterfat; they claim that most margarines contain significant amounts of trans fatty acids. Some of these aspects are also discussed in CHAPTER 3.

These examples highlight the difficulties, and also serve as a note of caution, of/to those (in international and national agencies) responsible for issuing nutrition education information/guidelines/policy in getting the right balance in their recommendations without being unduly influenced by the offensive/defensive research/promotion of vested interests in the food industry on nutrition matters.

It was also decided in this project to look at the type of nutritional information being issued by a sample of promotional agencies; these were chosen mostly in the dairy and meat areas (Table 2). While it is recognised that these largely aim at consumer education and 'winning over' consumers, they nevertheless have an impact on those back along the line i.e. researchers, nutritionists, policy makers etc as these people are, of course, also consumers and undoubtedly can be swayed (at least to an extent) by skilfully presented nutritional information. The data showed that three of the agencies gave extensive scientific information on human nutrition/health issues (Table 2). For example the UK Butter Information

TABLE 2: Classification of nutritional information disseminated by a sample of food promotion agencies

| Agency | Information | | |
	Scientific	Popular	Recipe
Dairy Bureau (Canada)	**	***	*
Butter Info. Council (UK)	***	***	***
Milk Marketing Board (UK)	*	**	**
Meat & Livestock Comm. (UK)	***	***	-
Dairy Produce Adv. Bd (UK)	-	*	**
National Dairy Council (UK)	-	**	-
National Dairy Council (IRL)	-	**	-
National Dairy Council (USA)	***	-	***
Irish Livestock & Meat Board (IRL)	-	*	-
Irish Sugar Company (IRL)	*	***	-
CMA (FRG)	-	*	***
Synergal (GR)	-	*	**
Danish Dairy Federation (DK)	-	*	*
OFIVAL (F)	-	*	-
Office Nat. Debouches Agr. + Hort. (B)	-	*	**
New Zealand Lamb Info. Bureau (NZ)	-	-	**

*** extensive; ** moderate; * small

Council publishes 'Diet and Health' on a monthly basis which contains critical reviews of health issues; they also issue booklets on the scientific aspects of cholesterol, fat, the lipid hypothesis etc. The UK Meat and Livestock Commission have prepared a major document on 'Meat: the health issue in perspective' which contains a response to the recommendations of the COMA committee report (6) in addition to comprehensive information on 'background to health issue', 'the medical view', 'the advice available'. The US National Dairy Council has published a 22 page catalogue entitled 'Nutrition Education Materials 1985-86' the foreword of which reads as follows:

"Americans are more concerned about what they eat, how they feel, and how they look than they have ever been. Yet many of us are overweight or don't eat a balanced diet. And all of us are vulnerable to the recent blizzard of nutrition misinformation.

Since 1915, the Dairy Council has been a non-profit organisation devoted to nutrition research and education. In those 70 years, we have developed a reputation for producing scientifically accurate and educationally sound nutrition materials and programmes.

Our catalogue for 1985-1986 features all of our award-winning, scientifically sound, nutrition education materials for health professionals, educators, and consumers. Each year these materials are revised to reflect current research in the young, growing science of nutrition." (Catalog, Courtesy of National Dairy Council, USA.)

The information classed 'popular' in Table 2 is more in the realm of nutrition/consumer education although some of it could influence the thinking of health professionals. The data (Table 2) also show that some promotion agencies issue only cookery recipe information. Inspection of the information given by the promotional agencies listed in Table 2 reveals that overall it is accurate and is presented in an unbiased fashion.

1.2.4   Government Departments/Agencies, WHO, FAO, EEC, OECD

These are shown in boxes E and F in Figure 1 and they obviously influence CHNT through commissioning research, setting up expert groups, hosting conferences/workshops/seminars, and by issuing dietary guidelines and nutrition policy.   Examples of recent major European Commission activities influencing CHNT include a Symposium on Nutrition, Food Technology and Nutritional Information in London in 1980 (37), a DG Vl major publication on 'The influence on health of different fats in the diet' (38) and a 250 page study entitled 'The problem of fats in the EEC (available, June 1986).   These departments/agencies often play a major role in consumer education on nutritional matters in some countries.   This may be in the form of literature or through an office or bureau.   Examples include the Nutrition Education Office in the Netherlands and the Health Education Bureau in Ireland.   These agencies also have a role in coordination of the sections in the CHNT matrix (see 1.2.7 and Fig. 1).

1.2.5   The media/consumer organisations

The role of the media is more in the area of consumer education than in formulating CHNT although they serve some function in CHNT; for example review articles on nutrition items in magazines such as WHICH and TIME and also in some newspapers undoubtedly have an effect on CHNT.   Most European countries also have TV programmes on diet and health but these are generally aimed at the general population.

Consumer organisations can influence CHNT through lobbying and back pressure. The recent banning of growth hormones in beef animals in the EEC is an example (see CHAPTER 3).   Such pressure on this and other matters can often cause the scientists to 'think again' and perhaps modify their original ideas or proposals.

1.2.6   The "New Class"

This is shown in box O in Figure 1 and is discussed in detail in CHAPTER 2. Kahn (39) traced the emergence of a new social group in advanced capitalist countries which he labelled the 'New Class'; he claims the group is largely composed of upper middle class intellectuals who derive their influence and income from possession and mastery of verbal, symbol and 'persuasive' skills engendered more by formal academic and analytical training than by practical training and experience. Kahn suggests that this 'New Class', which spans the entire political spectrum, is out of touch with reality and tends to be strongly represented in the media and Government Agencies; for these reasons they exert undue influence in public policy-making even to the extent that they tend to create the environment in which such topics are discussed. The core of Kahn's article represents an interesting hypothesis concerning the origin of many of the public policy issues of the 70s and 80s. It is likely that the 'New Class' or similar groups will have a considerable influence on CHNT in the 1980s and into the 1990s.

1.2.7   Interactions and coordination

The content of sections 1.2.1 to 1.2.6 above together with Figure 1 bring home the complexity of the CHNT matrix. While responsibility for the primary nutrition information which leads to CHNT resides largely with groups A-D and to a lesser extent E, F and G, H, nevertheless all sections in Figure 1 make a contribution. There are also many interactions which are impossible to separate. The coordination of all the different aspects in Figure 1 is a major task and is probably outside the capability of any individual agency or group; however, it is likely that some of the elements could be coordinated - perhaps through the EEC. For example there is still a great need for a more interdisciplinary approach where medical scientists, nutritionists and industrial food technologists can have dialogue - not just meeting at a conference for one day - but on a more continuous basis. Perhaps this can be brought about by the EEC; however, it must be realised that the problems of formulating CHNT are inter-disciplinary and span different directorates (DsG 111, Vl, Xll) within the EEC. This, therefore, may also require a new coordinated approach within the EEC itself in order to develop the necessary mechanisms to achieve this goal.

1.2.8 Nutrition education

The sections above have shown some of the pitfalls and difficulties in the CHNT area. The final product in the chain is the passing of reliable nutrition information to the consumer; however, the consumer must have the necessary knowledge and background in nutrition matters in order to understand and assimilate the information. For this reason more extensive nutrition education programmes are desirable in all EEC countries. The scientists and other generators of new nutrition information have a responsibility to ensure that they pass down the message in a comprehensible way and that the media report it in a balanced rather than in a dramatic fashion. Matters can be helped by better scientist/media interaction. For example, if a scientist prepares a press release, his results are more likely to be reported accurately than if he sends a copy of his scientific paper or article to the media.

The Commission of the EEC should, therefore, promote programmes for nutrition education of consumers in all EEC countries.

1.3   STATUS OF FOOD COMPONENTS/KEY ISSUES

The status of intrinsic food components of nutritional significance are strongly linked, at least in people's minds, to a whole range of conditions/diseases such as coronary heart disease (CHD), hypertension, cancer, obesity and others. This in turn reflects on these components and turns them into controversial issues such as the fat and cholesterol issue, the salt issue, the dietary fibre issue and others. However, it is extremely important to stress at this point that most, if not all, the so-called diseases of affluence have multiple causes and diet is only one of these. It is difficult to quantify the individual contribution of a given factor as a causal agent for most of these diseases and it is even more difficult (or perhaps impossible) to pinpoint interactive or synergistic effects. This raises the major question:

*is the role of diet as one of the causative factors of the so-called diseases of affluence over-emphasised?

An attempt will be made to address this question in this section.

Food is eaten for enjoyment, sustenance and health (40, 41). However, increased activity and awareness in the areas of food and health in the last decade brought about by the health professionals and taken up by the media has resulted in unprecedented interest in the effect of diet on health by consumers in the developed countries. People ask "is this food good for me", "might it cause cancer or CHD" (42), or on a broader base "how can I have a healthy and sensorically pleasurable diet and still remain slim"; the near obsession with slimness and fitness of many people has already been referred to (11).

It is against this background that the current status of food components/key issues is discussed in this section.

1.3.1   RDAs/Nutrient intakes

The nutritional needs and the nutritional situation in the EEC have been discussed in detail by Mariani (43) as have the evolution of eating habits (44) and dietary regimes (45).

Tables giving recommended dietary allowances (intakes) (RDA) have now been prepared in many developed countries. Figures for the RDA of some nutrients, e.g. protein, ascorbic acid, calcium and iron, have changed over the years. For these nutrients there is uncertainty how to define both adequate and optimal nutritional status (46). The committee on International Dietary Allowances of the International Union of Nutritional Sciences (47) published a report which compared RDAs in 20 countries; the changes from the 1930s were summarised by Truswell in 1976 (48) while the RDAs for European countries are assembled in the report of the Second European Nutrition Conference (49).

Identification of particular nutrients, as possible problem ones, based on low (or high) dietary intakes can alert specialists in food, nutrition, and public health to take action before consequences become serious. However, agreement is lacking on the level of intake that signifies a dietary problem which may lead to a health problem. The USA Food and Nutrition Board states that the Recommended Dietary Allowances (RDAs) are set high enough "to meet the nutritional needs of practically all healthy persons" (NAS/NRC, 1980). RDAs are daily amounts of nutrients recommended for populations grouped by sex and age over a period of time - they are not requirements for specific individuals. Variations in requirements among individuals are relatively unknown (50). The confusion and conflict regarding RDAs hit new heights in the USA in 1985 as indicated by the following report from the New York Times:

"Academy Won't Back Revised RDAs"

___"In an unusual move, the National Academy of Sciences announced ___ that some of the nation's most eminent scientists were in an irreconcilable conflict over proposals to alter the recommended levels of certain vitamins and minerals in the human diet. Frank Press, president of the academy, said the organisation would therefore be unable to issue a new set of recommended dietary allowances (RDAs) 'at this time'. The report had been expected (in the summer of 1985). The decision to defer the report, he said, 'stems primarily from an impasse' that resulted from 'scientific differences of opinion' about the levels of certain vitamins and minerals needed to maintain health ___ The Academy's Committee on Dietary Allowances drafted a detailed report, but 'many of the committee's conclusions and recommendations did not gain the full support of scientists who reviewed it', Press said. The committee's confidential draft report proposed reducing the allowances for magnesium, iron, zinc, and vitamins A, C, and B6, and raising the allowance for calcium."

Robert Pear in New York Times
8 Oct 1985

The current situation regarding RDAs is highlighted in a recent paper by Munro (51). He concluded that determining nutrient requirements is an evolving art as evidenced by the perceived need to have new additions of the RDA handbook every five years and suggests the following as the main research needs:

a) the interaction of one nutrient with another requires to be integrated into the process of recommending levels of nutrient intake

b) bioavailability of nutrients

c) the scientific basis of the RDA should continue to be explored

Nutrient intakes are normally measured by weighing the food in question and referring to food composition tables such as McCance and Widdowson (52). A publication of the United Kingdom Meat and Livestock Commission entitled 'Fat from meat - current consumption levels' criticises this approach and claims that the contribution of meat to fat intake in the UK diet according to the NACNE report at 30g (fat from meat) daily is too high and that the true figure could be about 24g. It is claimed that some of the discrepancy is due to out-of-date food composition values, i.e. the conversion factors in the computer are based on analyses of limited numbers of samples purchased and analysed some years ago. Since then, consumer preference has been for leaner meat, and both animals and meat merchandising practices have changed. So it is likely that the level of fat being purchased today is over-estimated. The above is just an example, presumably there are others (see CHAPTER 3). It also raises the further issue of compatibility of nutrient data banks in Europe; fortunately this subject is being tackled by 'Eurofoods'. A paper by West (53) describes developments in Europe since the establishment of Eurofoods in 1982. A review of food composition tables in individual European countries is included together with several background papers. A summary of recommendations made at the initial

Eurofoods Workshop in Wageningen in May 1983 and a review of subsequent progress are presented in West's paper.

The data in this section show that the area of RDAs is an evolving art. While it is important that scientists continue to explore what exact requirements are, the practical situation is that 'ball-park' values will suffice in most cases in developed countries. This is all the more so if the concept of a balanced diet is preached and also an increased emphasis on the intake of fresh foods rather than highly formulated products. It is suggested that the area of RDAs in Europe should be coordinated further through Eurofoods.

1.3.2 Food energy/overnutrition

Since a degree of over-nutrition is prevalent in most, if not all, European countries it follows that a degree of overweight occurs also. Overweight, and in its more severe form obesity, has dual implications; firstly it affects the appearance of the individual (a social implication) and secondly it may affect his/her health (11). Based on the laws of thermodynamics the answer to overweight is eat less and/or exercise more which implies appetite control and other mechanisms of weight homoeostasis (54) and/or an exercise programme . However appetite control and dieting on a long term basis is very difficult for most people (11). Different mechanisms of energy use/disposal seem to exist for different people. For example, what about people who eat a lot and stay slim versus those that eat less and remain overweight?; Garrow (55) has suggested that if two people who are in energy balance on the same diet both increase their intake by the same amount, but one (lean) gains less weight than the other (obese) there is a limited number of ways in which this can be explained:

(a)   Lean might absorb less energy from the gut than obese

(b)   Lean might use more energy assimilating the excess intake, or might
        store it in a form which involved greater metabolic work, so less
        energy remained for storage than with the thermodynamically more
        efficient process used by obese

(c)   If lean stored more of the excess intake as protein, and less as fat,
        this would have the effect of increasing his resting metabolic rate
        more than that of obese for a given weight gain.

(d)   Under conditions of overfeeding lean might become more sensitive
        than obese to thermogenic stimuli such as exercise, cold or anxiety.

Garrow (55) suggests that (a) can be dismissed immediately because in
normal people $95 \pm 3\%$ of dietary energy is absorbed and this percentage does
not differ between lean and obese subjects. However, the present author
queries this, e.g. is the suggestion of Garrow food specific or does it
apply to all foods; is there a 'standard' human gut and if not what is the
interaction between food types and 'guts'; are some foods, and especially
items such as resistant starches (see 1.3.3.1) likely to be 'carried
through' undigested in subjects who have short bowel transit times - it
seems likely; presumably the 'enzyme cocktail' within the gut varies from
person to person and there may also be genetic aspects. Therefore it may
still be premature to eliminate the so-called 'bad converter' from the
lean/obese issue. Concerning (b), although Shetty et al (56) demonstrated a
larger increase in metabolic rate following a meal in lean than in obese,
or post-obese subjects, the total energy expenditure of the lean subjects
was less than that of the obese subjects at every stage of the study.
Therefore, even if it was agreed that obese people have a smaller thermic
response to food than lean people, this would not in itself provide an
explanation for their obesity (55). If (c) is the mechanism then lean
people should have a higher resting metabolic rate than fat people.
However, Nair et al (57) have shown the opposite to be the case.

Some researchers postulate additional mechanisms, such as thermogenesis in brown fat, to explain the non-storage of excess energy in lean man. The present situation concerning white versus brown adipose tissue (WAT vs BAT) has been reviewed by Nechad (59) who concludes that the presently available data clearly demonstrate that BAT and WAT are two different tissues. While WAT is primarily an energy store, the function of BAT is the opposite, that is, to dissipate energy as heat. Himms-Hagen (60) states that thermogenesis in brown adipose tissue induced by cold or by diet can, under certain conditions, be a major component of overall energy expenditure. One or another type of defect in control of thermogenesis in brown adipose tissue has been identified in most animal models of obesity. The consequent deficit in energy expenditure is believed to contribute to a high metabolic efficiency and thus to the development of obesity in these animals (for a review see Himms-Hagen, (61) (62)). In studies with lean and obese mice the thermogenic activity of BAT was substantially increased by feeding maize oil in both mice types and it was concluded that energy balance in lean and obese mice is influenced by dietary lipid composition; this may involve a stimulator effect of PUFAs on thermogenesis in BAT (63). Obviously this result would be of considerable significance as would be those of Himms-Hagen above if the same principle applied in humans. Cunningham et al (64) on assessing the respiratory capabilities of the total perinephric fat found in non-obese man indicated that in the average adult this fat would account for less than 0.2% of the increase in oxygen consumption during noradrenaline stimulation.

In the rodent, 25% of the total brown fat is perirenal (65). Although the proportions of brown fat located in the different depots of adult man have yet to be precisely determined, the dissections (64) of whole man and the work of others (66, 67) would indicate that the perinephric area is the major site of brown fat in man. One would have to assume, unrealistically, that other depots of brown fat had an aggregate thermogenic capacity more than one-hundred fold greater than the perinephric site for this tissue to have relevance to any thermogenic defect in obese man. The situation in man contrasts with that in rodents, where brown fat thermogenesis accounts for almost all the extra heat produced in response to noradrenaline both in cold adaptation (68) and in overfeeding (69). It seems, therefore, at this point in time that thermogenesis involving BAT is less likely (70) to be the major explanation for the non-storage of excess energy in lean man.

Dietary fibre has also been implicated in 'weight control' through its possible effects on rate of gastric emptying, appetite control, satiety, and rate of carbohydrate absorption (71), and its affect on bowel transit time (72) and on fermentation in the gut. However, although in the final analysis obesity is related to a disturbance in energy balance, the mechanisms by which this process occurs, or could be reversed by dietary fibre, are not clear. In short-term studies, fibre-rich diets or supplements (fruits, vegetables, whole grains and probably guar gum) have been shown to achieve increased satiety (reported subjectively) and, in a very few studies, to contribute to modest weight loss. There is little information on whether these high fibre diets or fibre preparations would be acceptable for long-term use. The evidence to date is in no way sufficient either to establish weight reduction as a physiological effect of dietary fibre, or to determine the role of dietary fibre in weight loss preparations. Therefore, long-term controlled clinical studies testing the effects of different forms of dietary fibre in uncomplicated obesity are urgently needed (22).

The importance of maintaining ideal body weight for health has been

stressed by a number of expert groups (see CHAPTER 2) and the recent NACNE
report (5) suggests that even mild overweight is, on a public health basis,
important; a panel of nutritionists and doctors met at the National
Institute of Health in 1985 and concluded that even being 20% above
desirable body weight constituted an established health hazard (11).
However, not all evidence points in this direction. For example, in none
of the areas of the 7 - countries study (73) was overweight or obesity a
major risk factor for death or for the incidence of CHD and the conclusion
was made that overweight and obesity are much less serious risk factors
than popularly supposed and suggested by the older reports from the life
insurance industry; similarly Oliver (74) showed that when relevant
covariables (fat, cholesterol, salt) were factored out in a multivariate
analysis, obesity had a weak relationship to CHD. The US Committee on
Diet, Nutrition and Cancer (32) says of total caloric intake:

"neither the epidemiological studies nor the experiments
in animals permit a clear interpretation of the specific
effect of total caloric intake on the risk of cancer".

There is also some doubt as to what is ideal weight. For example a new
'ideal' weights table introduced by Seltzer in 1983 (75) revealed that
adults can weigh more than their 1959 counterparts and still expect
favourable longevity; however, in a debate highlighted in the International
Herald Tribune Walford said that long term undernutrition (as distinct from
malnutrition) retards ageing and extends the maximum lifespan of warm
blooded animals; he concludes that this finding is applicable to humans
because it worked in every animal species thus so far studied.

Despite the amount of research carried out on the response to over-
nutrition in man, there is no clear answer to the precise mechanisms

operating. This will remain a topic of extreme importance in the future.
It is likely that genetic factors may play a major part in individual
response to food intake. However, as overweight can be such a major social
and health problem in developed countries, it is essential that
mechanisms/pathways of energy use in humans should be studied further. Van
Itallie (76) points out that it is widely assumed that obesity has adverse
effects on health and, as a corollary, that the prevention or successful
treatment of obesity has distinct health benefits. But when these facile
assertions are examined critically, it is found that, like so many other
generalities, they must be qualified when applied to specific situations.

1.3.3   Carbohydrate and dietary fibre

1.3.3.1 Carbohydrate: Most   modern   reports   on   dietary
guidelines/recommendations for developed countries (see CHAPTER 2) suggest
an increased consumption of complex carbohydrate. High protein low calorie
diets in vogue in the late 1960s and early 1970s gave carbohydrates a bad
name as 'fattening, lots of calories' etc. However, carbohydrates from
unrefined whole foods (complex carbohydrate) are not a concentrated source
of energy. The status of complex carbohydrate in human nutrition terms is,
therefore, now high. However, excessively high carbohydrate intakes can
induce hypertryglyceridemia and raise VLDL (very low density lipo-protein)
fractions (77). A crucial issue not yet resolved is whether the rise in
triglycerides that occurs when carbohydrate is substituted for fat is
transient or permanent. Most epidemiologic data suggest it is transient.
Evidence for a relationship between hypertryglyceridemia and CHD is
inconclusive and the topic is being actively studied and debated. Much of
the   current   interest   centres   around   rate   of   absorption;   complex

carbohydrates in whole foods in addition to being complex molecules which have to be broken down before absorption are also 'packaged'. For example in potatoes the starch grains are in cells and so are not immediately accessible for attack by digestive enzymes; energy is thus released more slowly; this has been illustrated clearly in the classical apple experiment of Haber et al (78) in which insulin response decreased in going from apple juice to purée to whole apples. Heaton (71) claims that any dietary change which leads to increased insulin secretion deserves to be considered fattening. On this basis, ingestion of complex carbohydrate reduces insulin response while refined carbohydrate does the opposite. Gee and Johnson (79) have studied the in vitro digestion of a number of starches and the results (Table 3) show that the rates vary considerably.

TABLE 3: Carbohydrate content and rate of hydrolysis

Food	Free sugars (g 100 g^{-1})	Starch (g 100 g^{-1})	Dietary fibre content (g 100 g^{-1})	Half time for hydrolysis (min)
Potato starch	1.96	98.0	0	2.8
Maize starch	0	90.3	0	1.0
White rice	0.34	88.9	1.8	2.1
White bread	6.50	75.4	4.3	19.5
Porridge oats	2.80	67.4	9.4	8.0
Potatoes	5.53	88.9	9.9	1.2
Peas	22.50	12.1	19.0	60.0
Lentils	3.04	49.2	26.0	68.0
Butter beans	3.74	38.8	31.3	156.0
Red kidney beans	6.20	31.4	36.6	58.0
Baked beans (tinned)	15.80	34.6	49.4	120.0

Data of Gee and Johnson, J. Sci. Food Agric., 1985, 36, 614-620.
Results on a dry matter basis

This provides strong support for the view that the observed variation in the human glycaemic response to various starch-rich foods depends primarily upon differences in the rate of starch hydrolysis. Furthermore, the digestion method facilitated the comparison of initial rates of carbohydrate release and indicated that these may vary more markedly between different foods than the studies by other workers have suggested. This is particularly important in the light of experimental evidence demonstrating that the initial rate of glucose absorption governs the rate of appearance of glucose in the blood and the consequent hormonal response in man. However, it must be stressed that these were in vitro studies. The slow, and in some cases incomplete, hydrolysis of starch in some foods suggests the presence of resistant forms of starch which would escape degradation in the small intestine but would be estimated chemically as starch. This could lead to incorrect assessment of the energy available from the diet and influence the microflora of the large intestine (see 'bad converter', section 1.3.2). These results could have application also in the case of the wide range of hydrocolloids (e.g. xanthan gum) now being added to foods for water control and mouth feel. Presumably these also have relatively slow hydrolysis rates and could affect the rate of absorption of free sugars in the same system.

Dreher et al (80) have carried out a major review on 'the starch digestibility of foods - a nutritional perspective' containing 463 references. This extensive bibliography in itself is a reflection of the complexity of this area. They conclude that dietary starch varies greatly in digestibility; poor digestibility of starch may have negative effects on the utilisation of protein and minerals but is likely to reduce the requirement for B-vitamins; this may be due to the increased synthesis of B vitamins by intestinal microorganisms in the presence of low-soluble starches.

A recent paper by Jenkins et al (81) concludes that to a very large extent the energy from carbohydrate foods is made available after absorption at some point along the gastrointestinal tract either as sugars (e.g. glucose, fructose, galactose, etc) in the small intestine or as short chain fatty acids (SCFA) (together with alcohol and lactate) in the colon. The distinction between dietary fibre and 'available carbohydrate', although of great importance, must be seen in these terms.

The undesirable health effects of carbohydrates have largely been ascribed to the excessive consumption of sucrose which has been cited as a major factor in the aetiology of dental caries, obesity, diabetes and CHD. The consumption of sucrose in a solid sticky form between meals increases the incidence of caries (82). Carbohydrates per se are not more likely to result in obesity than fats when consumed in excess; however, excessive consumption of sucrose-rich foods can displace other foods which supply essential nutrients. The available epidemiological evidence does not support the concept that excessive sugar consumption is a factor in producing diabetes (83); more recently complex carbohydrate (84, 85) has been used to successfully treat mild forms of diabetes. Neither has a relationship been found between sugar consumption and CHD (86); however, in turn sugar could lead to obesity thereby predisposing the person to CHD. Carbohydrates are not implicated (32) directly in carcinogenesis; however, excessive carbohydrates can contribute to caloric excess, and this in turn has been implicated as a modifier of carcinogenesis.

The message for the future is, therefore, that complex carbohydrate is good for the human system. However, carbohydrate intakes above 60% of calories, especially when displacing fat, may be undesirable in view of the tendency towards hypertriglyceridemia and increasing VLDL levels. The adverse effects of excessive sugar intake are dental caries and a risk of obesity.

Further aspects of sugar and glucose syrups will be discussed in section 1.5.

1.3.3.2   Dietary fibre (DF): is largely composed of complex carbohydrate and is undoubtedly one of the major issues to take the developed world by storm in recent years.   The present status of DF among nutritionists is high and intakes in the region of 30 g/head/day are being advocated by expert groups (See CHAPTER 2).   The 'fibre hypothesis' of Burkitt and Trowell (3) suggested that the consumption of unrefined, high fibre carbohydrate foods protected against many 'Western' ailments including: colon cancer, diverticular disease, appendicitis, constipation, hemorrhoids, hiatus hernia, varicose veins, diabetes, heart disease, gallstones, obesity and many others. As they stood, these claims appeared too extensive to be valid.   For example, rates for colon cancer and diverticular disease in Japan are still, despite recent post war changes, some of the lowest in the World and the rates for cancer in migrants change to those of the host country within one or two generations (87).   Fibre cannot be the only reason for these low rates as intake of DF in Japan at 20 g per head per day is no greater than in the UK, USA and New Zealand which have the highest colon cancer rates in the world (88).   In addition many nutritional differences exist between Western nations and the more primitive communities in which Burkitts' observations originated.   Thus the exact importance of dietary fibre per se will be debated for some time to come.   Extensive basic laboratory data and clinical evidence has been gathered in support of the hypothesis and has had an impact on the management of constipation, diverticular disease, diabetes, hyperlipidemia and obesity (72).

The name dietary fibre (DF) itself is even under question and is now sometimes defined as non-starch polysaccharide with lignin (88); however, the term DF will continue to be used in this paper. Many terms are applied to fibre, for example dietary fibre, crude fibre (CF), acid detergent fibre (ADF), neutral detergent fibre (NDF) and others. However, these terms reflect different analytical methodologies and not physiologically-distinct types of dietary fibre. The fibre term most used is dietary fibre (DF) and the DF content of a food is usually greater, and in the case of some foods much greater, than the corresponding CF, ADF or NDF values. Therefore, it is difficult to compare the fibre content of a food that is reported as DF by one laboratory and as ADF by another.

The food source influences the composition of DF. For example, wheat bran contains about 48% DF (89); the DF is mostly hemicellulose, cellulose and lignin - it contains no pectin. In contrast, DF from fruit and to a lesser extent from vegetables contains pectin.

The beneficial effect of DF in the diet has received extensive media coverage over the last few years and will not be enlarged upon here. In summary, it increases faecal weight, reduces bowel transit time and may protect against certain diseases of the digestive tract (3); bran is particularly effective in this respect.

The multiplicity of analytical procedures for DF itself continue to confuse, and results vary dramatically depending on the method used; collaborative trials by Cummings et al (95) illustrate this point clearly.

Soluble DF is being regarded as increasingly important.   Some of this type of DF is hemicellulosic in nature;   that contained in oats (β-glucans) is being advocated as the possible key constituent in oats in relation to controlling some forms of diabetes (90).

More recently it has been shown that certain forms of DF, (pectin for example) can reduce serum cholesterol in humans (91); dietary fibre is being used increasingly in the control of late maturity onset diabetes (78, 85, 92).

The   properties of DF such as water holding capacity and its interactions with available carbohydrate, protein and fat make it useful in weight control and in calorie diluted products.   Interactions of DF with minerals are generally only modest.   So serious depletion is not a problem in individuals consuming a good mixed diet; however, these interactions must be carefully monitored in the different food/fibre systems since certain groups or individuals within the population may be at, or near, marginal intakes of some minerals (93). A review on DF and bioavailability by Staub et al (93) suggests that although no risks are seen it is prudent to continue experimental and clinical observations with fibre/fibre-containing products at realistic levels of intake.

There is a problem where measuring DF is concerned.   DF is almost a philosophical   concept rather than a biological material.   Chemical compositions are often variable and unknown.   Hence assay procedures are often empirical and sometimes produce different results from laboratory to laboratory.   The kernel of the problem is to obtain an 'enzyme cocktail' which degrades a given food in a similar fashion to the human digestive tract.   A number of enzyme and related procedures have been used and these have been reviewed by Asp and Johansson (94) and compared by Cummings et al

(95). One of the most recent systems is semi-automatic and uses a larger sample size - which is a big advantage - it is called the Tecator Fibretec E and uses a heat stable, broad-specificity protease and a heat-stable amylase preparation (Termamyl) (96). The procedure measures both soluble and insoluble DF and can be applied to a wide range of food products; it gives results similar to other methods. In starchy foods, such as bread, the assay is more complex because of the difficulty in removing all the starch and also because 'resistant' starch may be formed during baking. It is possible that some of the 'resistant' starch may be indigestible and so would contribute to the DF content of a food.

Asp et al (97) have described procedures for measuring resistant starch in wholemeal flour and in bread. A similar situation may occur during the toasting of bread where interactions between starch and protein result in an indigestible residue which is classed as DF.

Dietary fibre is used extensively in food product formulation (98). For example, bran is added to flour and the great upsurge in the use of extrusion and extrusion cooking has led to a wide range of products containing bran and other forms of DF. One look at the breakfast cereal counter in the supermarket illustrates this point clearly. There is also an increasing use of gums in a wide range of food products as stabilisers, thickeners, and for other purposes. These include guar, arabic, tragacanth, alginate, xanthan, and other gums. They contribute to the DF content of the food system into which they have been incorporated.

A number of studies (98, 99) have shown that the DF content of foods is usually increased by processing/cooking. This may be due to condensation reactions between constituents in the food - notably carbohydrates and proteins. However, DF fractions may also be lost during cooking as in the case of water soluble pectin in the cooking of fruits. The action of processing or cooking on the physical nature of DF may be more important than the small increases/losses mentioned above. Much of the action of DF is 'physical/chemical' and may depend on physical sites being available in the fibre matrix for the various functions of DF, for example water and mineral binding. The effects of cooking/processing foods on the 'physical/chemical' properties of DF have not been quantified satisfactorily and more research is needed in this area.

In addition to using dietary fibre sources/concentrates such as bran as a food ingredient, purified fibre supplements are also used. There is some concern (22) that insoluble cellulosic components may selectively deplete colonic flora of specific bacterial types; purified cellulose decreases faecal water and causes uncomfortable defaecation (100) while micro-crystalline cellulose has been reported to be persorbed into the circulation (101). There are also reports that dietary agar (102) or corn bran (103) added to the diet of rodents may enhance, rather than retard, the development of chemically-induced colonic tumours. These data serve warning that certain forms of DF could have toxicological effects.

Despite the amount of work on the subject there is still insufficient hard information available on the direct effect of DF on specific diseases and we still have to use phrases such as 'it seems that __' or 'DF may influence__' etc. The following are excerpts from a 1985 report (22) of the Expert Advisory Committee of Canada on DF which relate to effects of DF on specific diseases:

a) certain cereal fibres can be effective, in the short term in
   normalising colonic function by preventing or treating constipation,
   and possibly in the long term in reducing the incidence of
   diverticular disease

b) the type of fibre ingested determines hypocholesterolaemic action;
    in general gelling fibres are most effective in lowering <u>blood
    lipids</u> and in flattening the post-prandial glucose curve

c) raising DF and carbohydrate levels in the diabetic diet gives
    improved <u>diabetic control</u> and reduced serum <u>cholesterol levels</u>

d) fibre rich diets have been shown to achieve increased <u>satiety</u> and,
    <u>in a very few studies</u>, to contribute to <u>modest weight loss</u>.

e) at the present time, the effects of DF on the <u>availability</u> of
    minerals other than Ca, Mg, P, Zn and Fe have not been systematically
    investigated and so no conclusions can be drawn

f) potential toxicological effects of some forms of DF need to be
    studied/confirmed

The report (22) summarises succinctly the present status and future issues in the DF area and concludes that more information is urgently needed on all the issues debated. Specific areas include: comparison of different methods of analysis, physiological effects of fibre in foods, effects of fibre on the absorption of macro-minerals, trace elements and vitamins, and possible toxic effects of fibre. In addition, further information is required to allow accurate prediction of the effects of purified fibre added to foods.

1.3.4   Protein

Relative to carbohydrates and fats there is less controversy about the current status of protein in the diet in developed countries. In these countries intakes are usually in excess of requirements, although in any population there will be groups who are deficient. The image of protein is that of a growth and tissue builder but a large excess of protein in the diet may be undesirable.

The NACNE report (5) states that it would do people 'no harm' (in the UK that is) to eat a little less protein and that more protein should be eaten from plant sources as animal protein is often associated with fat. The Committee on Diet, Nutrition and Cancer USA (Assembly of Life Sciences) (32) states that evidence from both epidemiological and laboratory studies suggests that high protein intake may be associated with an increased risk of cancer at certain sites. The problem from an epidemiological approach is correlations between food constituents. For example Armstrong and Doll (104) examined the incidence rates for 27 cancers in 23 countries and mortality rates for 14 cancers in 32 countries and correlated them with per capita intake of a wide range of dietary/constituents and environmental factors. However, they found that the correlations of total protein and animal protein with total fat were 0.70 and 0.93 respectively. Significant correlations have been found for protein intakes and the incidence of certain cancers but the inseparable relationship of protein with fat must be borne in mind all the time. Examples of cancers associated with protein intakes (and in some cases more specifically meat protein intakes) are breast (105, 106), large bowel (107) and pancreatic (108).

In experiments on laboratory animals, the relationship of dietary protein to carcinogenesis seems to depend upon the level of protein intake (32). In most cases carcinogenesis was suppressed by diets containing levels of protein at or below the minimum required for optimum growth. Chemically-induced (109) (for example, feeding aflatoxin) carcinogenesis appears to be enhanced as protein intake is increased up to 2-3 times the normal requirement; however, higher levels of protein begin to inhibit carcinogenesis.

While it is claimed that, at least in some countries, protein intakes have remained relatively static in recent times (110) there is evidence that the meat component of this has increased significantly (111, 112).

This could be of significance in relation to the discussion above.

Extremes of protein intake in man can be very damaging; for example high protein/low calorie diets have caused death in some instances, and diets and/or foods which promote this concept should be used with great care (9). It has been shown that high protein and fibre diets may also affect mineral metabolism (113). In recent studies volunteers on a high protein diet retained more zinc than they retained from a low protein diet but those on the high protein diet also had a higher zinc requirement.

Because of the relative paucity of data compared with fat and the problems with the epidemiology outlined above, the US Committee (32) was unable to arrive at a firm conclusion about an independent effect of protein on cancer. However, based on this and some of the other discussion above the inquiring observer is left with a slightly uneasy feeling about the desirability of high protein intakes and must pose the question:

*has too much emphasis been put on fat intakes and too little on an upper limit for protein intake (and also protein source) in developed countries? The answer is probably yes.

1.3.5 Fat and cholesterol

Of all the health issues, these are probably the most debated in present times. The major questions are what is the effect of fat/cholesterol on the development of atherosclerosis, CHD and cancer. These issues have been debated again and again with volumes written about them. However, the purpose here is not to give an exhaustive treatment of the subject but rather to seek some of the current highlights. Scientific precision relating to making a minimum recommendation for fat intake is limited but any community which wishes to feed well and in a civilised tradition should obtain at least 20% of its energy from fat (113). Edible fats are of nutritional significance in several respects. Firstly, they are a carrier for fat soluble vitamins A, D, E and K; secondly, they are a concentrated energy source providing 37 kJ per gram compared with 16 kJ per gram for carbohydrate and 17 kJ per gram for protein. In Western countries the high energy density of fat is often considered to be less desirable because of the prevalence of obesity. Fat does, however, provide a high degree of satiety, and there is no clear evidence that increased fat in the diet leads to an increase in total energy intake.

A third aspect of fat in nutrition is the supply of the essential fatty acids, linoleic acid and linolenic acid. These two polyunsaturated fatty acids must be supplied in the diet for the avoidance of deficiency symptoms. These symptoms include reduced growth in infants, abnormal skin conditions, increased susceptibility to infection, sterility and poor healing of surgical wounds. Essential fatty acid deficiency is very rare since it only occurs if the intake falls below 1% of total energy intake. A minimum of 3% of this energy should be supplied by the essential fatty acids to ensure the avoidance of deficiency disorders (114).

Many expert committees suggest a decrease in fat intake, from the high levels of ca 40% of energy intake pertaining in some European countries, and an increase in polyunsaturated (PUFA) to saturated fat (SF) ratio (see CHAPTER 2). There is a degree of consensus between experts in developed countries, therefore, that fat intakes are too high at this point in time. It is difficult to oppose this tide of opinion; however many of the aspects regarding the affect of SF and PUFA on human health are far from clearcut.

Similarly cholesterol has got a 'bad press' with many consumers seeking to shun foods containing cholesterol.

Major documents/books/publications dealing in depth with the fat issue, in addition to guideline/recommendations documents (see CHAPTER 2), include an EEC (DG VI) study on the 'Influence on Health of Different Fats in Food' (38), 'Fats and Health - why the experts don't agree' - WHICH Magazine (115), 'The Role of Fats in Human Nutrition' - a book edited by Padley et al (116), 'Fats in the Diet - why and where'? - a Scientific Status Summary by the Institute of Food Technologists' (USA) Expert Panel on Food Safety and Health (117), 'Prevention of CHD - Diet and the Food Supply' - AFT report (118). These are just a few of very many.

The summary and conclusions of the EEC document published in 1977 on fats (38) mentioned above make important reading. One of the main conclusions was that insufficient and contradictory information, at the European level, on the origins of CHD had left consumers in a confused state. The same sentiments have been voiced by Ahrens (29) in 1985, i.e. eight years after the EEC report, when he asks "The Diet Heart Question in 1985: has it really been settled"? It seems, therefore, that in 1986 the real position is still unclear.

1.3.5.1 Fat, cholesterol and CHD: A modification of the lipid hypothesis of Keys (119) as enlarged by Truswell (120) is shown in Fig. 2 and outlines some of the components involved in CHD and their possible interrelationship.

There are two ways in which fat can affect CHD. One factor leading to the occurrence of CHD is atherosclerosis which is a narrowing of the arteries caused by an accumulation of a variable combination of lipids,

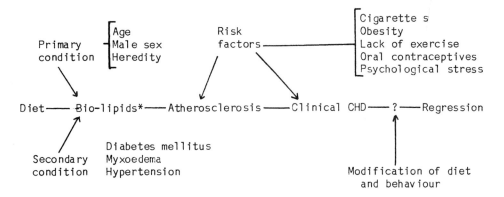

*Plasma cholesterol and the distribution of the cholesterol pool

Fig. 2: Augmented dietary fat hypothesis (According to Truswell, 120)

complex carbohydrate, blood and blood products, fibrous tissue and calcium deposits. Atherosclerosis does not appear overnight but over a long period of time (118). There is extensive epidemiological evidence (121) that populations that have high dietary saturated fat intakes have high cholesterol levels and high levels of CHD. However, there is a paucity of firm data that show clearly that high fat intake causes atherosclerosis in humans. In fact, there are some studies that suggest the opposite. The Boston/Ireland Heart Study (122) showed that Irish men had a higher caloric intake than their Boston brothers but fat percent of calories was virtually the same i.e. 38 vs 39%; the Irish ingested more of their fat from meat while blood pressure and smoking habits were the same for both groups. Yet, there was a higher mortality from atherosclerotic heart disease in Boston than in Ireland and the authors suggest that differences in physical activity seemed the likely cause of the effect, i.e. the Irish were much more active. These data also suggest that while the mean values for plasma cholesterol concentrations are often seen as related to incidence of CHD, the wide scatter within a population cannot be attributed to fat intake. Harper in the USA (123) suggests that there has been no dietary change in the USA which could account for any trends in heart disease mortality. He claims that mortality statistics in the USA show that CHD (or its equivalent) increased from the 1940s to 1968 and then fell; during this period animal fat and saturated fat intakes were static (124). Between 1968 (CHD re-defined) and 1980 when CHD declined, total fat intake continued to rise until 1972, declined slightly until 1980 (117) and then rose to a new peak in 1981.

More attention should be given to genetic aspects affecting atherosclerosis. The recent Nobel Prize winning study of Brown and Goldstein (125) highlights this point and shows the affect of an abnormal low-density lipoprotein receptor gene on cholesterol deposition and atherosclerosis. It also highlights the need for a much better understanding of the biochemistry of heart disease.

About 80% of cholesterol is synthesised in the body, the remainder being obtained from the diet. However, Keys (119) suggested that in adult man the serum cholesterol level is essentially independent of the cholesterol intake over the whole range of natural human diets. Results from the Tecumseh study (126) indicated a similar effect. i.e. that in the population in general, dietary cholesterol is not the principle element that controls the concentration of cholesterol in the blood. Brisson (127) reports results of a number of experiments indicating that ingestion of dietary cholesterol has little or no influence on levels in serum. These data challenge the prudence of the massive campaign now initiated in the USA (29) to reduce national plasma cholesterol levels - presumably by dietary means; the proposal is that the reductions be undertaken by everyone over two years of age. This step is also surprising in view of other evidence relating to cholesterol as a risk factor in CHD. For example, one of the conclusions of the 7 - countries study was that it appears that serum cholesterol concentration is a CHD risk factor at levels of 220 mg/dl or more; at levels below 200 mg/dl decreasing cholesterol concentrations tended to be associated with increasing rates of non-coronary death (73). On the basis of the Pooling project in the USA and correcting for age, Oliver (128, 129) suggested that the optimum serum cholesterol concentration is probably in the region of 200-220 mg/dl. This suggests that cholesterol lowering by dietary or other means is only desirable in those with values above 220 mg/dl. This is endorsed by recent criticism of the lipid hypothesis (that CHD will drop if plasma cholesterol levels are reduced) by Ahrens (29). He points out that over the past 25 years this hypothesis has been put to the test in more than 20 trials which attempted to lower plasma cholesterol levels by dietary manipulations or by the administration of plasma-cholesterol-lowering drugs. Only the Lipid Research Clinic's Coronary Primary Prevention Trial (LRC-CPPT) (130) produced evidence for benefit that was any more than suggestive. The CPPT was a drug and not a dietary trial. It should be noted that all of the 3806 men who entered the trial had cholesterol levels above 265 mg/dl. The cholesterol lowering (cholestyramine resin) resulted in a 24% reduction in risk of CHD death and a 19% reduction in risk of CHD disease and/or definite mycocardial infarction. The LRC-CPPT raises the issue of the actual regression of atherosclerotic lesions. Gotto in 1977 (131) claimed that the relationship between the concentration of plasma cholesterol and atherosclerosis is a continuous one but did not demonstrate regression in his arguments. In 1984 in a statement published in Nutrition Reviews (132) he outlined the two serious outstanding issues surrounding the lipid CHD hypothesis i.e. lack of evidence that regression of atherosclerotic plaque can occur if serum cholesterol is reduced and secondly a causal link between plasma cholesterol and incidence of CHD risk. Regarding the first he quoted results from a 1984 study as follows:

"In the NHLBI Type 11 Coronary Intervention Study," (Circulation 69: 313-337, 1984) 116 men with atherosclerosis and high plasma cholesterol were given a low fat diet designed to lower plasma cholesterol levels. Half of the men, in addition, took a cholesterol-lowering drug. This group experienced 21 percent lower cholesterol levels than did the controls. Although the researchers detected regression of the plaques in a few patients, it was clear that the growth of the plaques slowed or stopped in many patients. This was particularly true in the larger plaques that had narrowed the coronary arteries by 50 percent or more".

A personal communication from James (133) in 1986 indicated that there is still insufficient evidence to confirm that regression of atherosclerosis occurs upon lowering serum cholesterol. On the second point above Gotto (132) claims that the LRC-CPPT trial provides the first CONCLUSIVE evidence that reducing total serum cholesterol in high risk men can decrease the incidence of CHD death in men; he also claims that the results of this trial are the STRONGEST EVIDENCE to date that lipids have a causal role in the development of atherosclerosis and CHD.

One of the problems is the absence of good non-invasive screening techniques for measuring atherosclerosis in the coronary arteries. An angiogram will give the required information but it is not a screening technique and the test itself carries a degree of risk. Doppler ultrasound will measure atherosclerosis in the aorta and peripheral arteries but not in the coronary arteries. It seems, therefore, that non-invasory imaging of coronary arteries will not come 'on stream' for some years yet.

The second way in which fat can influence the development of CHD is by affecting the probability of formation of a blood clot - or thrombus - in the coronary arteries; it seems, therefore, that atherosclerosis on its own will not induce a heart attack (134). The saturated fat theory seeks to explain the increase in CHD largely in terms of an increase in atherosclerosis on a population basis. However, the work of Morris (135) based on the results of post-mortem examination of some 6000 patients aged 30-69 dying in London from 1908-1959 indicates that there was no deterioration in the coronary arteries of the population in the period 1908-1949 in spite of a 7 - fold increase in CHD over this period. Taylor (134) suggests that this increase may be due to an increase in thrombosis rather than atherosclerosis and so is influenced by platelet function. Platelet aggregation is promoted by thromboxanes (TXAs) and inhibited by prostacyclins, and a suggested biosynthetic pathway to these compounds is shown in Fig. 3; the '2' series originates from the 18:2 w-6 fatty acids and the '3' series from 18:3 acids. A recent review article (136) while supporting the general approach of Taylor above says that the precise mechanism by which the w-3 fatty acids exert their effect on platelet activity and VLDL biosynthesis is still unclear. Taylor (134) also points out that fatty acids of the w-6 series cannot be converted to acids of the w-3 series by man or the higher animals. It is important, therefore, that these be obtained in the diet as they confer anti-clotting properties in

Fig. 3: Metabolism of some polyunsaturated fatty acids

(According to Taylor (134))

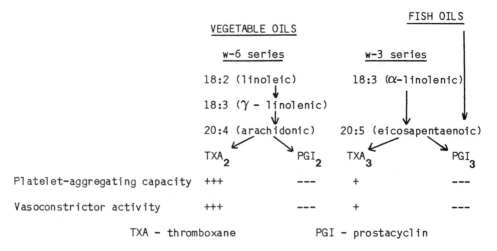

	TXA$_2$	PGI$_2$	TXA$_3$	PGI$_3$
Platelet-aggregating capacity	+++	---	+	---
Vasoconstrictor activity	+++	---	+	---

TXA - thromboxane   PGI - prostacyclin

Number of positive or negative signs indicate the potency of the compound in, respectively, promoting or inhibiting the particular physiological action

the blood (Fig. 3). It has been shown that Eskimos, whose diet is particularly rich in fatty acids of the w-3 series derived either directly or indirectly from fish, show a very long clotting time compared with the blood of Danes (137) who consume a Western type diet. The effect of the w-3 PUFA acids on platelet function has also been reviewed by Gottenbos (139). These findings suggest that one should encourage diets containing w-3 series PUFA rather than just a blanket PUFA recommendation. Crawford and Sanders at a recent symposium on Fats in Human Nutrition (UK, Society of Chemical Industry - Oils and Fats group) reported on by Gordon (138) spoke strongly in favour of a balance in dietary PUFA between the w-6 and w-3 acids. The ratio of w6/w3 acids in the UK in 1984 was about 13:1; this compares to a ratio of 4.8:1 in human milk. A low w6/w3 ratio is therefore desirable and Sanders claimed that the consumption of one mackerel/day would reduce the production of TXA_2 (see Fig. 3) thereby making the blood less likely to clot. The data (Table 4) show the fat composition of some common foods. The figures show that soft margarine and corn oil come out particularly badly on w6/w3 ratio while herring comes out very well.

TABLE 4: Fat content and composition of common foods[1] (g/100g food)

Foodstuff	Fat content	Saturated fat	w-6 acids	w-3 acids	P:S ratio	w-6:w-3 ratio
Corn oil	100	16.4	47.8	1.5	0.3	31.2
Soyabean oil	100	14.1	49.7	7.1	4.0	7.0
Butter	77.3	49.0	1.1	1.2	0.05	0.9
Margarine (hard)[2]	77.4	29.8	7.7	0.4	0.3	19.7
Margarine[2] (polyunsaturated)	77.5	19.1	41.6	1.5	2.2	77
Pork chop	27.1	11.7	2.0	0.25	0.2	8.1
Herring	16.3	3.7	1.2	7.0	0.9	0.2
Madeira cake	15.9	8.8	1.5	-	0.2	high
Ice cream (dairy)	6.2	4.3	0.1	0.1	0.05	1.7
Wholemeal bread	2.1	0.5	1.1	0.1	2.1	12.6

[1]Data in Table 4 according to Paul et al., 1st suppl. to McCance & Widdowson's The Composition of Foods, 1980, HMSO.
[2]Also contains trans unsaturated fatty acids

The benefits of fish in relation to CHD have also been noted in a recent study in the Netherlands (140) where men who ate fish regularly (2 dishes/week) had less CHD after 20 years than those that ate little. The fish eaten by the men was one third fatty and two thirds white. The importance of eicosapentaenoic and docosahexaenoic acids have been reviewed recently by Sanders (141); he also adds caution concerning consuming large amounts of fish oil notably from mackerel and herring as these oils contain a proportion of cetoleic (22:1 w-11) acid which can cause a transient mycocardial lipidolysis similar to that caused by erucic acid in several species of experimental animals. Eicosapentaenoic acid ('fatty fish acid') has also been shown to markedly reduce both systolic and diastolic blood pressure in normotensives; in hypertensive and hyperlipemic subjects only systolic blood pressure was reduced (142).

The use of PUFA - as in margarines - for reducing serum cholesterol and influencing atherosclerosis has received extensive coverage in recent years. The major National Diet Heart Study (National Diet Heart Study Group) used 100 healthy men and a P/S ratio which was four times higher than in the control diet (143, 127); this intake induced a drop in serum cholesterol of only 9% and Brisson (127) concludes:

> "It appears that such a drastic change in diet with such a little effect on serum cholesterol would be of little interest for the population at large especially in view of the fact that the very significance of the relationship between serum cholesterol and coronary heart disease is put to serious question".

and makes six points based on his own conclusions and those of Ahrens (144) in relation to possible adverse effects in the diet of excess linoleic acid and PUFA:

a) they may affect the permeability of cell membranes

b) they may bring about an imbalance between different prostaglandins which play a role in blood coagulation

c) they may bring about early ageing of certain types of cells

d) they may accelerate the development of cancer in mammary glands

e) PUFA tends to lower HDL cholesterol (high density lipoprotein cholesterol = "good cholesterol")

f) PUFA may interfere with the immune system

The material presented in this section (1.3.5.1) on fat, cholesterol and
CHD illustrates the lack of clarity and conclusiveness in most of the major
issues despite the vast volume of research (and money spent) worldwide on
the topic. The evidence suggests that while lowering cholesterol in people
with elevated levels may reduce CHD, the value of doing this on a population
basis seems small to non-existant. The future seems to lie in a better
understanding of the genetic aspects and the various lipoproteins
associated with cholesterol, and also to identify and then treat those
people who have high cholesterol values and may be at risk. Continuing
research on the antithrombotic effects of the w3-acids is a major priority.

1.3.5.2   Fat, cholesterol and cancer: Most of the research activity in
this field has hinged around epidemiological and laboratory animal studies.
Cancers most associated with fat intake are those of the breast, prostate
and large bowel. For example Doll and Petro (145) have shown the
correlation between fat consumption and breast cancer on a country basis
which ranged from about 26 per 100,000 of population in Holland to about 3
in Japan - an eight-fold difference. Corresponding fat intakes were about
145 and 42 g/person/day respectively. Ableson (146) claims that rancid
fats are one of the problems and account for a substantial fraction of all
the cancer deaths in the USA. Unsaturated fats are easily oxidised on
standing and in cooking to form mutagens, radical promoters and
carcinogens. Among the numerous products of such oxidations are fatty acid
hydroperoxides and cholesterol epoxide. Thus the colon and digestive tract
are exposed to many fat-derived carcinogens.

This has resulted in some caution about high intakes of PUFA in the
diet (5). Ahrens (144) has also warned about some of the possible dangers
of excess PUFA in relation to cancer. Comparisons of colonic cancer

incidence in Japan and the USA are striking. In Japan, where total fat constituted only 10% of calories in the daily diet, colon cancer incidence was about one fifth of the incidence in the USA where fat constitutes roughly 40% of daily calories (147). More and more Japanese are now following Western eating habits and, on average, fat is now 25% of daily calories and colon cancer is now increasing in Japan (together with an even more rapid reduction in stomach cancer) (158). Although the general correlation between fat intake and colon cancer is good, the correlation breaks down in neighbouring countries. As an example, in Finland, colon cancer mortality is about one quarter of the mortality in Denmark, whereas the Finns consume about the same amount of fat per day as do the Danes. However, another difference between the Finns and the Danes is that the Finns have more dietary fibre in their diet (149). It is known that a higher fat intake results in a greater excretion of bile acids in the faeces (150). It is also known that under the anaerobic conditions within the intestine, bile acids are metabolised by the anaerobic bacteria present into mutagenic compounds. Excretion of such compounds is indeed correlated with the incidence of colon cancer in several countries (151). In this context the research showing the ability of certain types of dietary fibre to bind bile acids (152) may be particularly relevant (148).

The relationship between dietary cholesterol and cancer is not clear. Many studies of serum cholesterol levels and cancer mortality in human populations have demonstrated an inverse correlation with colon cancer among men but the evidence is not conclusive. Data on cholesterol and cancer risk from studies in animals are too limited to permit any inferences to be drawn.

The whole area of nutrition and cancer has been reviewed by Jansen (153) and by the US Committee on Diet, Nutrition and Cancer (32). The committee concluded that of all the dietary components it studied, the combined epidemiological and experimental (animal studies) evidence is most suggestive for a causal relationship between fat intake and the occurrence of cancer.

1.3.6 Vitamins

An account will not be given here of the status, function and requirement of/for all the vitamins; these can be obtained in any general text (113). In any event the area of vitamins is so large that it could not be dealt with adequately in this section. Instead some of the newer developments will be outlined.

One of the first issues is the bioavailability of vitamins and this was reviewed in 1985 by Brubacher (154). In 1948 Everson et al (155) concluded that 'knowing the content of the diet is only one step towards knowing whether the individual consuming it is well fed'. This statement is still valid today. The term vitamin has a physiological rather than a chemical meaning. Different chemical compounds may give rise to the same kind of physiological activity and are often called vitamers. Vitamins may occur in a food bound to other components. For example, in the case of niacin it has been shown (156) that the major part of the nicotinic acid in cereal grains is in a bound form that is practically unavailable as a source of the vitamin. It was then found (157) that bound niacin in cereals is as an ester with glucose and this is embedded in a glycopeptide macromolecule. Since the ester linkage is alkali labile, nicotinic acid may be liberated by treatment with alkali. This is what occurs in the traditional Central American food practice of exposing maize flour to lime during tortilla manufacture. Factors enhancing or diminishing vitamin absorption are found in all kinds of foods. The absorption of β-carotene and its conversion to vitamin A for instance depends on a diversity of factors, among which the physical/chemical state and the presence of oil are of high importance. β-carotene in raw carrots is very poorly absorbed, whereas β-carotene in an oily solution has a high absorption and conversion rate. Other factors which may influence the bioavailability of vitamins may be the amount of the vitamin ingested. Very high doses of vitamin B_1, B_{12} or vitamin C are only absorbed to a small extent.

From a practical point of view the problems of bioavailability of vitamers, provitamins A, vitamin B_2, folic acid and vitamin B_6 should be urgently investigated. More of scientific interest are questions on vitamins which are partly synthesised in the intestinal tract or in the body, such as vitamin K, vitamin B_2, biotin, folic acid, and niacin.

There has been considerable interest in recent years in the possible inverse link between vitamin A status and the occurrence of certain forms of cancer. Hirayama (158) in a 10 year prospective study of over 250,000 Japanese adults found an association between frequency of green and yellow vegetable consumption and rates of mortality from cancer of different sites. In Japan, green and yellow vegetable consumption accounts for an average 44 and 23% of the typical dietary intake of vitamins A and C respectively. This and other studies (159-161) suggested that vitamin A might be exerting a protective role. However, in all of these studies it is not clear whether it is carotene or another micronutrient which provides the protective effect. However, a currently endorsed hypothesis for a mode of action for carotenoids in cancer prevention is their ability to quench singlet oxygen and in the absence of the latter, as an antioxidant (162, 163).

Fruits and vegetables that contain carotenoids also contain other substances such as plant sterols, phenols and other micronutrients, some of which are also antioxidants (e.g. vitamin C and selenium). These substances as yet have not been ruled out as possible anticancer constituents (161). Ames (164) stresses that just as foods contain anticancer agents, they also contain naturally occurring mutagens and carcinogens. It is likely, therefore, that several substances in the food supply are involved and that it is the relative balance of these in the diet of individuals and populations that determines the outcome. There is also extensive interest in the administration of retinoids at pharmacological levels (165) to inhibit cancer induction; these are usually synthesized and so are not of dietary origin and will not be considered here. Underwood (166) in 1985 suggested that the evidence for an association between vitamin A status and cancer is not yet clearly documented. This is due in part to the unavailability of a good indicator of relative levels of vitamin A in tissues. However, clinical trials now in progress may provide more definitive evidence in the near future. Clearly there is need for additional research to determine the true nature of the association between vitamin A status and cancer prevention before public policy can be reliably made and advice to the public confidently given (166). In the interim, the promotion of a high intake of green and yellow vegetables in European countries will do no harm. Vitamin C also occurs alongside carotene in most green and yellow vegetables; however, very few actual epidemiological data identify vitamin C as the specific factor in fruit and vegetable consumption that accounts for cancer risk reduction (167).

In another context vitamin C has long been known to have a marked stimulating effect on iron absorption but only recently has it emerged from a series of meticulous studies by Hallberg (168) that the vitamin C content of a meal largely determines the amount of non-haem iron absorbed. Sullivan (171) recently suggested that iron storage might be the explanation for the marked sex difference in the incidence of heart disease, with women only showing an increase in the rate of heart disease after the menopause. In traditional terms therefore one can consider the presence of ascorbic acid in diets to be an advantage because it aids iron absorption and prevents anaemia. Vitamin C may also be an important partner for vitamin E as a free radical scavenger which could have a possible link with heart disease (172). James suggests (169) that the finding of Morris et al (86) that individuals consuming whole grain cereals are protected in some way from heart disease could be due to vitamin E which occurs in the germ; vitamin E is an antioxidant and can scavenge free radicals. Substantial falls in vitamin E intake have coincided with the reduced intake of wheat germ (170, 173). Free radical production coupled with iron accumulation could account for membrane damage and might explain not only thrombotic tendencies of platelets but perhaps even the atherosclerotic event itself (169). It is of interest in this context that the fumes of a cigarette are known to be a rich source of free radicals and that smoking is a potent risk factor for coronary artery diseases in countries where the diet is similar to the current British diet. In other countries, e.g. Mediterranean, the oils consumed are low in saturated fats but rich in vitamin E and the rate of heart attacks amongst smokers is little more than in non-smokers (73).

Vitamin K (a naphthoquinone) is noteworthy as it may be involved in bone mineralisation (174). Recently it has become apparent that some elderly people with very fragile bones and fractures (175) (osteoporosis) have a markedly reduced blood concentration of vitamin K. This condition has hitherto been treated with a high calcium diet and sex hormones to reduce the rate of bone resorption. It is now suggested (169) that vitamin K (brassicas, spinach, soya beans, pork, beef liver and kidney are good sources) may be an important factor.

In any discussion on the status of vitamins <u>folic acid</u> must be included as folate deficiency is one of the most common vitamin deficiencies in developed countries especially in women. Diets in many countries are marginal in their folate content. A recent survey (176) concludes that women who use oral contraceptives have impaired folate metabolism, although the effect is mild.

In the future, therefore, research must continue on the deficiency diseases/symptoms associated with low vitamin intakes. However, the greater challenge lies in research probing further the possible role of certain vitamins such as A, E and C in preventing certain forms of cancer and protecting against CHD; the vitamin K/osteoporosis link must also be pursued. The possible major roles for these vitamins shows the importance of eating a balanced diet to ensure an adequate supply. This also poses a major challenge to the area of food processing technology to ensure that techniques used result in maximum vitamin retention.

1.3.7 Minerals and trace elements

As in the case of vitamins only the newer and more recent developments will be discussed. The issue of salt - both sodium and potassium - in relation to hypertension is discussed in section 1.5. It is often said that more is known of the trace element requirements of animals than of humans and this was definitely true in the past but perhaps not so much in the recent past.

Of the major minerals, the role of calcium in osteoporosis and hypertension is receiving increasing attention. The condition of osteoporosis has already been referred to (see 1.3.6) in connection with vitamin K; in a number of European countries at least 10% of people over the age of 50 - and especially women - suffer from this condition. It is caused by accelerated loss of bone and increased susceptibility to fractures. In pre-menopausal women some scientists suggest (177) that the parathyroid hormone stimulates the release of calcium from bone; this releasing effect increases as oestrogen levels fall and the best approach to reducing osteoporosis may be to encourage a balanced diet with adequate calcium during childhood and childbearing years when hormone balance most favours bone growth. Calcium absorption is also influenced by vitamin D. Surveys in several countries have indicated that elderly populations may have an intake of calcium below the RDA (177). However, studies aimed at showing that those with lifelong low-calcium have an increased risk of fractures have generally been unsuccessful with the exception of a Yugoslavian study which revealed a high incidence of hip fractures in a low calcium region (350-500 mg/day) compared to a high calcium intake region (1000-2000 mg/day). In contrast a recent Danish study indicated that calcium supplementation (1000-2000 mg/day) had little effect on loss of calcium from the bones in the early years after menopause. Based on these data it is not possible to say what are the real causes or the real preventive measures for osteoporosis.

65

The recent interest in calcium as an anti-hypertensive agent largely stems from work in the early 1970s which addressed the relationship between increasing water hardness and a reduced incidence of heart disease. At that time some studies suggested a relationship (180-182), others found none (183). Progress in the 'water story' was reviewed in the British Medical Journal (184) in 1978, and by others (178), and many of the examples cited were convincing of an effect; however, Vahouney (185) in 1982 stated that although suggestive and provocative, the ecological studies relating water hardness in general, or specific trace elements in drinking water supplies, to deaths from CHD have been less than convincing. More extensive epidemiology studies on a European scale would be useful in this context. In relation to hypertension it has been hypothesised that a defect in the vascular metabolism of calcium may underlie the abnormal vasoconstriction that characterises high blood pressure. Consequently, it has been postulated that maintenance of calcium balance might either afford protection against increases in arterial pressure for those at risk of developing hypertension or actually lower pressure in those already afflicted (186). Epidemiologic observations, as well as studies in human and experimental models of hypertension lend support to this postulate as outlined in a major review article by Parrott-Garcia and McCarron in 1984 (187). However, they hasten to point out the important possible interface between calcium and sodium in blood pressure regulation (189). In their analysis of the HANES 1 data (Health and Nutrition Examination Survey, USA), McCarron et al. (189) found that higher blood pressure in a representative sample of the US population was associated with a reduced sodium and calcium diet. The way in which the data base from HANES 1 was used by McCarron et al. to obtain their findings has been criticised by

Feinleib et al in a letter published in 'Science' in 1984 (190); however, the criticisms were refuted by McCarron et al. (191) in a reply letter.

Perhaps the most intriguing evidence that implies an interaction between dietary calcium and sodium in blood pressure regulation comes from the preliminary results of a dietary intervention trial in the SHR (spontaneous hypertensive rat) and its normotensive control (192). The provision of a high-calcium diet in conjunction with an increased sodium content effectively prevented the characteristic onset of hypertension in the SHR. Moreover, the cohort exposed to the reduced-sodium/high-calcium regime experienced only an insignificant lowering of blood pressure, suggesting that the antihypertensive effects of calcium are sodium-dependent. Finally, both normotensive and hypertensive animals consuming the low-sodium/low-calcium diet experienced an elevation in blood pressure response. Based on these findings the authors concluded (192) that sodium restriction may exacerbate blood pressure in hypertensives and normotensives or blunt the beneficial effect of high calcium exposure. Conversely, adequate sodium exposure may be a requisite for the full expression of the antihypertensive effect of calcium.

Moreover, the general recommendations from several voluntary and governmental health agencies for modifying lipid intake in the interests of lowering cardiovascular risk raises the concern that some individuals may consequently restrict their intake of certain food groups (such as dairy products) known to be important sources of calcium. Likewise, sodium restriction advised by some for society in general and hypertensives in particular may effect similar results in terms of calcium restrictions (193). If, as suggested above, the protective actions of calcium are sodium dependent, then caution must be exercised in reducing dietary levels of sodium lest the efficacy of calcium be diminished or lost completely (187).

The nutritional significance of dietary essential trace elements have been reviewed recently by Sattar and Khalid (194) and by Mertz (195). Essential trace elements are required by man in amounts ranging from 50 micrograms to 18 milligrams per day. Acting as catalytic or structural components of larger molecules, they have specific functions and are indispensible for life (Table 5). Research during the past quarter of a century has identified as essential six trace elements whose functions were previously unknown. In addition to the long-known deficiencies of iron and iodine, signs of deficiency for chromium, copper, zinc, and selenium have been identified in free-living populations. Marginal or severe trace element imbalances can be considered risk factors for several diseases of public health importance, but proof of cause and effect relationships will depend on a more complete understanding of basic mechanisms of action and on better analytical procedures and functional tests to determine marginal trace element status in man.

There is always concern about the availability of trace elements especially in diets high in dietary fibre and in diets of particular groups in the population, e.g. vegetarians. However, research in 1980 by Freeland-Graves et al. (196) has shown that food consumed in the vegetarian diet can provide adequate amounts of zinc and copper. Foods that contain high concentrations of these minerals include legumes, soy products, hard cheeses, whole grains, cereals, nuts, seeds and sprouts. However, the low mineral to fibre ratios that are found in many of these foodstuffs may reflect the poor bioavailability of these minerals. Thus vegetarians should consume some of the foods that are highest in trace mineral

TABLE 5: Classification of the essential trace elements*

Element	Function
Fluorine	Structure of teeth, possibly of bones; possibly growth effect
Silicon	Calcification; possible function in connective tissue
Vanadium	Not known
Chromium	Potentiation of insulin
Manganese	Mucopolysaccharide metabolism, superoxide dismutase
Iron	Oxygen, electron transport
Cobalt	As part of vitamin B_{12}
Nickel	Interaction with iron absorption
Copper	Oxidative enzymes; interaction with iron; cross-linking of elastin
Zinc	Numerous enzymes involved in energy metabolism and in transcription and translation
Arsenic	Not known
Selenium	Glutathione peroxidase; interaction with heavy metals
Molybdenum	Xanthine, aldehyde, sulfide oxidases
Iodine	Constituent of thyroid hormones

*According to Mertz (195)

concentration but lowest in fibre. Recommended are such foods as hard cheeses and products derived from soy protein such as tofu. Research in the U.K. in 1979 (197) indicated that the West of Scotland diet contained less Zn than the recommended daily allowance possibly indicating the need for a revision of the allowances or a change of diet. The change could be made simply by the substitution of wholemeal flour for the presently preferred white flour. Other changes in diet could be used but they are unlikely to be acceptable. Even with these changes the requirement of pregnant or lactating women is unlikely to be met and these women may have a temporary deficiency as part of their condition.

TABLE 6: Trace elements and cardiovascular function*

Trace element intake	Reported beneficial effects	Reported detrimental effects
Cadmium	Reduces serum cholesterol	Induces hypertension; enhances capillary sclerosis and atherosclerosis; induces ventricular hypertrophy; affects cardiac conduction; interferes with copper metabolism
Zinc	Protects against Cd-induced hypertension; regulates insulin release	Interferes with copper metabolism, resulting in elevated serum cholesterol
Copper	Required for elastin cross-linking	Deficiency results in increased serum cholesterol and hepatic cholesterogenesis
Chromium	Protects against atherosclerosis; increases cholesterol catabolism; protects against diabetes	
Cobalt	Protects against atherosclerosis (orally)	Enhances atherosclerosis (injection)
Vanadium	Reduces plasma and aortic cholesterol levels	
Manganese	Protects against atherosclerosis	
Selenium	Protects against Cd-induced hypertension: protects against cardiac and pancreatic necrosis	Induces hypertension

* Modified from Masironi (198)

Trace elements and risk factors in relation to CHD have been reviewed by Vahouney (185) and some additional suggested effects to those shown in Table 5 are given in Table 6. Vahouney concludes that the evidence for the role of specific trace elements and trace element interactions in one or more aspects of experimental atherosclerosis or human CHD is far from complete. Obviously, the concentrations of these substances are relatively small and their interactions are complex. This complicates long-term nutritional studies and requires elaborate control of all environmental factors. Nevertheless, it seems likely that trace elements play important roles in specific aspects of the genesis and/or enhancement of the atherosclerotic process. Masironi (198) synthesized the existing information on alleged beneficial or detrimental effects of trace elements in relation to cardiovascular disease. This has changed little in the past decade and, with some modification, is summarized in Table 6.

The overall material and data presented in this section suggest that there is no room for complacency regarding the position of certain minerals and essential trace elements in the diet. A major priority is the continuation of studies on the desirable levels of, and interaction or synergism between, Ca and Na in relation to hypertension in view of current trends/advice to limit salt intake and also intakes of dairy products (this will, indirectly, reduce Ca intake). An extensive input is also required into investigating further the many subtle roles of trace elements in human nutrition.

1.4   FOODS OF PLANT, ANIMAL AND MARINE ORIGIN

The current status of nutrients in human health terms has been outlined in section 1.3. However, these nutrients are not normally consumed individually but in a mixed or balanced diet situation.

1.4.1   Balanced/prudent/healthy/varied diets

The concept of balanced diets stems from the recognition that an appropriate mixture of food items will provide the minimum requirements of protein, minerals and vitamins needed by the body. By ensuring that several different foods are consumed, the idea was that one item rich in a particular nutrient would 'balance' the lack of this nutrient in another food. The balanced diet is therefore a term which has developed from a concern that a diet should prevent the development of deficiency. While deficiency may still apply to sub-groups within the European population the overriding situation is one of overnutrition and more attention is being focused on carbohydrate to fat ratios and to a lesser extent protein. Within carbohydrates the intake of complex to refined is now being increasingly recognised as is the ratio of poly to saturated fat. This tends to reduce the importance of the so-called food groups i.e. milk, meat, fruit/vegetable, and cereal/potato so frequently referred to in dietary advice leaflets. If one was to define 'new broad food groups' more in line with developed countries and overnutrition they might be as outlined (and subdivided) in Table 7, i.e. there would be three broad groups each of which should be significantly represented in the diet if not on a daily basis at least on a twice weekly basis. However, each of the subdivisions of the main group should also be represented. For example, in the animal sources group some of the meat eaten should be poultry and/or game as these are low fat meats. Within the fish group oily fish should be eaten to obtain PUFA. In the plant group salads should be dressed with oils to obtain PUFA, fruits have pectin as a dietary fibre fraction, cereals do not, i.e. there are different forms of protein, fat, dietary fibre and carbohydrate and each has/may have a different functionality in human nutrition terms. In addition some vitamins may be common to foods from the three sources, however, they may be more available from meat than from a plant source (see 1.4.2 on availability); also an increased intake of protein from plant sources may be desirable (mentioned in section 1.3.4). Taking into account current recommendations for an increased intake of complex carbohydrate and a reduced level of fat (see CHAPTER 2) in the diet and noting the data in Tables 9, 11, 12 and 13 a shift in food intake towards food from plant and fish sources at the expense of animal seems desirable/necessary/inevitable.

It is desirable that 'whole foods' should be eaten when convenient for two reasons:

a) key nutrients are retained

b) nutrients are 'diluted'

Some key nutrients may be lost during processing; however in fairness in processed foods this problem is often overcome by restoration. The question of nutrient dilution may also be important. For example some constituents of foods may be physiologically and/or chemically very active, e.g. ascorbic acid and some PUFAs; but, in nature they are diluted by the other constituents in the food, presumably for a good reason. However, man acts against this principle by taking macro quantities of ascorbic acid or drinking fish oil in order to obtain a large concentrated intake of these so called 'good-for-you' substances. For example, some essential dietary components such as vitamins can be very toxic when taken in excess (199) confirming that 'everything' is a poison, but it is only the dose that makes it poisonous. Natural foods therefore need not necessarily mean healthy foods. In another context the so-called food concentrates i.e. sugar, concentrated fats, alcohol represent the same situation as they have an over-concentration of 'undiluted' readily available calories (see section 1.5).

Obviously it is not convenient to eat 'whole' foods all the time and the above discussion is not a criticism of processed foods; it is a suggestion, however that the diet where possible should contain 'whole' foods or 'whole related foods' and that consumers should be aware of this.

TABLE 7: Re-definition of food groups in relation to an over-
nutrition situation

Foods from:		Suppliers of:
PLANT SOURCES	- fruits	DF, V, M
	- leafy vegetables	DF, V, M
	- root vegetables	DF, CC, V, M
	- cereals	DF, CC, P, M, PUFA, V
	- oil crops	PUFA, P, F
	- legumes	DF, CC, V, M, P
ANIMAL SOURCES	- beef	P, F, M, V
	- mutton	P, F, M, V
	- pork	P, F, M, V
	- game	P, PUFA, M, V, F
	- poultry	P, M, V, F
	- milk	P, F, M, V
MARINE SOURCES	- white fish	P, M, V
	- oily fish	P, PUFA, M, V
	- shellfish	P, M, V, PUFA

DF (dietary fibre), V (vitamins), M (minerals), F (fat), CC (complex
carbohydrate), P (protein), PUFA (polyunsaturated fatty acids).

That many consumers are aware of this is seen from the increasing sales and popularity of fresh (chilled) foods (200), wholemeal breads and health foods. The concept of 'freshness' is also increasingly seen in processed foods as evidenced by in-store bakeries and in-store sausage making (179). Gibney (201) asks how long must we wait before the committees of experts reach the conclusion that a good diet is a balanced diet and that there are no villain foods or good foods; he concludes there are villain diets and good diets, and a good diet contains a bit of everything. Hollingsworth (110) suggests that our concern for diet and health should be about lifestyles rather than a drastic dietary change. Such a conclusion accords with the wisdom of the School of Salernum - "If you would be free from physicians, let these three be your physicians, a cheerful mind, rest, and a moderate diet". The question does natural equal healthy often arises;

however, the general assumption that 'natural' foods must mean better is questioned (201). Many natural foods, e.g. eggs and legumes contain indigenous toxins as well as contaminants such as aflatoxins and botulinum toxins.

The data in Table 7 refer largely to primary products of agriculture. Food products have not been considered in this framework as many of them contain constituents from two, or perhaps three, of the sources given in Table 7 and may, in some cases, represent a balance of nutrients far from that found in a primary agricultural product.

In view of the general recommendation (see CHAPTER 2) to reduce calories from fat to less than 35% of total calories the composition of a 'sample lunch' has been drawn up in Table 8 containing soup, meat, two vegetables, potatoes, apple pie, coffee and biscuits. Certain items are then removed and others added to study the effect on the percentage of

TABLE 8: Composition and calorie content of 'sample lunch'

Lunch	Portion (g)	Weight (g) Carbo.	Prot.	Fat	Calories
Oxtail soup	250	12.8	6.0	4.3	111
Gammon steak	73	–	21.5	8.9	166
Carrot	112	4.5	0.7	–	20
Cabbage	91	2.1	1.5	–	14
Boiled potatoes	213	42.0	2.9	0.2	172
Apple pie	80	45.4	3.4	12.4	290
Double cream	25	0.5	0.4	12.1	113
Milk (coffee)	35	1.6	1.2	1.3	23
2 Cream biscuits	24	16.7	1.2	6.3	125
Totals	903	125.6	38.8	45.5	1034

TABLE 9: Effect of omission or replacement of items in the 'sample lunch' (Table 8) on the % of calories as carbohydrate, protein, fat

Option	Total calories	Carbo.	Protein	Fat
Sample lunch	1034	45.6	14.5	39.8
1. Potatoes omitted	862	36.4	16.0	47.6
2. (-) Potatoes (+) Chips (213g)	1397	43.7	12.2	44.1
3. Cream omitted	921	51.0	16.1	32.9
4. Cream + pie omitted	631	47.5	22.2	30.3
5. (-) Cream (-) pie + apple (160g)	704	52.7	20.1	27.1
6. (-) Gammon (+) steamed cod (73 g)	928	50.9	12.7	36.5

calories coming from fat (% CF). Despite the fact that the lunch contained two vegetables and also potatoes the % CF was 39.8%. Removal of potatoes (which often happens - "I'll have the meat and veg. please but no potatoes") exacerbates the position and raises % CF to 47.6. Replacement of the potatoes with chips (French fries) raises total calories and also % CF in comparison with the sample lunch. Removal of cream drops the % CF to 32.9 while removing the apple pie only drops % CF to 30.3 despite the fact that the pie contains 12.4 g of fat; this small reduction is due to the high carbohydrate content of the apple pie (Table 8). Replacement of the apple pie and cream with an apple gives the lowest % CF figure of 27.1; replacing gammon steak with steamed cod gave a % CF value of 36.5% (Table 9). The lunch in Table 8 is far from representative of lunches (dinners) in different countries of the EC but might be reasonably close to the norm for the UK and Ireland.

TABLE 10: Food items in 'sample breakfast' and 'sample tea'

Breakfast:	Orange juice (175 g), porridge (195 g), All Bran (35 g), milk (220 g - for coffee and cereal), boiled egg (50 g), 2 slices wholemeal bread (64 g), margarine (13.3 g), marmalade (26 g), sugar (8 g)
Tea:	Milk (105 g - for 3 cups of tea), 3 slices wholemeal bread (95 g), margarine (20 g), lettuce (50 g), tomato (25 g), cheddar cheese (42 g), sardines in tomato sauce (30 g)

76

TABLE 11: Effect of omission or replacement of items in the 'sample breakfast' (Table 10) on the % of calories as carbohydrate, protein, fat

Option	Total calories	% of calories from:		
		Carbo.	Prot.	Fat
Sample breakfast	851	52.7	14.3	32.9
1. Margarine omitted	755	59.5	16.2	24.4
2. Milk-skim for whole	777	58.4	15.2	26.4

TABLE 12: Effect of omission or replacement of items in the 'sample tea' (Table 10) on the % of calories as carbohydrate, protein, fat

Option	Total calories	% of calories from:		
		Carbo.	Prot.	Fat
'Sample tea'	641	26.0	18.3	55.7
1. Margarine omitted	497	33.6	23.5	42.9
2. Cheddar omitted	474	35.2	16.0	48.7

TABLE 13: Calories from carbohydrate, protein and fat for the 'sample breakfast, lunch and tea'

'Sample meal'	Total calories	Number of calories from:		
		Carbo.	Prot.	Fat
Breakfast	851	449	122	280
Lunch	1034	472	150	412
Tea	641	167	117	357
Total	2526	1088	389	1049
% calories from:		43.1	15.4	41.5

Similarly models of a 'sample breakfast and tea' have also been made (Table 10). The sample breakfast has % CF of 32.9 (Table 11) which is reduced considerably if margarine is omitted or if skim milk replaces milk. The standard tea has a % CF value of 55.7 (Table 12) which is also reduced if margarine or cheddar cheese are omitted. The total effect of the three 'sample meals' is shown in Table 13 with an overall % CF figure of 41.5%. These model data serve to show the complexity and the permutations and combinations involved in having a varied diet and still targeting for a % CF value below 35. The data show the difficulty in meeting the % CF figure of 35 while using full fat dairy products or margarine and indicate the potential for low-fat spreads in this regard; in these data margarine can be replaced by butter without influencing the % CF figures (see further discussion of butter and margarine in section 1.5). This subject is also addressed by Fallows and Wheelock (202). The data in Tables 8, 9, 11, 12, 13 were compiled using values from McCance and Widdowson (52) and g to calorie conversion figures of 3.75, 4 and 9 for carbohydrate, protein and fat respectively.

Dietary advice in the future is likely to return increasingly to a balanced diet comprising daily intakes of foods of plant, animal and marine origin rather than to saying 'eat a lot of this and none of that'; there will be emphasis on increased intakes of food of plant and marine origin at least in some countries. Superimposed on this will be a greater emphasis on consumption of fresh, unprocessed 'whole' foods with emphasis on moderation in everything. Healthy eating should follow the 'rule of one' or the 'rule of two' in most cases, but seldom the 'rule of three or more' i.e. have one or two drinks - not three; eat meat once or twice a day - not three times; have one or two biscuits at coffee time - not three, eat cream cake when visiting - but only one slice; supplement one meal per day with added bran — not every meal. This advice is broadly in agreement with current recommendations of expert committees (see CHAPTER 2).

1.4.2   Availability

One area where foods of plant, animal and marine origin may differ is in the bioavailability of some of their nutrients.

Few natural phenomena have been assessed in as many diverse ways and studied so intensively with so little progress towards a practical objective as the availability of nutrients. Suttle (203) points out that to merit universal acceptance a concept of availability must satisfy five conditions: it must be definable, distinct from terms already accepted, appropriate to all nutrients, measurable and above all useful. For example of the nutrient ingested, only a proportion may be absorbable (e) and only a part of this may be absorbed (d). The product ed gives the proportion of the ingested nutrient which flows to the tissues and its maximal value should be universally regarded as AVAILABILITY (203). This is a 'gastrointestinal' concept of availability and the two coefficients as its dietary (e) and consumer (d) components. The dietary component will largely be determined by chemical composition and in particular by:

a)   the form in which the nutrient is present
b)   the digestibility of the matrix in which the nutrient is consumed
c)   other constituents affecting the proportion which remains absorbable.

The consumer component will be influenced mainly by the genetically determined efficiency of the absorptive process and the need for and capacity to absorb the nutrient (203). Some details of the availability of different nutrients in specific foods are given in section 1.4.

1.4.3   Food from plant sources

Emphasis in this and succeeding parts of section 1.4 is on highlighting some of the possible advantages and disadvantages, from a human health point of view, of food of plant, animal and marine origin. No detailed treatment of the nutrient content of the foods is given as this can be found in standard textbooks and food composition tables.

The different foods of plant origin are listed in broad outline (Table 7) and items such as potatoes and bulb crops are included under the heading root vegetables even though, botanically, they are not so. These foods are collectively suppliers of complex and simple carbohydrate, dietary fibre, protein, fat and PUFA, vitamins, minerals and other constituents.

Fruits, vegetables and cereals are the major suppliers of DF and complex carbohydrate; animal foods supply none with the possible exception of some mucopolysaccharides. The DF in fruit and vegetables differs from that in cereals in that cereal fibre does not contain pectin. Fruit DF has a high pectin content (204) while fibre from leafy vegetables and some of the root vegetables contains less pectin and more cellulose. Durrington et al. (205) have shown that pectin and guar gum administered 'neat' reduced serum cholesterol in humans and in an extension of this work Gormley et al. (91) have shown that eating two apples per day, in addition to the normal diet, reduced serum cholesterol and raised high density lipoprotein cholesterol (HDL) (the 'good' fraction of cholesterol). The maximum reduction in cholesterol was 8% while the % HDL cholesterol rose from 18 to 24%. These results must be viewed in the light that this reduction was achieved in subjects with relatively low serum cholesterol levels and by the increase of a single dietary component. Robertson et al. (206) found an 11% reduction in cholesterol in subjects who consumed raw carrots for breakfast. The mechanism for cholesterol lowering may be via bile acid binding by pectin. In theory this could also have application in cancer prevention seeing that intestinal cancer may be associated with bile acids (207).

Legumes also have a cholesterol lowering effect as indicated by a fall of 7% in subjects consuming 30 g of freeze dried peas in addition to their normal diet (208); HDL cholesterol rose from 21.5 to 24.4%. The mechanism by which peas exert their hypocholesterolaemic effect is not clear. Hellendoorn (209) points out that the consumption of beans results in a more rapid bowel transit time and a greater excretion of bile acids. The faster transit time may be due to the formation of volatile fatty acids by fermentation in the intestine which stimulate the peristaltic action of the intestine. Potter et al. (210) have suggested that dietary saponins (steroid compounds) can exert a hypocholesterolaemic action; peas also contain saponins (Table 14) and this may be a contributory factor to the cholesterol reduction. Oakenfull (211) has shown that dietary saponins increase faecal excretion of the bile acids. This means that the body's pool of bile acids has to be replenished by metabolising cholesterol from the liver. Thus, in conjunction with other dietary modifications, foods rich in saponins are likely to be useful in reducing the risk of heart disease. Soya beans are the most commonly accepted food known to have a significant content of saponins and this may explain the hypocholesterolaemic effect of soy-proteins. Saponins occur widely in legumes (Table 14) which may be one of the benefits of consuming legumes in the diet. A number of other studies also demonstrate the hypocholesterolaemic effect of legumes (209, 212, 213)) including the suggestion that soy lecithin has the ability to raise HDL cholesterol (214).

TABLE 14: Commonly eaten saponin-containing plants/foods*

Cereal	Legumes	Leafy vegetables
Oats	Soya beans Chick peas Mung beans Peanuts Broad beans Kidney beans Lentils Garden peas	Spinach Silver beet Asparagus

* Oakenfull (211)

Claims are made for some other vegetables also in relation to CHD/cholesterol. For example Baghurst et al. (215) have shown in a dietary trial that the rate of platelet aggregation was significantly greater after a 'fat' meal compared with the control but when onion was included in the meal the results were not significantly different from the control; neither the high fat nor the onion meal had any significant effect on the extent of platelet aggregation. Kinderlehrer (214) also suggests that onions and garlic influence platelet aggregation and may be protective against CHD. A recent study (216) has confirmed the presence of both arachidonates and eicosapentaenoate in garlic. In view of the earlier reference to the thrombotic aspect of CHD (see section 1.3.5) these results could be of considerable importance.

Cereal fibre has some different properties to that from fruit and vegetables. For example, wheat bran enhances stool weight and reduces transit time but has little or no effect on serum cholesterol or faecal bile acids (217). However, it is in the area of oats that most of the recent interest has revolved. Gould et al. (90) have shown the hypocholesteraemic effect of oats especially when 100 g of a coarse oat fraction is consumed daily; HDL cholesterol levels were raised. They claim that the effect is due to the β- glucan fraction which is often termed soluble dietary fibre. The coarse oat fraction is obtained by 'sieving off' oatflour from ground groats using a 400 μ sieve; oat flour comprises about 60% and coarse oat about 40%. The data (Table 15) show the composition of the different oat fractions and illustrate the high DF content of the coarse oat fraction. Workers in the Netherlands (218) also found that rolled oats (140 g/day) reduced serum cholesterol in humans; however, this represents a very large intake by any standards. Gormley et al. (219) could not produce a lowering in cholesterol in humans consuming the porridge equivalent of 43 g of oatmeal daily and concluded that this 'normal portion' was not sufficiently large to produce an effect. Cereals, therefore, with the exception of oats (in large quantities) don't have the cholesterol lowering capacity of fruit and vegetables.

TABLE 15: Analytical values [1] for oat fractions (Kinsealy Research Centre, IRL, 1986)

Sample	Fat %	Dietary fibre[2] %	Protein %
Oatflour	6.87	5.24	8.68
Coarse oat fraction	9.02	16.00	13.72
Ground oatmeal	7.73	8.34	10.92

[1] Data are on an 'as is' basis (moisture levels 10.5%)
[2] Dietary fibre by 'Fibretec'

It has already been noted above that cereals, potatoes and some other plant foods supply complex carbohydrate and confer satiety. A study in Ireland (220) in the 1970s is noteworthy in this respect. Twenty three volunteers consumed 1 kg of boiled/baked potatoes for 10 weeks. Four gained weight (1-3 kg per person), six subjects showed no change while 13 lost from 1-5 kg. This trial clearly indicates that the potato is not fattening and that its energy value of 750 cal/kg is not in fact high in relation to its satiety value.

Plant foods notably cereals, legumes and oil seed crops are good sources of protein. However, the proteins are not as available as animal protein (greater than 80% available) (221). The data (Table 16) show the eight essential amino acids and indicate that egg, fish and red meat protein are best in terms of their content of essential amino acids in comparison with the standard/guideline values of the Food and Agricultural Organisation (FAO). Whole egg is a perfect protein as is milk protein. The plant proteins are all deficient in methionine and tryptophan while wheat is also deficient in lysine. However, they are still high quality proteins and Sinclair (222) points out that mixing plant proteins can give a biological value as good as some animal proteins. For instance taking egg protein as the standard with a protein score of 100 (FAO, 1957), wheat protein is 53 and soy flour 73. But a mixture of 70% wheat flour and 30% soy flour has a score of 72. Rye has a score of 80, oats 79, cow's milk 78 and fish only 70.

Beans are also deficient in methionine and tryptophan (Table 16) and some have poor digestibility which partly accounts for their low net protein utilization (NPU) compared with proteins of animal origin. Rat assay NPU values ranged from 45 to 66 for a number of bean types (223)

TABLE 16: Grams of protein per 16 grams of nitrogen

FAO standard	Acid	Whole Egg	Red Meat	Fish flesh	Wheat	Beans (dry)	Soya* isolate
4.2	Isoleucine	8.0	4.7	5.0	4.9	5.3	4.8
4.5	Leucine	9.2	8.0	9.2	6.9	8.1	7.8
4.2	Lysine	7.2	8.5	10.6	2.5	6.1	5.9
2.2	Methionine	4.1	2.5	2.7	1.2	1.1	1.0
2.8	Phenylalanine	6.3	4.5	4.7	4.4	5.2	5.5
2.8	Threonine	4.9	4.6	5.5	3.9	4.0	3.7
1.4	Tryptophan	1.5	1.1	1.4	1.2	0.9	1.3
4.2	Valine	7.3	5.5	5.8	4.5	5.3	4.8

Source: Principles of Food Science, Vol. 2, by G. Borgstrom,
         Macmillan Co., N. York, 1968, page 17.

*Proteins as Human Foods, R.A. Lawrie, Butterworths, London, 1970, page 351.

compared with a value of 83 for milk. Similar values are shown in a major review of dried beans by Despande et al. (224).

Oilseeds also contain significant protein contents, e.g. soyabean 38%, lupinseed 35% and rapeseed 20%. Proteins are extracted as 'isolates' and those from lupinseed and rapeseed are increasing in use now that problems with toxic substances have been overcome. Soy protein usually ends up as textured vegetable protein (TVP) but is a good quality protein (Table 16) and can provide high quality protein in human diets at a cost lower than that from animal origin.

As already pointed out protein intakes are, if anything, considerably in excess of requirements in all the EC countries and protein deficiency is not a problem except in sub-groups. However, plant proteins make a big contribution in the European diet and perhaps even larger intakes of protein from plant sources should be encouraged in view of the fact that there may be an association (however weak) between certain cancers and animal protein intake (32).

Foods of plant origin supply considerable quantities of fat to the diet with oilseeds and olives among the foremost; much of the fat is PUFA. Most of the fat in the European diet from plant sources comes from oilseeds and olive oil while cereals provide most of the remainder; within cereals the oat is particularly rich in fat (Table 17) and also contains a

TABLE 17: Fat (%) and PUFA content of some cereals

| Cereal | Fat (%) | P/S | PUFA (g/100 g fatty acid) | | | |
			Total	18:2	18:3	20:4
Oats	8.2	2.3	42.9	40.7	2.2	Tr
Wheat flour(wholemeal)	2.0	3.1	63.7	59.4	4.1	0.2
Rye	2.0	3.4	65.6	56.8	8.8	0
Rice	1.0	1.6	42.3	41.2	1.1	Tr
Barley	1.7	2.6	63.5	57.4	6.1	0

Source: McCance and Widdowson (52); data in Tables 17-21 are reproduced with permission of the Controller, HMSO.

significant amount of PUFA. In view of its affect on cholesterol noted above and also its PUFA content, consumption of oats should be promoted within Europe either as porridge or muesli. In these forms oats are one of the most natural, additive free and nutritious foods available (225).

Plant foods are an important source of vitamins; however, vitamin A is only present in animals but green plants are rich in β- carotene but in many cases this is not readily absorbed from them. These aspects may be of importance in view of the inverse association noted above between retinoids and incidence of certain forms of cancer. Vitamin D only occurs in animals but plants and especially wheat germ (133 mg of vitamin E/100 g) are rich sources of vitamin E. The possible importance of vitamin E as a free radical scavenger has already been mentioned (see 1.3.6). Water soluble vitamins are more prevalent in vegetable foods and animal foods are poor sources with the exception of liver and kidney. However, pork contains significant amounts of thiamin (0.89 mg/100 g) and cow's milk is a good source of riboflavin (0.19mg/100 g). Vitamin C and folic acid occur mostly in fruit and vegetables while vitamin B_{12} is contained only in animal foods. These data show clearly the need for a balanced diet in order to ensure the requirement of the different vitamins.

A similar situation exists for minerals. Animal foods, with the exception of milk tend to be low in calcium. Many plant foods are also low but spinach and watercress are good sources of calcium. Meat and organs are good sources of available iron; spinach and some legumes also contain significant amounts but it is not so readily absorbed. On balance, trace elements tend to be more abundant in animal than in plant foods. However, there is concern that DF may bind some of the minerals and trace elements (226) and people on high fibre diets such as vegetarians could be deficient; these people therefore need to consume an adequate quantity of foods high in minerals and trace elements.

1.4.4. Food from animal sources

In terms of the European diet milk and meat are the two main items of interest although there are other by-products such as blood and gelatin which are used as foods. However, the discussion here will be confined to milk and meat. The preceding section on plant foods included details on animal products as suppliers of protein (Table 16), minerals, and vitamins in comparison with plant foods and so the issue of fat from animal foods will be the main topic in this section.

1.4.4.1.   Milk: Cow's milk is a good source of protein, fat, calcium and vitamin A.   Its composition in comparison with goats and human milk is given in Table 18.   The main difference is that human milk has more

TABLE 18: Composition of different milks

Milk type	%				PUFA (g/100 g fatty acid)	
	Carb.	Prot.	Fat	P/S	18:2	18:3
Cow	4.7	3.8	3.3	0.05	1.4	1.5
Goat	4.6	3.3	4.5	0.03	2.3	-
Human	7.2	1.3	4.1	0.16	7.2	0.8

Source: McCance and Widdowson (52)

carbohydrate, less protein and more of its fat as PUFA than cow's or goat's milk; it also has a higher w-6 to w-3 ratio.   Milk from vegan mothers has four times the linoleic acid content than that from omnivore mothers (227).

With increasing pressure to lower fat and cholesterol intakes in European diets, milk and its products have come under severe attack in recent times and there is a gradual shift towards low fat and skim milks in most developed countries.   Based on an intake of 0.5 litres of milk a day these three milk forms represent fat contents of 19.0, 9.5 and 0.5 g respectively with corresponding calorie values of 324,245 and 165; 0.5 litres of milk contains 70 mg of cholesterol which is about 13% of the average Irish daily intake of cholesterol. In the 'sample meals' shown in Table 13 milk represented 9.3% of all calories and 11.7% of the calories from fat. However, milk itself is hypocholesterolaemic as shown by Howard and Marks (228). Their results showed that milk contains a hypocholesterolaemic factor, a hypothesis which is supported by the greater hypocholesterolaemic effect of skimmed milk. This result was confirmed when an equivalent weight of butterfat and calcium produced a highly significant rise in serum cholesterol. These findings were partly endorsed by the work of Connolly et al. (229) who compared data for upper and lower quartiles for intake of dairy products (milk, butter, cheese). The cholesterol for both quartiles was similar while the upper quartile had a higher HDL and a lower LDL than the lower quartile. When the data were re-analysed on the basis of upper and lower quartiles for milk intake, milk had a hypocholesterolaemic effect in females but not in males; HDL levels were raised in the upper milk quartile for both males and females. A similar effect was obtained when the data were re-analysed based on upper and lower quartiles for butter intake. However, it should be noted that the number of individuals in the quartiles was as low as 3 and 1 in some cases.

Mann (230) in 1977 has shown that yoghurt was hypocholesterolaemic but not milk itself; however he used only four volunteers. He suggested that the yoghurt bacteria produce a substance which blocks cholesterol production in the liver.

Based on these data the case for cutting milk intake or changing to low fat or skim is rather weak. The situation, however, is different in the case of butter and certain forms of cheese. These will be discussed in section 1.5. Some of the implications of reducing milk intake or switching to low fat milk have been outlined by Fallows and Wheelock (202); this is also discussed in CHAPTER 2.

A number of studies have been carried out to increase the PUFA content of milk by protecting the feed rations (containing sunflower seed) against biohydrogenation in the rumen. This raised the linoleic acid content of the milk fat by 10-22% (231). However, this milk has to be protected against oxidation and butter and cheese made from it were less acceptable than that from ordinary milk. Hodges et al. (232) carried out a major study where groups of volunteers were fed diets containing milk, butter, ground beef, other beef, and lamb which was obtained in polyunsaturated form by 'protected' lipid feeds for the animals in comparison with normally produced products. The design allowed for four dietary groups: (a) saturated diet (normal products) for 20 weeks, (b) PUFA diet ('protected feed') for 20 weeks, (c) saturated for 10 weeks, PUFA for 10 weeks, (d) PUFA for 10 weeks, saturated for 10 weeks. Linoleic to total saturated fatty acid ratios for the saturated and PUFA diets were 0.09 and 0.74 respectively. The main effect of the diets on cholesterol was a mean 5.5% decrease in cholesterol as a result of the PUFA diet and an increase of 4% due to the saturated diet; this 'swing' represents 18 mg/dl of cholesterol and does not warrant the production of PUFA foods from animals.

Breeding animals for lower milk fat (see CHAPTER 3) is another way of attacking the milk fat issue.

1.4.4.2 Meat: Much of the problem of high fat low PUFA meat has been of man's making brought about through domestication and intensive feeding of farm animals (233). Crawford et al. have shown that the higher the fat content in animals the lower the PUFA content (234). The whole meat from intensively reared beef has a P/S ratio of 0.10 compared with 1.3 for giraffe and 0.82 for woodland buffalo meat. Animal breeding also played a part in this as selection was made for fast weight gain based on high energy feeds; this inevitably means more fat. Fortunately this has now changed and emphasis is also being placed on leanness in animal breeding (see CHAPTER 3). The intensive feeding regimes have also had an effect on broiler chickens; their fat content has increased significantly in the last 10 years (235). A similar situation occurs in pigs; for example pig fat contains 8-12% linoleic acid whereas the wild pig has 35% of its fat as PUFA and a P/S ratio of 1.7 (236). This of course is a reflection of the animals diet. In ruminants the carcase fat has always a low P/S ratio because of biohydrogenation in the rumen. However, what happens here is not so much the P/S ratio as the total amount of fat, which in a large number of wild species averages at only 2-3%.

If one wishes to comply with the general recommendation for less fat and more PUFA in the diet then the following options are available in relation to fat from meat.

a) eat less meat
b) remove visible fat
c) eat leaner types of meat

These issues and related ones have been discussed by Fallows and Wheelock (202). One must also consider not only fat and PUFA content but also the ratio of w6/w3 acids. On the basis of recent evidence a low ratio is desirable (see section 1.3.5.1).

Fat and cholesterol values for meats and organ meats are given in Tables 19 and 20. These figures must be interpreted in the broadest sense in view of the difference between different parts of the carcase within each meat type. The amount of fat left on the meat has a huge bearing on fat content as shown in the example of beef, lamb and pork in Table 19.

TABLE 19: Fat and cholesterol content of different meats

Meat type	Fat (%)	Cholesterol (mg/100 g)	PUFA (%)[1]	Ratios P/S	Ratios w6/w3
Sirloin (roast, lean)	9.1 (21.1)[2]	82	4.3	0.13	1.4
Lamb (roast, lean)	8.1 (17.9)[2]	110	5.0	0.10	1.0
Pork (roast, lean)	6.9 (19.8)[2]	69	8.3	0.12	8.2
Venison (roast)	6.4	-	-	-	-
Rabbit (steamed)	7.7	71	34.0	0.78	2.1
Chicken (roast)	5.4	97	14.9	0.55	19.3
Goose (roast)	22.4	-	-	-	-
Grouse	5.3	-	62.2	2.53	1.1
Partridge	7.2	-	25.1	0.91	1.6
Duck (roast)	9.7	160	12.7	0.44	21.0
Pigeon (roast)	13.2	-	-	-	-

[1] % of total fatty acids
[2] (lean + fat)

Source: McCance and Widdowson (52)

TABLE 20: Fat and cholesterol content of some organ meats

Meat	Fat (%)	Cholesterol (mg/100 g)
Brain (calf, boiled)	11.2	3100
Heart (sheep, roast)	14.7	260
Kidney (lamb, fried)	6.3	610
(pig, stewed)	6.1	700
Liver (calf, fried)	13.2	330
(chicken, fried)	10.9	350
(lamb, fried)	14.0	400

Source: McCance and Widdowson (52)

Roast goose has the highest fat content followed by pigeon. Duck is also 'fat' and the fat content of lamb, beef and pork depends on one's ability to remove all the fat. Chicken and grouse have the lowest fat contents.

Grousemeat is exceptional from a PUFA point of view in that it has a high P/S ratio and also a very favourable w6/w3 ratio. Duck and chicken also have good P/S ratios but their w6/w3 ratios are unfavourable. Beef, lamb and pork have favourable w6/w3 ratios but the P/S ratio is low and their overall content of PUFA is small. Of the meats listed (Table 19) grousemeat best meets the 'requirement' for a low fat meat with a high P/S ratio and a favourable w6/w3 ratio.

The data (Table 20) show that kidney has the lowest fat content of the organ meats listed but with the exception of brain has the highest cholesterol content. The organ meats have much higher cholesterol contents than the 'ordinary' meats (Table 19).

The data in Tables 19 and 20 must be taken in the context of overall food intake. For example in the UK 25% of saturated fat comes from meat, 33% from dairy products and the remainder from margarine, cakes, biscuits, pies (237). Cholesterol has already been discussed and many would agree that the importance of dietary cholesterol has been overemphasised (238). Some interesting developments are taking place in the restaurant business in the USA in relation to meat. For example, cooperating restaurants of Steak House Associates in Houston are serving low cholesterol dinners (238) based on the following practices.

a)   ground beef fat max 15%

b)   lean cuts used

c)   all visible fats trimmed

d)   skin removed from chickens

e)   margarine - not butter

f)   PUFA coffee creamer used

g) skim milk used in food preparation

h) low fat cheeses used

This may be an indication of more widespread developments to come in reducing cholesterol and fat intakes from foods by the catering trade.

1.4.5   Food from marine sources

White fish has long been recognised as a supplier of important vitamins, minerals and high quality protein.   Since it contains little or no carbohydrate and very little fat it is also a relatively low calorie food.   However, most of the recent interest has centred around the oily fish in view of the fact that they are a good source of w-3 acids and especially eicosapentaenoic acid.   The possible importance of this in relation to thrombosis has already been discussed (see section 1.3.5.1). All the fish types listed (Table 21) have good w6/w3 ratios indicating high linolenic and eicosapentaenoic acid contents relative to linoleic and

TABLE 21: Fat content of fish

Fish	Fat (%)	PUFA* (%)	Ratios	
			P/S	w6/w3
Cod (raw)	0.7	56.8	2.2	0.25
Haddock (raw)	0.6	45.3	1.5	0.44
Herring (raw)	18.5	19.6	0.9	0.24
Mackerel (raw)	16.3	27.1	1.0	0.35
Crab (boiled)	5.2	43.8	2.6	0.15
Shrimps (boiled)	2.4	43.3	2.0	0.12
Mussels (raw)	1.9	31.5	1.3	0.55
Oysters (raw)	0.9	43.7	1.4	0.21

* as % of total fatty acids   Source: McCance and Widdowson (52)

arachidonic acids. However, in absolute terms herring and mackerel contain much more w-3 acids because of their high overall fat content. The inclusion of oily fish in the diet will, therefore, increase overall P/S ratios and also contribute the w-3 acids which may be protective against CHD (see section 1.3.5.1). Crab and shrimp have a high proportion of their PUFA content as eicosapentaenoic acid but their total fat contents are small relative to mackerel and herring. Eicosapentaenoic acid has also been shown to reduce blood pressure in humans (142) which may be another reason for consuming oily fish in the diet.

1.4.6   Vegetarians vs omnivores vs carnivores

A good indication of the adequacy of a plant food vs an animal food diet for good health can be obtained from the literature on vegans and a comparison of the health of vegetarians and carnivores. The majority of vegetarians eat milk and eggs, and must be distinguished from vegans who after weaning eat no animal food. By contrast Eskimos on their traditional diet are almost entirely carnivorous. A classic comparison was made by Orr and Gilks (239) of the Masai and Akikuyu. The former are largely carnivorous, consuming milk, meat and raw blood; the Akikuyu were mainly eating porridge made of maize, legumes and plantains, and gruel of millet flour. The Masai were taller, heavier and stronger than the Akikuyu, but had more intestinal stasis and rheumatoid arthritis. The vegetarian tribe had more bone deformities with low plasma calcium, more dental caries, anaemia, tropical ulcer and pulmonary infections.

Sanders and Ellis (240) showed that vegans had lower cholesterol (4.1 m mol/l) and serum triglycerides (0.95 m mol) compared with omnivores (6.1 and 1.35 m mol). A review of studies on the health and nutritional status of vegans in the 25 years prior to 1978 was carried out by Sanders (227). He concluded the following: vegans compared with omnivores are lighter in weight for the same height because they are less obese; they have lower serum cholesterol and triglyceride concentrations. Breast milk from vegan mothers contains about four times as much linoleic acid as that from omnivore mothers and the erythrocyte lipids of infants breast fed by vegan mothers contain more linoleic acid and its long-chain derivatives, and less of the long-chain derivatives of α-linolenic acid, than those from infants breast fed by omnivore mothers. A vegan diet seems to be adequate provided it comprises a mixture of unrefined cereals, pulses, nuts, fruit and vegetables and is supplemented with vitamins B_{12} and D. The evidence suggests that people following such diets enjoy good health. The vegan diet is probably protective against ischaemic heart disease (241) and cancer of the colon and a vegan-type diet may be of therapeutic value in the treatment of angina pectoris, ischaemic heart disease and certain hyperlipidaemias. However, Truswell (242) points out that while on the whole vegetarians appear to have a lower risk of obesity and 'modern' diseases much of the evidence for this comes from groups such as the Seventh Day Adventists who have a more healthy lifestyle than average in other ways.

In the context of carnivores Eskimos (222) are particularly interesting in view of their diet which traditionally is extremely high in fat (relatively highly polyunsaturated) and meat, but very low in carbohydrate and plant fibre, and low in tocopherols and ascorbic acid. Yet, as already mentioned, they are almost free of 'Western' diseases characteristic of those subsisting on 'Western' diets such as Eskimos living in Denmark as already mentioned in section (1.3.5); this may be due to their high intake of PUFA from fish.

These data show that it is possible to live healthily on diets which are highly vegetarian or high in meat although groups such as the Eskimos and the Masai may have become 'adapted' (243) to these dietary regimes. However, it would not be prudent to recommend these extreme forms of diet to a European population and the motto based on the above evidence, and on that in the previous sections, should be a varied diet of plant, animal and marine foods with emphasis on an increased consumption of foods of plant and marine origin in some EEC countries - especially those in Northern Europe.

1.5   THE CONCENTRATES

The concentrates refer to fat spreads, cheese, oils, sugar, alcohol and salt. These items are 'so called' in this document because they contain energy (carbohydrate or fat) or in the case of salt, sodium chloride, at levels far above that found in foods in nature, i.e. man has concentrated them. As such they can present problems in a healthy varied diet in that they may provide an excess of calories (salt excepted) in the form of carbohydrate or fat. The 'concentrates' are of major significance in the European diet and some of them are highly controversial.

1.5.1   Fat spreads

The main items are butter, margarine and the low fat spreads. Butter and margarine contain about 80% fat and their effect on calories when spread on bread is shown in Table 22. The bread slices used in Table 22 represent the thickness found in the standard sliced pan in Ireland, i.e. about 11 mm. Obviously the % CF values will decrease as slice thickness increases so to spread on thicker slices is one way of reducing the amount of spread consumed at a given meal. Butter and margarine promotions in recent years have sometimes used 'slim with butter' or 'slim with margarine' themes.   In view of the data in Table 22 this claim can only be

TABLE 22: Weight (g) and calorie content of margarine (M) and/or jam (J)
           spread on 3 slices of wholemeal bread (WMB)

| Slice thickness (11 mm) | Calories (11 mm slice) | % CF [1] | |
		11 mm slice	22 mm slice [2]
3 slices WMB (95 g)	198	9.1	9.1
3 x WMB (95 g) + M-light (13 g)	293	38.6	26.7
3 x WMB (95 g) + M-normal (20 g)	344	47.7	33.6
3 x WMB (95 g) + M-liberal (34 g)	446	59.6	44.0
3 x WMB (95 g) + J-light (27 g)	268	6.6	-
3 x WMB (95 g) + J-normal (40 g)	302	5.9	-
3 x WMB (95 g) + J-liberal (54 g)	339	5.3	-
3 x WMB (95 g) + (M+J) normal	448	36.6	-

[1] CF = calories from fat
[2] 3 slices = 190 g

made if the bread consumed is sliced thickly rather than thinly.   For example when three slices of bread were covered with the minimum quantity of spread this still amounted to 13 g; normal spreading was 20 g and liberal 34 g.   In relation to a target of 35% of calories from fat as the maximum value, bread and butter or margarine gives a % CF figure above this for 11 mm thick bread - even at the lowest spreading level.   However, the position improves considerably if slice thickness is increased to 22 mm. These data show the importance of consuming the bread at a meal as thick rather than as thin slices.This may be difficult to achieve in many cases as many breads are sliced to a thickness of about 11 mm.   The data (Table 22) also show the need for low fat spreads; some of these are now on the market with half the fat content of butter or margarine.

Epidemiological evidence (Joossens, 244) from Belgium suggests that butter (consumed in the south) may be the reason for a higher CHD and total mortality in the south compared with the north (margarine consumed). Saturated fat and PUFA consumptions were 58 and 17 g in the south versus 47 and 24 g in the north. Joossens cites similar evidence from France. As already noted above some studies (228) show that butter raises cholesterol whereas others (229) show no effect but with HDL levels raised; so once again the position is not clearcut.

Many studies have shown that PUFA margarines reduce cholesterol but the impact of this on CHD and mortality is far from clear (see section 1.3.5.1). While the claims made that butter is a natural pure food are correct the position is different regarding margarines. Some of them contain a very high level of PUFA relative to that found elsewhere in nature. For example mackerel contains about 4% PUFA as eaten, a low fat PUFA spread about 12% and a soft PUFA vegetable margarine about 18%. In view of the possible link between high intakes of PUFA and cancer (see section 1.3.5.2) there must be some concern about ingesting large quantities of these margarines. In addition, margarines have been 'tampered' with to the extent that some of them contain a high percentage (up to 50%) of trans fatty acids (245); these may be harmful to the heart muscle in that they reduce the capacity of its cells to produce energy (246). The health aspects of dietary trans fatty acids have been reviewed recently in the FASEB report (257). While no major adverse effects are noted most of the results cited are based on animal studies. Soft margarines also have very unfavourable w6/w3 ratios (Table 4). Taylor (134) sees no justification for recommending the widespread substitution of w-6 rich polyunsaturated margarines for ordinary margarine or butter. The

August 1985 issue of New Health (245) contains an excellent review of margarines and oils; Kochhar and Matsui (246) also reviewed this subject.

1.5.2   Cheese

Cheese is an excellent source of protein and calcium but it also contains fat. This can vary extensively depending on the type of cheese. High fat cheeses include cream (47%), Stilton (40%), Cheddar (33%) and Caerphilly (31%). Cottage cheese (4%) and Ricotta (5-10%) are low fat cheeses. Current and future dietary advice should ensure a good demand/market for a wide range of low fat cheeses flavoured in a variety of ways for use as spreads and on salads and other dishes.

1.5.3   Oils

Most of what has been said of margarine can be said about vegetable oils except that they are not hydrogenated. They are all over 97% fat and so are a high source of calories. The typical fatty acid contents of the principal oils are given in Table 23. All the vegetable oils have unfavourable w6/w3 ratios. Even though it has a low PUFA content olive oil has been claimed to have a favourable effect on atherosclerosis in regions where it is used extensively in the diet (73). An account of the patterns of refined fat usage and practical constraints has been drawn up by Crawford (34). Rapeseed oil is one of the newer oils to come on the market. It is very low in saturated fat. The vegetable oils only contain traces of cholesterol but have a significant vitamin E content, i.e. sunflower oil 630 ppm, rapeseed oil 300 ppm, maize oil 240 ppm, soyabean oil 150 ppm, groundnut 100 ppm. As oils they are mainly ingested from cooking (deep frying), or when used as dressings or as ingredients in food products.

TABLE 23: Typical fatty acid composition of the principal vegetable oils and animal fats

Oil or Fat	% of Total Fatty Acids		
	Monounsaturated	Polyunsaturated	Saturated
Soybean oil	24	61	15
Cottonseed oil	19	54	27
Corn oil	28	58	14
Peanut oil	48	32	20
Olive oil	72	11	17
Safflower oil	13	78	9
Sunflower oil	18	70	12
Palm oil	40	10	50
Coconut oil	6	2	92
Palm kernel oil	14	2	84
Lard	47	12	41
Beef Tallow	46	3	51
Rapeseed oil*	64	30	6

Source: Food Processing, May 1985, 60
*data for rapeseed oil from trade literature

1.5.4 Sugar

Claims that sugar (sucrose) is a pure natural product are correct. However, like fat it represents a large amount of energy on a weight basis. When used in drinks it is readily absorbed and so leads to increased insulin secretion which in turn leads to fat deposition. However, when sprinkled on cereal or used in other foods containing dietary fibre or complex carbohydrate its rate of absorption is likely to be slowed down and so a much smaller insulin response results. This slower release of energy may enable more of the energy to be used as it is released rather than having it stored (71). The data presented earlier in this document (see section 1.3.3.1) suggest that sugar does influence obesity and the development of dental caries but has no other major effect on health.

Other sugar related materials such as glucose syrups, being longer molecules are probably absorbed more slowly on ingestion than sugar. Sugar in jams may also be more slowly absorbed because of the presence of pectin, however, there is little work carried out in this area. Honey contains about 75% carbohydrate which is readily absorbable. The data (Table 22) show the large number of calories that come from jam spreads on bread. Even a light spreading amounts to 27 g (based on three slices of bread).

1.5.5   Salt

The role of salt in cardiovascular hypertension (HT) has been the subject of books (247) and many scientific papers and yet despite the amount of work carried out there are still doubts about the actual role of salt in HT (in this document HT and high blood pressure HP are used interchangeably) and of the need for dietary restriction of salt on a population basis. The low sodium foods business has become large, especially in the USA, where low sodium foods were valued at $169 billion in 1981-82 (248). A scientific status summary by the US Institute of Food Technologists' Expert Panel on Food Safety and Nutrition and the Committee on Public Information (249) says of salt:

> "As in the case with many dietary components, there are levels of salt which cannot be exceeded without placing vulnerable individuals 'at risk.' (Potential hazards also exist for the individual who reduces his intake below his requirements, although this is unlikely in North America).
>
> Salt requirements and tolerances are specific for each individual. The potential hazard of salt intakes above the requirement are therefore specific for each person

based on a number of interrelated factors such as genetic vulnerability, other attendant pathologies, stress, nutritional status, and - perhaps especially - obesity. For those whose genetic make-up leads to medical vulnerability, clearer labelling and access to information concerning sodium content of all ingestible substances is highly desirable.

In addition, the unique functions filled by the sodium ion in food processing and preservation mean that decisions to restrict or eliminate salt from specific products must take into account the effects on food safety and on the free choice of food products for that majority of consumers who are not "at risk". © IFT, USA.

These statements agree largely with those of Boon and Aronson (250) and with those presented by Robertson (251) at the 1985 Nutrition Congress in Brighton. Robertson suggests that tolerable and realistic dietary salt restriction (i.e. down to some 60-100 mmol/day) probably is effective in lowering blood pressure in a substantial number of patients with moderately severe essential hypertension (i.e. fifth phase diastolic of 110 mm and upwards). Robertson claims that this benefit is not seen in every case but is often useful and may reinforce the antihypertensive effects of drugs. He suggests that long term value of such salt restriction in supervised patients is worthy of a strict long-term trial in which an assessment of morbidity and side-effects should be carried out, in much the same way as the study would be carried out using antihypertensive drugs. The value of salt restriction in more mild hypertension is more doubtful. Certainly the effects can vary greatly from one individual to another. The value of salt restriction as a preventive measure is also quite uncertain and is not supported by any major study in practice (251).

The presence of 'adequate' sodium for a possible calcium/sodium effect in regulating BP has already been referred to in section 1.3.7. These data suggest that sodium restriction should be confined to those with moderately severe HT and not to a whole population. However, this does not mean that everyone should start using the salt cellar; obviously restraint is desirable in this respect. But it questions the need for a wide range of reduced sodium foods for the population at large; this is even more the case if consumers turn increasingly to a balanced diet. Recommendations for salt intakes by various groups are given in CHAPTER 2.

Potassium/sodium balance in the body may also be important. Some studies have supported a theory that increased intake of potassium chloride can reduce the blood pressure of hypertensive patients, even in the presence of excess sodium chloride (252). Potassium chloride has been reported to exert a protective action against sodium-induced hypertension in animals, and to reduce the blood pressure of diabetic children taking excess salt in their diets.

Some consumers, particularly those on moderately reduced sodium diets, may benefit from the use of mixtures of sodium and potassium chloride for 'salting' their food. Excessive amounts of dietary potassium should, of course, be avoided (except under a physician's instructions) because of potential toxicity at high levels of intake.

The decreased incidence of cancer of the stomach in industrialised countries could be due to the replacement of salt and smoking by refrigeration for food preservation.

1.5.6   Alcohol

Epidemiological evidence (253) shows that individuals who consume moderate levels (e.g. 2 whiskies or equivalent/day) of alcohol may be less susceptible to mycocardial infarction than those who are total abstainers; this may be due to higher HDL cholesterol levels in the former.   Alcohol may also reduce stress which could be beneficial. At the other extreme the effects of excess alcohol are well known to all.

1.6   OTHER AREAS/ASPECTS

There are many other areas/aspects that are not included in this report.   For example, little information has been presented on actual food intakes but the BRADFORD team (see foreword) will provide much of this information in their project. They will also provide essential information on nutritional labelling, a topic which is overlapping and complementary to many of the items discussed and presented in this report.

Two other areas worthy of special mention are naturally occurring food toxicants (164, 252, 254) (see CHAPTER 3) and food intolerance/food allergy (255, 256).   The latter should be the subject of another study as it represents one of the major problems facing food producers and processors. Many of its manifestations are sub-clinical which further complicates the issue.

1.7   REFERENCES

1.   Yeomans, L. (1985). Food nutrition in Europe. Fd. Manufacture Internat.   July/August: 41-47.

2.   Hetzel, B.S. (1983). Diet, nutrition and health. Fd. Technol in Australia, 35: 519-522.

3.   Trowell, H.C. and Burkitt, D.P. (1975). Concluding considerations. In: Refined Carbohydrate Foods and Disease: Some implications of dietary fibre, D.P. Burkitt and H.C. Trowell Eds, Academic Press, London: 333-345.

4.   Nesheim, M.C. (1985). Evaluation of research opportunities to solve national problems in human nutrition through changes in the agricultural/food system, USDA/Cornell University, Agreement No. 58-32 U4-4-772, 35 pages.

5.   NACNE Report (1983): Proposals for nutrition guidelines for health education in Britain, 40 pages.

6.   COMA Report (1984): UK Committee on Medical Aspects of Food Policy, 32 pages.

7.   Schutz, H.G. and Judge, D.S. (1986). Changing needs and lifestyles in developed countries. Proc. 13th Int. Cong. Nutr. Brighton, T.G. Taylor and N.K. Jenkins Eds, John Libbey, London and Paris: 862-865.

8.   Anon. (1984). Americans' diet consciousness. Fd Processing, Sept: 8.

9.   Clydesdale, F.M. (1984). Culture, fitness and health. Fd. Technol. (USA), Nov: 108-111.

10. Anon. (1985). Fitness fattens US profits. Fd Processing, Nov: 27-29.

11. Toufexis, A. (1986). Dieting: the losing game. Time Magazine, Jan 20: 42-48.

12. Gray, J. (1985). How safe is your diet. Chem. & Ind. March: 146-148.

13. James, W.P.T., Powles, J. and Williams, D.R. (1981). The prevalence of diet-related Western diseases in Britain. In: Preventive Nutrition and Society. M.R. Turner ed. Academic Press, 1-54.

14. Laing, W.A. (1981). The cost of diet related diseases. In: Preventive Nutrition and Society.   M.R. Turner ed. Academic Press, 55-76.

15. Wodicka, V.O. (1971). Fd Chemical News, 1 March.

16. Hall, R.L. (1971). Information, confidence and sanity in the food sciences. The Flavour Industry, August: 455-457.

106

17. Miller, S.A. (1985). Food safety and health: a scientific and
legislative perspective. Paper presented at the 13th Int. Cong.
Nutr. Brighton. (Not reported in the proceedings).

18. Hawthorn, J. (1985). Personal communication.

19. Beckers, H. (1985). Incidence of food borne disease in the
Netherlands. J. Fd Protection, 48: 181-187.

20. Todd, E.C.D. (1985). Economic loss from foodborne disease outbreaks
associated with food service establishments. J. Fd Protect. 48:
169-180.

21. Irvin, M.S. and Hegsted, D.M. (1971). Conspectus of research on
protein requirements of man. J. Nutr. 101:. 385-430.

22. Report of the Expert Advisory Committee on Dietary Fibre (1985),
Health Protection Branch, Health and Welfare, Canada, 29 pages.

23. Of mice and men (1984). The benefits and limitations of animal
cancer tests: A Report of the American Council on Science and Health,
March: 25 pages.

24. Beynen, A.C. and West, C.E. (1986). The suitability of animal models
for research in human nutrition. Workshop No. 25. Proc. 13th Int. Cong.
Nutr. (see Ref. 7): 58-59.

25. Derry, B.J. and Buss, D.H. (1984). The British National Food Survey
as a major epidemiological resource. Br.M.J.., 288: 765-767.

26. Diet and cancer (1984). The benefits and limitations of animal
cancer tests: A Report of the American Council on Science and Health,
March: 25 pages.

27. Truswell, A.S. (1983). The development of dietary guidelines.
Fd Technol. in Australia, 35: 498-502.

28. Oliver, M. (1985). Consensus or non-consensus conferences on coronary
heart disease. Lancet, 1: 1087-1089.

29. Ahrens, E.H. (1985). The diet-heart question in 1985: has it really
been settled. Lancet, 1: 1085-1087.

30. Recommendations for a Food and Nutrition Policy in Ireland (1979).
Report prepared by the Food Advisory Committee. 21 pages.

31. Prevention of coronary heart disease (1982). Report of a WHO Expert
Committee.

32. Diet, nutrition and cancer (1982). (Executive Summary). Committee
on Diet, Nutrition and Cancer, Nutrition Today, July /August:
20-25.

33. Dietary fibre: current developments of importance to health (1978).
Proc. 3rd Kellogg Nutr. Symp. (K.W. Heaton ed), Biddles Ltd., U.K.
158 pages.

34. Crawford, R.V. (1985). Patterns of refined fat usage and practical constraints. In: The role of Fats in Human Nutrition. Padley et al eds, Ellis Horwood, U.K. 62-83.

35. Hornstra, G. (1979). Effect of dietary fats on arterial thrombosis: rationale for dietary primary prevention of coronary artery disease. Symposium on Prevention of Coronary Heart Disease. Coronary Prevention Group, U.K. November.

36. Facts on Fat. Butter Information Council, U.K. (undated booklet), 12 pages.

37. Symposium on Nutrition, Food Technology and Nutritional Information, London. (Held 1980, Proc. published 1981). Commission of the European Communities, Report Eur 7085EN.

38. Influence on health of different fats in food (1977). Commission of the European Communities. DGVI, No. 40.

39. Kahn, H. (1979). The world at a turning point: New Class attitudes. In: Crit. Fd Issues of the Eighties, M. Chou and D.P. Harmon eds, Pergamon Press, New York: 5-17.

40. Kramer, A. (1973). Food and the Consumer. Avi Publishing Co. Inc., Westport, Conn., 256 pages.

41. Anon (1972). Food facts can be fun. Food and Nutr., 2:8.

42. Derby, G. (1981). Nutrition and Health. CEC Symposium (see reference 37): 67-69.

43. Mariani, A. (1981). Nutritional needs and the situation in the European Community. CEC Symposium (see reference 37): 5-38.

44. McKenzie, J. (1981). Evolution of eating habits in countries of the EEC. CEC Symposium (see reference 37): 39-60.

45. Hendrikx, A. (1981). Evaluation of dietary regimes. CEC Symposium (see reference 37): 61-66.

46. Passmore, R. and 4 authors (1974). Handbook on Human Nutrition Requirements. FAO Nutritional Studies No. 28. Rome, FAO.

47. RDIs in 20 countries (1975). Comm. Int. Dietary Allow. of Int. Union of Nutr. Sci.

48. Trusswell, A.S. and Hansen, J.D.L. (1976). In: Kalahari Hunter - Gatherers, R.B. Lee and De Vore eds, Harvard Univ. Press, 167.

49. Zollner, N., Wolfram, G. and Keller, C. (ed) (1977). Second European Nutrition Conference, Nutr. Metab. 21: 210.

50. Crocetti, A. and Guthrie, H.A. (1981). Food Consumption patterns and nutritional quality of US diets: a preliminary report. Fd Technol. (USA), 35: 40-57.

51. Munro, H.N. (1985). Evolving scientific bases for the recommended dietary allowances - a critical look at methodologies. J. Amer Clin. Nutr. 41: 149-154.

52. McCance and Widdowson's - The Composition of Foods (1978, 4th Edn), Paul, A.A. and Southgate, D.A.T., HMSO/Elsevier - North Holland Biomedical Press.

53. West, C.E. (1985). Eurofoods: towards compatibility of nutrient data banks in Europe. Annals of Nutr. and Metabolism, 29: 72 pages.

54. James, W.P.T. (1985). Appetite control and other mechanisms of weight homoeostasis. In: Nutritional Adaptation in Man, K. Blaxter and J.C. Waterlow Eds, J. Libbey, London and Paris: 141-154.

55. Garrow, J.S. (1985). Responses to overnutrition. In: Nutritional Adaptation in Man, K. Blaxter and J.C. Waterlow Eds, J. Libbey, London and Paris: 105-110.

56. Shetty, P.S. and 4 authors (1981). Postprandial thermogenesis in obesity. Clin. Sci. 60: 519-525.

57. Nair, K.S., Halliday, D. and Garrow, J.S. (1983). Thermic response to isoenergetic protein, carbohydrate or fat meals in lean and obese subjects. Clin. Sci. 65: 307-312.

58. Blaza, S. and Garrow, J.S. (1983). Thermogenic response to temperature, exercise and food stimuli in lean and obese women, studied by 24h direct calorimetry Br. J. Nutr. 49: 171-180.

59. Nechad, M. (1986). Distinction between white and brown adipose tissue. Proc. 13th Int. Cong. Nutr. (see Ref. 7): 344-346.

60. Himms-Hagen, J. (1986). Brown adipose tissue and obesity. Proc. 13th Int. Cong. Nutr. (see Ref. 7): 325-327.

61. Himms-Hagen, J. (1984). Thermogenesis in brown adipose tissue as an energy buffer. New England J. Med,. 311: 1549-1558.

62. Himms-Hagen, J. (1985). Brown adipose tissue metabolism and thermogenesis. Ann. Rev. Nutr. 5: 69-94.

63. Mercer, S.W. and Trayhurn, P. (1985). Influence of high fat diets on energy balance and brown adipose tissue thermogenesis in obese mice. In: Abstracts from 13th Int. Cong. Nutr.Brighton: 99.

64. Cunningham, S. and 8 authors (1985). The characterisation and energetic potential of brown adipose tissue in man. Clin. Sci. 69: 343-348.

65. Foster, E.O., Depocas, F. and Frydman, M.L. (1980). Noradrenaline induced....(long title). Can. J. Physiol. and Pharmacology, 58: 915-924.

66. Heaton, J.M. (1972). The distribution of brown adipose tissue in the human. J. Anatomy, 112: 35-39.

67. Tanuma, Y., Yamamoto, M. and Yokochi, C. (1975). The occurrence of brown adipose tissue in perirenal fat in Japanese, Arch. Histologica Japonica, 38: 43-70.

68. Foster, E.O. and Frydman, M.L. (1978). Comparison of microspheres and 86 Rb(+) tracers of the distribution of cardiac output of 86 Rb(+) based measurements, Can. J.Physiol. and Pharmacol. 56: 97-109.

69. Rothwell, N.J. and Stock, M.J. (1981). Influence of noradrenaline on blood flow to brown adipose tissue in rats exhibiting diet induced thermogenesis, Pflugers Archiv. 389: 237-242.

70. Andrews, F. (1986). Personal communication.

71. Heaton, K.W. (1978). Fibre, satiety and insulin - a new approach to overnutrition and obesity. Proc. 3rd Kellogg Nutr. Symp. (K.W. Heaton ed), Biddles Ltd., U.K. 158 pages.

72. Hill, M.J. (1983). Bacteria, dietary fibre and chronic intestinal disease. In: Dietary Fibre, G.G. Birch and K.J. Parker eds, Applied Science Publishers, London and New York, 255-274.

73. Keys, A. et al. (1980). Seven countries: A Multivariate Analysis of Death and Coronary Heart Disease. Harvard Univ. Press, Cambridge, Mass. and London, U.K.

74. Oliver, M.F. (1981). Diet and coronary heart disease. Med. Bull 37: 49-58.

75. Seltzer, F. (1983). Untitled paper presented at U.S. Dept. of Health and Human Services Nutrition Symp., Washington DC, March 15.

76. Van Itallie, T.B. (1979). Obesity: adverse effects on health and longevity. Am. J. Clin. Nutr., 32: 2723-2733.

77. Ahrens, E.H. Jr. (1986). Carbohydrates, plasma triglycerides, and coronary heart disease. Nutr. Rev., 44: 60-64.

78. Haber, G.B., Heaton, K.W., Murphy, D. and Burroughs, L. (1977). Depletion and disruption of dietary fibre. Effects on satiety, plasma glucose and serum insulin, Lancet, 2: 679-682.

79. Gee, J.M. and Johnson, I.T.(1985). Rates of hydrolysis and changes in viscosity in a range of common foods subjected to simulated digestion in vitro. J. Sci Fd Agric. 36: 614-620.

80. Dreher, M.L., Dreher, C.J. and Berry, J.W. (1984). Starch digestibility of foods: a nutritional perspective. CRC Rev Fd Sci. and Nutr. 20: 47-71.

81. Jenkins, D.J.A. and 4 authors (1986). Variations in the availability of carbohydrates. Proc. 13th Int. Cong. Nutr. (see Ref. 7): 242-246.

82. Wei, S.H.Y. (1979). National Symposium on Dental Nutrition. An update on nutrition, diet, cariogenicity of foods and preventive dentistry. University of Iowa Press, Iowa City.

83. Southgate, D.A.T. (1981). Role of carbohydrates in the diet of industrialised countries. Biblthca Nutr. Dieta, No. 30: 124-130.

84. Reaven, G.M. (1986). The effect of carbohydrate on the metabolism of patients with non-insulin dependent diabetes mellitus. Nutr. Rev., 44: 65-73.

85. Mayne, P.D. and 5 authors (1982). The effect of apple fibre on diabetic control and plasma lipids. Ir. J. Med.Sci. 151: 36-41.

86. Morris, J.N., Marr, J.W. and Clayton, D.G. (1977). Diet and heart: a postscript Br. Med. J. 2: 1307-1314.

87. Haenszel, W. and Kurihara, M. (1968). Studies of Japanese migrants. Mortality from cancer and other diseases among Japanese in the U.S.A. J. Nat. Cancer Inst. 40: 43-68.

88. Bingham, S.A. (1986). Dietary fibre as a protective factor in human large bowel cancer. Proc. 13th Int. Cong. Nutr. (see Ref. 7): 567-569.

89. Downey, G. (1979). Wheat bran: the analysts view. Fd Ireland, 10: 26-28.

90. Gould, M.R., Anderson, J.W. and O'Mahony, S. (1980). Biofunctional properties of oats. In: Cereals for Food and Beverages, Inglett and George eds, Newman Publ. Co. Ltd.: 447-460.

91. Gormley, T.R., Kevany, J., Egan, J.P. and McFarlane, R. (1977). Effect of apples on serum cholesterol. Ir. J. Fd Sci. Technol. 1: 117-128.

92. Kiehm, T.G., Anderson, J.W. and Ward, K. (1976). Beneficial effect of a high carbohydrate high fibre diet on hyperglycaemic diabetic man. Am. J. Clin. Nutr., 29: 895-899.

93. Staub, H.W., Mardones, B. and Shah, N. (1983). Modern dietary fibre product development and nutrient bioavailability. In: Dietary Fibre, Birch and Parker eds, Appl. Sci. Publ. London and New York, 37-60.

94. Asp, N.G. and Johansson, C.G. (1984). Dietary fibre analysis. Nutr. Abs and Reviews, Review in Clinical Nutrition, Series A, 54: 734-752.

95. Cummings, J.H., Englyst, H.N. and Wood, R. (1985). Determination of dietary fibre in cereals and cereal products - collaborative trials. Part 1: Initial trial. J. Assoc. Publ. Analysts, 23: 1-35.

96. Halvarson, H. and Alstin, F. (1984). Dietary fibre determination methods, Cer. Fds World, 29: 571-574.

97. Asp, N.G., Johansson, C.G. and Siljestrom, M. (1983). Dietary fibre analysis for the estimation of wholemeal flour in bread. Proc. 6th Int. Cong. Fd Sci. and Technol., Dublin, 3 (McLoughlin and McKenna eds): 7-8.

98. Johnston, D.W. and Oliver, W.T. (1982). The influence of cooking technique on dietary fibre of boiled potato. J. Fd Technol., 17: 99-107.

99. Anderson, N.E. and Clydesdale, F.M. (1980). Effects of processing on the dietary fibre content of wheat bran, puréed greenbeans and carrots, J. Fd Sci. 45: 1533-1537.

100. Wrick, K.L. and 6 authors (1983). The influence of dietary fibre source on human intestinal transit and stool output. J. Nutr. 113: 1464-1479.

101. Grasso, P. (1976). Persorption - A new long-term problem. Fd Cosmet. Toxicol. 14: 497-498.

102. Glauert, H.P., Bennick, M.R. and Sanger, V.L. (1983). Dietary agar induced changes in colon topography as seen with scanning electron microscopy, Nutr. Rep. Int. 27: 271-277.

103. Barnes, D.S. and 4 authors (1983). Effect of wheat, rice, corn and soybean bran on 1,2-dimethylhydrazine-induced large bowel tumorigenesis in F-344 rats, Nutr. and Cancer, 5: 1-9.

104. Armstrong, B. and Doll, R. (1975). Environmental factors and cancer incidence and mortality in different countries with special reference to dietary practices, Int. J. Cancer, 15: 617-631.

105. Knox, E.G. (1977). Foods and diseases, Br. J. Prev.Soc. Med. 31: 71-80.

106. Hems, G. (1980). Associations between breast cancer mortality rates, child-bearing and diet in the United Kingdom, Br. J. Cancer, 41: 429-437.

107. Gregor, O., Toman, R. and Prusova, P. (1969). Gastrointestinal cancer and nutrition Gut, 10: 1031-1034.

108. Lea, A.J. (1967). Neoplasms and environmental factors. Ann. Rep. Coll. Surg. Engl. 41: 432-438.

109. Madhavan, T.V. and Gopalan, C. (1968). The effect of dietary protein on carcinogenesis of aflatoxin. Arch. Path. 80: 123-126.

110. Hollingsworth, D.F. (1979). What do we know and believe about diet. Biologist, 26: 61-65.

111. Frank, J.D. (1985). International Food Consumption Levels, Food Policy Res. Univ. Bradford, U.K.: 7 pages.

112. Frank, J.D. (1985). Food Consumption Patterns in the U.K. from 1880 to 1980. Food Policy Res. Univ. Bradford, U.K.: 16 pages.

113. Davidson, S., Passmore, R., Brock, J.F. and Truswell, A.S. (1979 - 7th Edn). Human Nutrition and Dietetics, Churchill Livingstone, Edinburgh, London, New York: 57.

114. FAO/WHO (Rome) (1977). Dietary fats and oils in human nutrition.

115. Fat and Health (1985). WHICH Magazine, June: 263-266.

116. The Role of Fats in Human Nutrition (1985). F.B. Padley et al eds, Ellis Horwood, U.K., 172 pages.

117. Fats in the diet: why and where (1981). Scientific status summary by the Institute of Food Technologists' Expert Panel on Food Safety and Nutrition. Fd Technol. (USA), Dec: 33-38.

118. Connolly, J.F. (1977). Prevention of coronary heart disease - diet and the food supply. The Health Advisory Committee of An Foras Taluntais, Dublin: 28 pages.

119. Keys, A. (1956). Diet and development of coronary heart disease. J. Chronic Diseases, 4: 364-380.

120. Truswell, A.S. (1976). Diet in the pathogenesis of ischaemic heart disease. Post-grad.med.J. 52: 424-432.

121. Ahrens, E.H. Jr. and 8 authors (1979). The evidence relating six dietary factors to the nations health. Am. J. Clin. Nutr. 32: 2621-2748.

122. Brown, J. and 18 authors (1970). Nutritional and epidemiologic factors related to heart disease. Wld Rev. Nutr. Diet. 12: 1-42.

123. Harper, A.E. (1983). Coronary heart disease - an epidemic related to diet. Am. J. Clin. Nutr. 37: 669-681.

124. U.S. heart disease and fat intake trends. Health Bulletin, No. 1: 5 pages (date not available).

125. Brown, M.S. and Goldstein, J.L. (1984). How LDL receptors influence cholesterol and atherosclerosis, Scientific American, Nov: 58-66.

126. Nichols, A.B., Ravenscropf, Lappbeird, D.E., and Ostrader, L.D. (1976) Daily nutritional intake and serum lipid levels. The Tecumseh study. Am. J. Clin.Nutr. 29: 1384-1392.

127. Brisson, G.J. (1984). Fats and human health. Natl Renderers Assoc. Bull. No. 766: 5-8.

128. Oliver, M. (1976). Dietary cholesterol, plasma cholesterol and coronary heart disease. Br. Heart J. 38: 214-218.

129. Oliver, M.F. (1981). Serum cholesterol - the knave of hearts and joker. Lancet, 2: 1090-1095.

130. The Lipid Research Clinic's Coronary Primary Prevention Trial Results. (1984). I. Re-education in incidence of coronary heart disease. *JAMA*, *251*: 351-364.

131. Gotto, A.M. (1977). Atherosclerosis and heart disease: role of the plasma lipoproteins. International Conference on Atherosclerosis, Milan, 8 pages.

132. Gotto, A.M. (1985). Statement on : lowering blood cholesterol to prevent heart disease. *Nutr. Rev. 43*: 286-287.

133. James, W.P.T. (1986). Personal communication.

134. Taylor, T.G. (1980). Diet and coronary heart disease. *Proc. IFST* (U.K.), *13*: 45-50.

135. Morris, J.N. (1951). Recent history of coronary disease. *Lancet*, *260*: 1-7 and 69-73.

136. Anon. (1985). Reduction of plasma lipids and lipoproteins by marine fish oils. *Nutr. Rev. 43*: 268-270.

137. Dyerberg, J. and Bang, H.O. (1979). Haemostatic function and platelets-polyunsaturated fatty acids in Eskimos *Lancet, 2*: 433-435.

138. Gordon, M. (1984). The role of fat in human nutrition. *Nutr. Fd Sci.* No. 89: 10-11.

139. Gottenbos, J.J. (1985). The role of linoleic acid. *In*: The Role of Fats in Human Nutrition. Padley et al eds, Ellis Horwood, U.K., 117-131.

140. Anon. (1985). Mortality from CHD is inversely related to fish consumption in the Netherlands. *Nutr. Rev. 43*: 271-273.

141. Sanders, T.A.B. (1985). The importance of eicosapentaenoic acid and docosahexaenoic acids. *In*: The Role of Fats in Human Nutrition, Padley *et al* eds, Ellis Horwood, U.K. 101-116.

142. Singer, P., Wirth, M., Godicke, W. and Heine, H. (1985). Blood pressure lowering effect of eicosapentaenoic acid-rich diets in normotensive, hypertensive and hyperlipidaemic subjects. *Experentia, 41*: 462-465.

143. National Diet-Heart Study Research Group (1968). National Diet-Heart Study final report. *Circulation* 37, 38: Suppl. 1.

144. Ahrens, E.H. (1979). Dietary fats and coronary heart disease: unfinished business. *Lancet, 2*: 1345-1348.

145. Doll, R. and Petro, R. (1981). The causes of cancer. OUP - *J. Natl. Cancer Institute, 66*: 1191-1308.

146. Ableson, P.H. (1983). Dietary carcinogens. *Science, 22*: 1255.

147. Wynder and 4 authors (1969). Environmental Factors of Cancer, 23:
     1210-1220.

148. Anon (1977). Dietary fibre as a binder of bile salts. Nutr. Rev.,
     35: 183-185.

149. Int. Agency for Res. on Cancer Intestinal Microecology Group (1977):
     Dietary fibre, transit-time, faecal bacteria, steroids and colon
     cancer in two Scandinavian populations, Lancet, ii: 207-211.

150. Cummings, J.H. and 6 authors (1978). Influence of diets high and low
     in animal fat on bowel habit, gastrointestinal time, faecal micro-
     flora, bile acid and fat excretion. J. Clin. Invest. 61: 953-963.

151. Hill, M.J. (1978). Bacterial metabolism and colon cancer. Symp. Food
     and Cancer, Maribou, Naringsforskning 22 suppl. 16: 34-39.

152. Story, J.A. and Kritchevsky, D. (1976). Comparison of the binding
     of various bile acids and bile salts in-vitro by several types of
     fibre. J. Nutr. 106: 1292-1294.

153. Jansen, J.D. (1982). Nutrition and cancer. Wld Rev. Nutr. Diet. 39:
     1-22.

154. Brubacher, G. (1986). Bioavailability of vitamins. Proc. 13th Int.
     Cong. Nutr. (see Ref. 7): 250-254.

155. Everson, G., Wheeler, E., Walker, H. and Caulfield, W.J. (1948).
     Availability of riboflavin of ice cream, peas and almonds judged by
     urinary excretion of the vitamin by women subjects. J. Nutr. 35:
     209-223.

156. Kodicek, E. (1962). Nicotinic acid and the Pellagra problem.
     Biblthca Nutr. Dieta, 4: 109-127.

157. Mason, J.B. and Kodicek, E. (1973). The chemical nature of the bound
     nicotinic acid of wheat bran: Studies of partial hydrolysis products.
     Cer. Chem. 50: 637-647.

158. Hirayama, T. (1979). Diet and cancer. Nutr. Cancer, 1: 67-81.

159. Bjelke, E. (1975). Dietary vitamin A and lung cancer. Int. J.
     Cancer, 15: 561-565.

160. Mettlin, C., Graham, S. and Swanson, M. (1979). Vitamin A and lung
     cancer. J. Natl. Cancer Inst. 62: 1435-1438.

161. Colditz, G.A. and 6 authors (1985). Increased green and yellow
     vegetable intake and lowered cancer deaths in an elderly population
     Am. J. Clin. Nutr. 41: 32-36.

162. Burton, G.W. and Ingold, K.V. (1984). Beta-carotene: an unusual type
     of lipid antioxidant. Science, 224: 569-573.

163. Peto, R., Doll, R., Buckley, J.D. and Sporn, M.B. (1981). Can dietary-beta carotene materially reduce human cancer rates. *Nature,* 290: 201-208.

164. Ames, B.N. (1983). Dietary carcinogens and anticarcinogens. *Science,* 221: 1256-1264.

165. McCormick, L. and Moon, R.C. (1986). The modulation of carcinogenesis by retinoids. *Proc. 13th Int. Cong. Nutr.* (see Ref. 7): 564-567.

166. Underwood, B.A. (1986). Vitamin A status, carotene and cancer prevention. *Proc. 13th Int. Cong. Nutr.* (see Ref. 7): 474-477.

167. Graham, S. and Mettlin, C. (1981). Fibre and other constituents of vegetables in cancer epidemiology. *In*: Nutrition and Cancer, Etiology and Treatment, G.R.Newell and N.M. Ellison eds, Raven Press, New York: 189-215.

168. Hallberg, L. (1981). Effect of Vitamin C on the bioavailability of iron from food. *In*: Vitamin C, Ascorbic Acid, J.N. Counsell and D.H. Hornig eds, Applied Science Publishers, London: 49-61.

169. James, W.P.T. (1984). Health policies in relation to the National Diet: the role of the horticultural industry. East Malling Res. Rep. (UK), 209-217.

170. Aykroyd, W.R. and Doughty, J. (1970). Wheat in human nutrition. FAO Nutritional Studies No. 23.

171. Sullivan, J.L. (1981). Iron and the sex difference in heart disease risk. *Lancet,* 1: 1293-1294.

172. Packer, J.E., Slater, T.F. and Willson, R.L. (1979). Direct observation of a free radical interaction between Vitamin E and Vitamin C. *Nature,* 278: 737-738.

173. Department of Health and Social Security (1981). Nutritional aspects of bread and flour. Report on Health and Social Subjects, No. 23, HMSO, London.

174. Hanschka, P.V., Lian, J.B. and Gallop, P.M. (1978). Vitamin K and mineralization. *Trends in Biochemical Sciences,* 3: 75-78.

175. Hart, J.P. and 6 authors (1984). Circulating Vitamin K levels in fractured neck of femur. *Lancet,* 2: 283.

176. Majid Sho Jania, J. (1982). Oral contraceptives: effect of folate and Vitamin B12 metabolism. *Can. Med. Assoc.* 126: 244-247.

177. Anon. (1985). Osteoporosis. *Nutrition and Health* - National Dairy Council (IRL) Newsletter, 1: 8 pages.

178. Gormley, T. R. and Egan, S. (1981). Water hardness in county Dublin. *Fm Fd Res.*, 12, 133-134.

179. Gormley, T.R. (1986). Fresh and chilled foods. Paper presented at 5th World Frozen Foods Congress, Lausanne, Switzerland, 20 pages.

180. West, R.R., Lloyd, S. and Roberts, C.J. (1973). Mortality from ischaemic heart disease-association with weather. Brit. J. Prev. Soc. Med. 27: 36-40.

181. Elwood, P.C., St. Leger, A.S., and Morton, M. (1977). Mortality and the concentration of elements in tap water in county boroughs in England, Br. J. Prev. and Soc. Med. 31: 178-182.

182. Knox, E.G. (1973). Ischaemic-heart-disease mortality and dietary intake of calcium, Lancet, 1, 1465-1467.

183. Roberts, C.J. and Lloyd, S. (1972). Association between mortality from ischaemic heart disease and rainfall in South Wales and in the county boroughs of England and Wales. Lancet, 1: 1091-1093.

184. Anon. (1978). Progress in the water story. Br. Med. J. 1: 264.

185. Vahouney, G.V. (1982). Trace elements and cardiovascular disease. In: Nutritional Toxicology, Volume 1, J.N. Hathcock ed, Academic Press, London and New York: 135-159.

186. McCarron, D.A. (1983). Calcium and magnesium nutrition in human hypertension. Ann. Intern. Med. 87: 800-805.

187. Parrott-Garcia and McCarron, D.A. (1984). Calcium and hypertension Nutr. Rev. 42: 205-213.

188. Webb, R.C. and Bohr, D.F. (1978). Mechanism of membrane stabilisation by calcium in vascular smooth muscle. Am. J. Physiol. 235: C227-C232.

189. McCarron, D.A., Stanton, J., Henry, H. and Morris, C. (1983) Assessment of nutritional correlates of blood pressure. Ann. Intern. Med. 98: 715-719.

190. Feinleib, M., Lenfant, C. and Miller, S.A. (1984). Hypertension and calcium, Science, 226: 384-389.

191. McCarron, D.A., Morris, C. and Cole, C. (1982). Dietary calcium and human hypertension. Science, 217: 267-269.

192. Hann, S.A., Shneidman, R.J. and McCarron, D.A. (1984). Prevention of genetic hypertension in the SHR: concurrent effects of Na^+ and Ca^{++}. Clin. Res. 32: 36A.

193. Engstrom, A.M. and Tobelmann, R.C. (1983). Nutritional consequences of reducing sodium intake. Ann. Intern. Med. 98: 870-872.

194. Sattar, A. and Khalid, Z.M. (1979). Nutritional significance of dietary essential trace elements. Lebensm. Wiss u. Technol. 12: 306-307.

195. Mertz, W. (1981). The essential trace elements. Science, 213: 1332-1338.

196. Freeland-Graves, J., Ebangit, M.L. and Bodzy, P.W.(1980). Zinc and copper content of foods used in vegetarian diets. J. Amer.Dietetic Assoc. 77: 648-654.

197. Lyon, T.D.B., Smith, H. and Smith, L.B. (1979). Zinc deficiency in the West of Scotland? - A dietary intake study. J. Nutr. 42: 413-416.

198. Masironi, R. (1969). Trace elements and cardiovascular disease. Bull. WHO 40: 305-312.

199. Anon (1985). Natural = healthy: true or false? Ind. Obst - Gemuseverwert. 70: 166-170.

200. Roper, J. (1985). Feeling the chill. Convenience Store, July: 23-24.

201. Gibney, M. (1983). Which polyunsaturates should we eat. Diet and Health, 7: 3-4.

202. Fallows, S.J. and Wheelock, J.V. (1983). The means to dietary change; the example of fat. J.R.S.H. 5: 186-202.

203. Suttle, N.F. (1986). A concept of availability and its technical implications. Proc. 13th Int. Cong. Nutr. (see Ref. 7): 232-237.

204. Gormley, T.R. (1981). Dietary fibre - Some properties of alcohol insoluble solids residues from apples, J.Sci Food Agric. 32: 392-398.

205. Durrington, P.N., Manning, A.P., Bolton, C.H. and Hartog, M. (1976) Effect of pectin on serum lipids and lipoproteins, whole gut transit time and stool weight, Lancet, 2: 394-396.

206. Robertson, J. and 5 authors (1979). The effect of raw carrot on serum lipids and colon function. J. Amer. Clin. Nutr. 32: 1889-1892.

207. Hill, M.J. and 5 authors (1975). Faecal bile acids and clostridia in patients with cancer of the large bowel. Lancet, 1: 535-573.

208. Gormley, T.R., Kevany, J., O'Donnell, B. and McFarlane, R. (1979). Effect of peas on serum cholesterol levels in humans, Ir. J.Fd. Sci. Technol. 3: 101-109.

209. Hellendoorn, E.W. (1976). Beneficial physiological action of beans, J. Amer. Dietetic. Assoc. 69: 248-253.

210. Potter, J.D., Topping, D.L. and Oakenfull, D. (1979). Soya, saponins and plasma - cholesterol, Lancet, 1: 223.

211. Oakenfull, D.G. (1981). Dietary fibre, saponins and plasma cholesterol. Fd Technol in Australia, 39: 432-435.

118

212. Luyken, R., Pikaar, N.A., Polman, H. and Schippers, F.A. (1962). The influence of legumes on the serum cholesterol level. _Voeding,_ _23_: 447-453.

213. Grande, F., Anderson, T.J. and Keys, A. (1965). Effect of carbohydrates and leguminal seeds, wheat and potatoes on serum cholesterol in man. _J. Nutr._ _86_: 313-317.

214. Kinderlehrer, J. (1978). Keeping off cholesterol. _Prevention,_ _21_: 56-60.

215. Baghurst, K.I., Raj, M.J. and Truswell, A.S. (1977). Onions and platelet aggregation. _Lancet,_ _1_ 101.

216. Afzal, M., Hassan, R.A.H., El-Kazimi, A.A. and Fattah, R.M.A. (1985). Allium Sativum in the control of atherosclerosis. _Agric. Biol. Chem._ _49_: 1187-1188.

217. Kay, R.M. and Truswell, A.S. (1977). The effect of wheat fibre on plasma lipids and faecal steroid excretion. _Br. J. Nutr._ _37_: 227-235.

218. de Groot, A.P., Lugken, R. and Pikaar, N.A. (1963). Cholesterol lowering effect of rolled oats. _Lancet,_ _2_: 303-304.

219. Gormley, T.R., Kevany, J., O'Donnell, B. and McFarlane, R. (1978). Investigation of the potential of porridge as a hypocholesterol-aemic agent. _Ir. J. Fd. Sci. Technol._ _2_: 85-91.

220. Flynn, J.F. Beirn, S.F. and Burkitt, D.P. (1977). The potato as a source of fibre in the diet. _Ir. J. Med. Sci._ _146_: 285-288.

221. Gormley, T.R. (1978). Some aspects of the nutritive value of plant foods. An Foras Talúntais, Dublin,: 21 pages.

222. Sinclair, H.M. (1979). The human nutritional advantages of plant foods over animal foods. _Qualitas Plantarum-Plant Foods for Human Nutrition._ _29_: 7-18.

223. Legumes in human nutrition (1982). FAO Food and Nutrition Paper 20: 150 pages.

224. Deshpande, S.S., Sathe, S.K. and Salunkhe (1984). Dry beans of Phaseolus. _CRC Crit. Rev. Fd Sci. Nutr._ _21_: 132-95.

225. Gormley, T.R. (1985). Oats - a human food par-excellence. _Fm Fd Res._ _16_: 89-91.

226. Ronaghy, H.A. and 6 authors. (1974). Zinc supplementation of malnourished schoolboys in Iran: increased growth and other effects. _Am. J. Clin. Nutr._ _27_: 112-121.

227. Sanders, T.A.B. (1978). The health and nutritional status of vegans. _Plant Foods for Man,_ _2_: 181-193.

228. Howard, A.N. and Marks, J. (1977). Hypocholesterolaemic effect of milk, _Lancet,_ _2_: 225-256.

229. Connolly, J.F. and 4 authors (1980). Dietary biochemical and anthropometric effects of dairy products on selected family groups. Ir. J. Fd. Sci. Technol. 4: 143-172.

230. Mann, G.V. (1977). A factor which lowers cholesteremia in man. Atherosclerosis, 26: 335-340.

231. Badings, H.T., Tamminga, S. and Schaap, J.E. (1976). Production of milk with a high content of polyunsaturated fatty acids. 2. Fatty acid composition of milk in relation to the quality of pasteurised milk, butter and cheese. Nethl. Milk Dairy J. 30: 118-131.

232. Hodges, R.E. and 10 authors. (1975). Plasma lipid changes in young adult couples consuming polyunsaturated meats and dairy products. Am. J. Clin. Nutr. 28: 1126-1140.

233. Crawford, M.A. (1968). Possible implications of atheroma. Lancet, 1: 1329-1333.

234. Crawford, M.A., Gale, M.M., Woodford, M.H. and Casperd, N.M. (1970). Comparative studies of fatty acid composition of wild and domestic meats. Int. J. Biochem. 1: 295-305.

235. Fisher, C. (1984). Fat deposition in broilers. In: Fats in Animal Nutrition, J. Wiseman ed, Easter School at Nottingham University: 471-479.

236. Crawford, M.A., Gale, M.M. and Woodford, M.H. (1970). Muscle and adipose tissue lipids of the warthog, Phacochoerus Aethiopicus. Int. J. Biochem. 1: 654-658.

237. Ball, K. (1984). Leaner meat means few coronaries. Inst. Meat Bull. No. 125: 17-18.

238. Scott, L.W. (1979). A low cholesterol menu in a steak restaurant. J. Amer. Dietetic. Assoc. 74: 54-56.

239. Orr, G.B. and Gilks, J.L. (1931). The physique and health of two African tribes. Med. Res. Counc. Spec. Rep.Ser. 155: 17-82.

240. Sanders, T.A.B. and Ellis, R.F. (1976). Serum cholesterol and triglycerides concentrations in vegans. Proc. Nutr. Soc. 36: 45A.

241. Sanders, T.A.B., Ellis, R.R. and Dickerson, J.W.T. (1978). Studies of vegans: the fatty acid composition of plasma choline, phosphoglycerides, erythrocytes, adipose tissue, and breast milk, and some indicators of susceptibility to ischemic heart disease in vegans and omnivore controls.Am. J. Clin. Nutr., 31: 805-813.

242. Truswell, A.S. (1985). ABC of nutrition: Adults young and old. Br. Med. J. 291: 466-469.

243. Waterlow, J.C. (1985). What do we mean by adaptation. In:
     Nutritional Adaptation in Man. K. Blaxter and J.C. Waterlow eds,
     John Libbey, London and Paris: 1-12.

244. Joossens, J.V. (1979). Food pattern and mortality. Paper presented
     at Symposium on Prevention of Coronary Heart Disease. Coronary
     Prevention Group, U.K. November.

245. Kee, M. (1985). Guide to nutrition - fats. New Health, August
     68-69.

246. Kochhar, S.P. and Matsui, T. (1984). Essential fatty acids and
     trans contents of some oils, margarine and other food fats. Fd
     Chem. 13: 85-101.

247. The Role of Salt in Cardiovascular Hypertension (1982). M.J. Fregly
     and M.R. Kare eds. Academic Press: 473 pages.

248. Nolan, A.L. (1983). Low sodium foods: Where are we headed.
     Fd Engineering, 55: 95-104.

249. Dietary salt (1980). A Scientific Status Summary by the Institute
     of Food Technologists' Expert Panel on Food Safety and Nutrition and
     the Committee on Public Information, Fd Technol. Jan: 85-91.

250. Boon, N.A. and Aronson, J.K. (1985). Dietary salt and hypertension.
     Br. M. J. 290: 949-950.

251. Robertson, J.I. (1986). Dietary sodium intake in relation to
     hypertension. Proc. 13th Int. Cong. Nutr. (see Ref. 7): 548-551.

252. Meneely, G.R. (1973). Toxic effects of dietary sodium chloride
     and the protective effect of potassium. In: Toxicants Occurring
     Naturally in Foods. Comm. on Fd Protection, Food and Nutrition Board,
     Natl. Res. Council, Natl. Acad. Sci. Washington DC. 26-42.

253. Marmot, M.G., Rose, G., Shipley, N.J. and Thomas, B.J. (1981).
     Alcohol and mortality: a U shaped curve. Lancet, i: 580-583.

254. Toxic constituents in legumes (1982). In: Legumes in Human
     Nutrition, FAO Food and Nutrition Paper 20: 35-44.

255. Food intolerance and food aversion (1984). A summary by J. Gray
     of the joint report of the Royal College of Physicians and the
     British Nutrition Foundation. BNF Nutrition Bull. 9: 135-142.

256. Perkin, J.E. and Hartje, J. (1983). Diet and migraine: a review of
     the literature, J. Amer.Dietetic Assoc. 83: 459-463.

257. Health aspects of dietary trans fatty acids (1985). In: Report
     prepared for the Centre for Food Safety and Applied Nutrition, FDA,
     USA. R.R. Centi ed., Federation of American Societies for
     Experimental Biology (FASEB).

258. Andres, C. (1985). Fats and oils in foods. Fd Processing, May, 60-61.

CHAPTER 2

REVIEW AND ASSESSMENT OF FOOD AND NUTRITION POLICIES

G. DOWNEY

- this chapter is based on reports from government and other relevant bodies in European and non-European countries that have such national policies and also on interviews with personnel working in this field. The reasons behind the call for and formulation of such policies are examined as are possible problems arising from their implementation.

2.1 INTRODUCTION

In this chapter, a transition is made from the experimental sciences to the pragmatic world of politics and government policy formulation. Such a transition is often an uncomfortable one for scientists who normally operate in a well-defined and controlled environment. However, the successful application of nutritional (and indeed all) science to the benefit of mankind should be an important goal for all of us and the complex environment in which public policy measures operate must not act as a total deterrent to action. The purpose of CHAPTER 2 of this study is therefore to outline the process through which diet has come to be viewed as a risk factor in the development of degenerative diseases, how governments assess risk (in this instance health risk) and how their perception of its magnitude conditions their response, and what some of the ramifications of a coherent food and nutrition policy framework would be in the context of the European Economic Community (EEC). Finally, examples of the approach of governments in a number of developed countries are discussed.

2.2   FOOD, NUTRITION AND HEALTH

There is growing interest and concern by people in all walks of life in food and its relationship to nutrition and disease (1-5). This interest is a relatively new phenomenon but the sensitivity of the issue and the articulate presentation of arguments by those who seek to change national dietaries ensures a generous coverage of debate by national and international news media.   What are the reasons for this concern with food supply and composition and who are the people seeking to change our eating habits?

2.2.1   Security of food supply

Security of food supply is a primordial concern which has been of major importance to nations and individuals alike.   However, most people now alive in developed countries do not remember times when an entire crop could be wiped out by unfavourable weather conditions or disease and, forgetting the destructive capabilities of nature, look upon her only as good, kind and safe.   Because of the success of agricultural science in ameliorating the effects of disease and inclement weather, food supply security is not generally perceived as a problem.   Instead, concern over quantity has been replaced by anxiety over quality (6).

2.2.2   Affluence and security

Up until the mid-1970s, the generation which grew up after World War 11 did so in a period of continuous growth in affluence and consumerism. Material living standards increased relentlessly and people were confident that science and technology would lead the way to a bigger and brighter future. Substantial efforts have been made in the USA to survey public attitudes to science and opinion polls conducted during the 1950s and 1960s showed considerable public support due to its perceived ability to achieve desirable goals rather than for its inherent interest (7). The effects of science and technology were clearly apparent in the range of processed foods appearing on supermarket shelves and in the increase in productivity recorded by agriculture during this period; the growth in total farm output in the EC of Six in the period 1968-73 was 2.1% per annum (7a) and in 1977, 4% of the US population fed in excess of 215 million people. In parallel, there was a movement of population from the land to urban centres and an increased separation of food producers from food consumers; labour productivity in the Six from 1968-73 increased at the rate of 7.6% per annum (7a). Advances in medicine and public health resulted in the almost complete abolition of nutrient deficiency states and infectious disease as a cause of death in developed countries. People were living longer and better lives and while infectious disease as a cause of death was replaced by degenerative diseases, it was accepted as natural and inevitable that medicine would seek to elucidate the cause and mechanisms of these conditions and work towards their avoidance or cure - people would therefore "die young as late as possible" (8a).

During the 1960s however, a number of events occurred which began to shake the confidence and optimism of consumers. Concern over the effects of chemicals on the environment began to be voiced, catalysed by Rachel Carson's Silent Spring, the appalling and well-documented effects of massive oil spillages close to coastal areas, urban smog and the spoilage of European forests which was linked to industrial air pollution by acid-rain. The energy crisis of the '70s and with it the realisation that science and technology alone could not provide for a secure future also seems likely to have played a part in eroding public confidence. The ensuing international pre-occupation with over-consumption in all its forms led to a psychological retreat into a form of neo-Calvinism which has as its main goal a reduction of all forms of consumption. Evidence to illustrate the changing public perception of science was obtained by surveys of public opinion conducted in the USA and Europe. American opinion polls during the 1970s (7-9) revealed a change in public appreciation of science with a decline in its unqualified support; research that was seen as increasing opportunities for personal control over one's destiny was regarded as positive while any activity which tended to reduce opportunities for the exercise of individual choice was not. For example, in a poll conducted for the National Science Foundation in 1972 (reported in 7), 72% of respondents expressed "satisfaction and hope" or "excitement and wonder" as their dominant emotional reaction to science and technology while "fear and alarm" was the response of only 6%. By 1979 (8), the percentage of subjects polled which was critical of the effects of science had risen substantially with a sharp reduction (from 87% in 1957 to 66% in 1979) in the numbers who agreed with the statement that "on balance, the benefits of scientific research have outweighed the harmful results" and a majority reacting positively to the assertion that "scientific discoveries make our lives change too fast". Surveys of European attitudes have been less frequent but four (10-13) have been carried out by the Commission of the European Communities (CEC) in 1977, 1979, 1982 and 1983 respectively. While the latter two were confined to the investigation of attitudes to energy (in 1982) and environment (in 1983), those conducted earlier related to science and technology in general and revealed a perception of science which, while mainly positive, was coupled with anxiety about increasing potential risks. Of the total sample polled in 1977 (10), 80% was "really concerned" about environmental pollution, 67% about automation and employment and 53% about the increased impact of "artifical things of all sorts" on daily life. A more recent survey (14) of UK adults commissioned by the New Scientist magazine generally confirmed the CEC findings but interestingly, science was ranked below medicine, the armed forces and the law as a social institution whose leaders were trusted by the public. (In the USA, science ranked second in public confidence, below only medicine (7)). 84% agreed that "scientists and technologists should pay more attention to the social implications of their work". Despite the notorious difficulties inherent in the interpretation of public opinion polls and the critical importance of the exact wording of questions, these reports all suggest that public attitudes to science in Europe and the USA are broadly similar while possibly differing in degree; the public give qualified support to it but are wary of some of its applications and groups in both regions identified food and medical issues as being of particular concern. In relation to food, specific unease was voiced over additives; an American poll conducted in 1979 (8) showed mixed feelings on the part of the public with 30% seeing harm and no benefit from their use. In a French opinion poll conducted in 1976 involving 2000 adults (> 18 years old), 45% considered that the quality of food had "deteriorated" in the recent past and the (unspecified) majority expressed vague unease in relation to food processing operations, feeling that traditional methods of preservation were safer than recently introduced techniques (15). A survey of Netherlands citizens (1) revealed that diet (49%) was placed second after stress (55%) as a major threat to health above smoking (45%) and the environment (43%); at the same time, 56% of respondents believed that their opportunities for prevention were related specifically in the area of diet as opposed to taking more exercise (53%), stopping smoking (42%) and relaxing (40%). Public unease was heightened, paradoxically, by advances in analytical chemistry which developed the capability to detect mutagenic materials in ever smaller amounts; food additives which were previously accepted as free of significant risk fell under suspicion and in the case of one (cyclamates) were banned by legislation. Thus the application of science began to be viewed with suspicion and food processing became associated in the minds of some with an increased rather than a decreased risk of disease.

In parallel with these events has been a change in the sensitivity of certain people in developed countries towards issues such as ecology, energy conservation and food production and processing methods. In the USA, Kahn (16) has suggested that changes in society during this post-war period have produced a stratum of influential people identified by him as the 'New Class'; this group is described as young, middle-class intellectuals who treat many issues as moral imperatives in contrast to the rest of society. They have also been described as "the most deeply individualistic generation in American history" (17). Kahn identifies these people as a group who make their living by mastery of language, aesthetic and analytical skills or through the manipulation of symbols — perhaps, most significantly they do not specialise in entrepreneurial, engineering or administrative skills and they are therefore according to Kahn, out of touch with reality. Because of their strong representation in the media and government, issues which they believe to be important tend to be constantly in the public eye and the terms of the discussion are formed by them. By implication, Kahn infers that media discussions in the USA about food safety and nutritional policy are not the real concerns of most people and therefore do not deserve the exposure they command.

One such group has been identified in Europe (10) as holding views divergent from the majority population; classified as "intellectuals with ecological inclinations", they expressed reduced confidence in science for the future and defined pollution control and alternative energy sources as priority areas for research. Most of this group were male, lived in towns, had a higher education and were strong opinion leaders; given, however, that they were quantified at about only 3% of respondents, their importance in the moulding of public opinion is questionable. An alternative explanation for public debate would be the logical result of increased concern about the application of science already noted, medical progress to a point where non-dietary causes of serious and widespread illness are small and steadily diminishing, agricultural advances which have ensured an abundance of food in the market-place and removed security of supply as a cause of public concern, and social evolution to a stage where public discussion of important national issues is commonplace. While particular individuals and groups spearhead and stimulate the debate, aided by a communications industry which is ever-vigilant for topical and controversial issues, it would appear that the link between diet and disease is real and of widespread concern throughout Europe and other developed countries (18).

2.2.3   Nutrition and health

Since the beginning of the century, the pattern of disease and mortality in developed countries has changed. One indicator of population health is life expectancy at birth - in the UK, this has increased by 20-25 years since 1901 (19) resulting in a life expectancy at birth of 70 years for men and 76 for women. Recent data on life expectancy at birth in EEC countries is shown in Table 1.

TABLE 1: Life expectancy at birth in EEC member states*

	Belgium	Denmark	France	FRG	Greece	Ireland	Italy
Males	70	72	71	70	72	69	71
Females	77	78	79	77	76	75	77
Year	1979/82	1982/83	1982	1981/83	1980/82	1979	1977/79

	Luxembourg	Netherlands	Portugal	Spain	UK
Males	70	73	69	73	71
Females	77	79	77	79	77
Year	1980/82	1982/83	1979/82	1980	1980/82

*taken from "Recent demographic developments in the member states of the
 Council of Europe", Strasbourg, 1985 CDDE(85)1

Reasons for this dramatic increase in longevity are improved public health

and hygiene, resulting in a reduced incidence of infectious diseases, and

the virtual disappearance of nutrient-deficiency states, although these are

still present among certain groups in society (20-24).   This is in marked

contrast to the disease pattern in developing countries, some of which are

still plagued by malnutrition caused by poor diets, food contamination and

infected water; as recently as 1977, diarrhoea was the major cause of death

in five South American nations and one of the five leading causes of death

in seven others (25).   One result of a population reaching greater age is

the increased incidence of deaths associated with ageing such as coronary

heart disease (CHD) (26) cerebrovascular disease and certain forms of

cancer.   As the number of people living to 70 years of age and beyond

increases, the absolute number of deaths due to such diseases rises

although the extent of their incidence varies from country to country e.g.

CHD death rates are 249 per 100,000 persons in Japan, 300-400 in France and

Canada, 400-500 in the U.S.A., Norway and Italy and more than 500 in

Germany, Great Britain, Finland and Ireland (26) (see also Table 2).

TABLE 2:   Death rates for coronary heart disease (ICD 410-414) for the
           fifteen highest ranking countries in 1978 (age standardised
           rates per 100,000; 35-74 year age group) (from ref. 177)

Males		Females	
Finland	664	Scotland	256
Scotland	656	Northern Ireland	233
Northern Ireland	653	Israel	207
Ireland	542	Ireland	200
England and Wales	533	New Zealand	196
New Zealand	529	USA	187
USA	506	Australia	186
Australia	499	Finland	177
Canada	457	England and Wales	173
Denmark	443	Hungary	168
Sweden	436	Bulgaria	162
Hungary	420	Canada	155
Norway	414	Denmark	141
Israel	395	Sweden	132
Netherlands	379	Austria	119

In attempting to establish valid trends, however, the use of age-
corrected data is essential. A major study (27) has recently revealed that
among women in the 45-64 age group, age-corrected death rates due to heart
disease (ICD 420-447 before 1967; 400-404, 410-429 after 1967) have
decreased in all EEC member states during the period 1950-1978.   For men,
such death rates increased in almost all countries (quite dramatically in
some) during the early part of this period although a decline is apparent
in most since the early 1970s. These trends are emphasised in the relative
importance of heart disease as a cause of death since the proportionate
mortality from this source has increased appreciably during this 28 year
period in most member states, thus heightening the popular conception of a
significant increase in deaths due to "heart attacks".   (Interestingly,
despite early increases and later decreases in heart disease mortality, no
change has occurred in the overall pattern of international differences in
this factor among men; this suggests that environmental components are of

decisive importance in the establishment of such differences). Outside Europe, age-corrected deaths from heart disease have not increased since 1950 and have in fact been in marked decline since the 1970s (27, 28) while Japan has witnessed a steady decline over the entire period.

In relation to cancer (all types), data (29) reveal an increase in the age-adjusted death rates for men (45-64 years of age) in the twelve EEC countries during the period 1950-1975; for women, the situation was more complex, with increases being reported for Greece, Ireland, Italy, Portugal, England and Wales and Northern Ireland. However, of the major cancers examined, only those occurring in the trachea, bronchus and lung showed any major increase in incidence over this period; this increase was much greater among men than women. Cancers of the prostate, breast and intestine all showed a slightly increased incidence while neoplasms of the stomach and rectum arose less frequently. Contrary to popular opinion therefore, the only cancer which has shown a significantly (in public health terms) increased incidence is that of the trachea, bronchus and lung; cancer in these sites has been specifically linked to a single environmental pollutant - tobacco smoke. Therefore, while degenerative diseases undoubtedly are a major public health problem, the use of words such as 'epidemic' to describe their incidence is misleading. Such terminology arises fundamentally from a mis-interpretation of epidemiological data but its use is fostered and encouraged by widespread public fear of contracting CHD, cerebrovascular disease or cancer. This fear may be due to the insidious nature of these diseases, developing as they do over a prolonged time-period (30) and becoming apparent with often little or no warning. In the case of CHD in particular the social effects of the disease are distressing especially given that CHD incidents usually occur dramatically to relatively young people (men for the most part) who appear outwardly healthy and often lead to death before medical help can arrive. After-effects of cerebrovascular accidents (CVAs) also give rise to considerable emotional upset while the apparent helplessness of modern medicine to facilitate remissions from neoplasms once established leads to a heightened fear of such disease states.

Degenerative diseases are multifactorial in cause. Suggested causal agents include dietary cholesterol, saturated fatty acid intake, hypertension, lack of dietary fibre, obesity, lack of physical exercise, stress, hereditary factors, consumption of tobacco and alcohol, food preparation techniques (See CHAPTER 1 for a full discussion of these relationships). Diet is therefore only one of a range of risk factors in their causation although it is arguably the one most associated with disease development in the public eye; this has probably stemmed in a general way from the advances in medicine and analytical chemistry and the sociological changes charted above and in particular from the identification of diet as a major causal factor by the McGovern Report (31) and others (32-34). Diet has been implicated largely through epidemiological studies which have highlighted the differences in incidence of degenerative diseases between developed and developing countries and in their respective national dietaries. Since these diseases have only come to prominence in developed countries during this century, the study of changes in the average diet obtaining in these countries since 1900 was initiated in the hope of identifying factors responsible for the incidence of degenerative disease states. The changes which have emerged are qualitatively the same in all countries with a 'Western' lifestyle and the predominant features are as follows:-

(a)   an increase in total energy consumption

133

(b)   an increase in the percentage of energy derived from fat

(c)   a decrease in the intake of complex carbohydrates (starch etc.)

(d)   an increase in the intake of simple carbohydrate (esp. sucrose)

(e)   an increase in the intake of animal protein at the expense of
       protein from vegetable sources - protein intake overall has
       remained constant.

A schematic representation of these dietary changes together with their relationship to national affluence is shown in Figure 1 using data from 85 countries (35).

Figure 1:   **Energy derived from fats, carbohydrates and proteins as a percentage of total calories according to income of countries (1962) - based on 85 countries (from (35))**

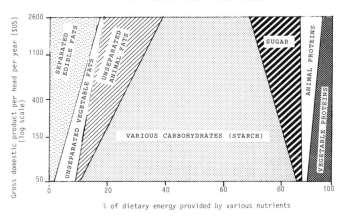

% of dietary energy provided by various nutrients

As a result of these findings, the changes themselves were suggested to be the reason for dietary risk in degenerative disease causation (31, 33, 34, 36) despite the serious reservations of some (28, 37) who drew attention to the fact that the 'Western' diet has been instrumental in facilitating the attainment of longevity, the virtual disappearance of significant nutrient deficiency states and the improvement of overall health. The Food and Nutrition Board of the US National Academy of Sciences has stated (38) that: "The American food supply is on the whole nutritious and provides adequate quantities of nutrients to protect essentially all healthy Americans from deficiency disease".

2.2.4   Implications for the future

There are unlikely to be any significant changes in the public perception of science and technology over the next 5-10 years; in the absence of any effective, sustained drive by scientists to improve public understanding of their goals and the possible risks attendant upon their achievement, it seems inevitable that fears over the application of scientific research will continue to grow, fuelled especially by developments in genetic engineering and in vitro fertilisation of human ova. In relation to degenerative diseases, it is reasonable to postulate that the public dread recently associated with them will decline due to advances in treatment regimes which will continue to reduce their associated mortality rates and clearer identification of the major risk and predisposing factors leading to a reduction in morbidity. However, with the link between diet and disease firmly established in the minds of many consumers, pressure is likely to continue for action by food producers, processors, retailers and governments to facilitate the general availability of foods which will permit the consumption of a diet less likely, in the opinion of many, to lead to disease. The over-riding need in the immediate future seems to be for a wide-ranging public debate, organised at a European level, both on the specific and wider issues touched on in the above sections. In particular, health professionals and research scientists need to know how they are perceived by the general public and what the specific concerns and informational requirements of the lay population are. For their part, the general public need to be educated about the complexities of the research tasks being faced and the concepts of risk and uncertainty. Such widespread, informed debate sponsored by the Commission would need to utilise the most efficient communications media and techniques in all countries of the Community to achieve the desired aim i.e. a clearer understanding of the problem of degenerative disease incidence and the mechanisms available for its solution. Public interest in science and medicine is apparent in, for example, the audience figures for UK television programmes such as Tomorrow's World (average 9.2 million for the 41 programmes in 1982-1983) and Your life in their Hands (average 5.5 million) (7) and the upsurge in television, radio and magazine articles dealing with the diet and nutrition. The time seems ripe for building on this interest through reasoned and widespread discussion.

2.3   DIETARY GUIDELINE DEVELOPMENT

Since the postulation of a linkage between diet and degenerative disease has gained widespread circulation, numerous expert committees have been convened in many national and international fora to examine the available evidence and draw their own conclusions. The end result of such activity has been in each case the promulgation of a set of dietary guidelines, adherence to which, it was suggested, would reduce the risk of developing these diseases.

2.3.1   General vs specific intervention

Mass population intervention is one strategy for attempting to reduce the incidence of degenerative diseases, especially heart disease. A complementary approach involves the detection (through screening programmes) of those individuals in the population who are judged to be at the greatest risk of contracting the diseases. In an ideal world both systems would be involved but given the economic constraints imposed on any such action, choices have to be made. Critics of the population approach point out the unimpressive results obtained from reported mass intervention trials using dietary manipulation while supporters of this strategy suggest that limitations in experimental design and/or the time-span of the studies have mitigated against any decisive outcome (39). Treatment of individuals at high-risk would appear, for coronary heart disease at least, to be more successful although the cost of general screening programmes is high. Whatever the arguments on either side may be, it would seem morally unacceptable to continue to permit disease to develop in a population and treat most of those subsequently at highest risk of developing it rather than to attempt to remove the causes; for this reason alone it seems that governments are unlikely to opt for screening programmes at the expense of any mass intervention activity.

The concept of dietary guidelines is not a new one but can be traced back directly to the U.K. Merchant Seaman's Act of 1835 which provided for the issuance of lime-juice for the prevention of scurvy. Since that time a number of dietary standards have been promulgated (40) which had the aim of preventing starvation diseases (1862), feeding the army and the nation (1918), maintaining health and working capacity (1933), marrying health and agriculture (1933, 1935) and facilitating "buoyant health" (1941). Interestingly, these represent an evolution of basic aims ranging as they do from the prevention of starvation, through the maintenance of working-capacity to the concept of buoyant health; dietary standards issued during the last 20 years have been concerned with the quality of health and the elimination of diseases which, paradoxically, earlier dietary standards have permitted to develop.

The promulgation of dietary guidelines has, however, been criticised (41, 42) as symptomatic of an attitude towards human behaviour which is derived largely from experimental chemical and biological sciences; in other words, they reflect a conception of man as an experimental animal participating in a life-long study rather than a free agent who consumes food for a variety of reasons many of which may not be defined. In addition, no indication of risk is attached to deviations from such specific intake levels which, given that few individuals actually consume the exact quantity of any particular nutrient specified, limits their utility in the assessment of risk at individual and population sub-group level. An alternative approach would be to describe limits to a zone of nutrient intakes and hence food consumption within which individual choice could be safely exercised. Such an approach would envisage statements defining intakes of each nutrient which represent the minimum and maximum levels within which it can be safely consumed on the basis of current scientific knowledge. Minimum safe intake levels would be those below which there is known to be an increased risk of loss of physiological function while maxima would be set at consumption levels for which there is a known risk of toxicity or disease. Such a strategy would make it easier to identify individuals and/or groups at risk within a population and would be more readily understood and applied by interested members of the public at large. To date, however, no committee has approached the problem in this way although, in spite of the possible difficulties associated with the definition of maxima, it would seem to represent a useful perspective.

Since 1968, approximately 51 reports dealing with dietary guidelines for developed countries have been published by groups in Scandinavia (43-47), USA (38, 49-60, 92), UK (61-65), New Zealand (66-69), Australia (70-76), Holland (77), Canada (78, 79), Republic of Ireland (80), Federal Republic of Germany (81), France (82), Italy (83), Japan (83), and Israel (84). International agencies have also been active in this field (85, 86) as have professional bodies (87-89). The guidelines contained in such publications range from those (the majority) which issue quite detailed advice on the intake of particular food constituents such as fat, salt and sugar to vaguer exhortations to, for example, "consume a diet which is in harmony with the climatic conditions and resource endowment of Japan" (83) or to "reduce caloric intake ..... by encouraging substitution within the livestock and fats sector, in particular the substitution of poultry for beef and veal" (83). The precise target group for such dietary recommendations also varies from report to report, with the majority catering for the general population and others (15%) for groups at high-risk; seven provide guidance for both.

2.3.2   Principal features of reports

The major proposals contained in each report are shown in Table 3 (modified from (90)) together with the target grouping at which each is aimed. Over the eighteen year period covered by the table, there has been relatively little change in the main recommendations which relate to consumption of total energy, fat (saturated + polyunsaturated) and complex carbohydrate while the advice with regard to sugar and salt has varied somewhat in emphasis. Admonitions relating to alcohol consumption have also been included in some while the importance attached to control of cholesterol intake and the replacement of saturated by polyunsaturated fat would seem to have declined somewhat in the last decade. In addition, a trend away from very clearly defined maximum intake levels for food constituents to much vaguer exhortations (for example, to reduce or increase their consumption) is apparent. It appears possible to identify a

TABLE 3: Selected dietary guidelines (based on (90))

Ref.	Country and organisation	General population (GP) or high risk (HR)	To prevent coronary heart disease (C) or broader advice (B)	Dietary total fat (% energy)	Increased polyunsaturated fat	Reduce Na or salt for GP	Dietary cholesterol (mg/day)
43	Scandinavia 1968	GP	B	25-35	Yes	-	
48	USA 1970: Inter-	GP)					-
	society Commission	HR)	C	<35	Yes	-	< 300
66	New Zealand 1971:	GP	C	Reduce	No	-	Reduce
	Royal Society	HR		Reduce	Medical use		Reduce
67	New Zealand 1971:	GP	C	35	-		Restrict
	Heart Foundation	HR		<35	Possibly	-	Reduce
70	Australia 1971: National Heart Foundation	HR	C	40	Yes	-	< 300
49	USA 1971, 1973: White House Conf.	GP	B	Reduce	Yes	-	300
50	USA 1972: FNB NRC- NAS: CFN.AMA	HR	C	Substantial decrease	Yes	-	Lower
51	USA 1972: American Health Foundation	GP	C	35	Yes	Yes	About 300
52	USA 1973: American Heart Association	GP	C	35	Yes	Probably	About 300
77	The Netherlands '73	GP	C	30-40	Yes	-	250-300
87	Int. Soc. of Cardiology 1973	HR	C	< 30	Yes	-	< 300
71	Australia 1974: Nat. Heart Foundation	HR	C	30-35	Yes	-	300
72	Australia 1975: Acad. of Science	GP	C	Approx. 35	Yes	-	350
81	Federal Republic of Germany 1974	GP	C	Reduce	Yes	-	Reduce
44	Norway 1975-76: Nutrition and food policy	GP	B	To 35 gradually	Should be increased	-	-
68	New Zealand 1976: Heart Foundation	GP	C	Reduce to	-	-	(Reduce)
		HR		35	Yes	-	Reduce
62	United Kingdom 1976: Royal College of Physicians	GP	C	Towards 35	Yes	-	(Reduce)
78	Canada 1976	GP	B	30-35	Yes	Yes	< 400
91	Prof. K. Norum 1976-78 questionnaire	GP	C	Less	Yes	Possibly	Less

TABLE 3 (cont'd): Selected dietary guidelines (based on (90))

Ref.	Country and organisation	General population (GP) or high risk (HR)	To prevent coronary heart disease (C) or broader advice (B)	Dietary total fat (% energy)	Increased polyun-saturated fat	Reduce Na or salt for GP	Dietary choles-terol (mg/day)
53	USA 1977: Dietary goals (1st edn)	GP	B	To approx 30	Yes	Yes	To 300
63	United Kingdom 1977: Truswell at Nutrition Soc.	GP	B	Decrease	(Yes)	Yes	(Reduce)
85	FAO/WHO 1977: Dietary fats and oils	GP	B	30-35	Yes	-	< 300
54	USA 1977: Dietary goals (2nd edn)	GP	B	To about 30	Yes	Yes	To 300
79	Canada 1977: Quebec's policy on nutrition	GP	B	Reduce by 25%	-	-	-
88	European Soc. of Cardiology 1978	HR	C	Towards 30	Yes	-	Reduced
55	USA 1978: American Heart Association	GP	C	30-35	Yes	Yes	< 300
64	United Kingdom 1978: DHSS Eating for health	GP	B	Cut-down	No	Possibly	-
65	United Kingdom 1979: Better British diet	GP	B	Reduce visible fats by 15%	-	-	-
73	Australia 1979: Commonwealth Dept. of Health	GP	B	Decrease	-	Yes	-
74	Australia 1979: National Heart Foundation	HR	C	30-35	Yes	-	Restrict
75	Australia 1979: Australian Assoc. of Dietitians	GP	B	Decrease	-	Yes	-
56	USA 1979: Surgeon-General's report	GP	B	Less	-	Yes	Less
57	USA 1979: American Soc. of Clinical Nutrition	GP	B	Less	?	Possibly	Less

TABLE 3 (cont'd): Selected dietary guidelines (based on (90))

Ref.	Country and organisation	General population (GP) or high risk (HR)	To prevent coronary heart disease (C) or broader advice (B)	Dietary total fat (% energy)	Increased polyun-saturated fat	Reduce Na or salt for GP	Dietary choles-terol (mg/day)
58	American Medical Assoc. 1979	HR	B	Regulation by physician	- -	Possibly -	Regulation by physician
		GP		Moderation	-	-	Moderation
59	USA 1980: USDA+ Dept. of Health Education and Welfare	GP	B	Reduction	-	Yes	Reduction
38	FNB/NRC-NAS 1980: Toward healthful diets	GP	B	< 40% Energy only	No	Yes	-
		HR		if obese and sedentary. Therapy under a physician's guidance.			
82	France 1981: Apports nutritionnels conseilles	GP	B	Reduce	-	Yes	-
76	Australian Nat. Heart Foundation 1982.	GP	B	Reduce	Partial replacement of saturated	Yes	Reduce
92	American Heart Association 1982		C	Reduce saturated to <10%	Partial replacement of saturated	Yes	< 300
60	USA 1982: Diet, nutrition & cancer	GP	B	To 30%	No	Yes	-
86	WHO 1982: Prevention of coronary heart disease	GP	C	Reduce to 10% saturated	Partial replacement of saturated up to 10% energy	Yes	< 300
69	NZ Nutrition goals 1982	GP	B	Eat less, especially saturated	No	Yes	No
46	Norway 1981: National Nutritional Council	GP	B	35%	Yes	-	-
47	Finnish Nutrition Committee 1981	GP	B	30-35%	Yes slightly	Yes	Yes
45	Sweden 1983: Expert Committee for Diet and Health	GP	B	30%	Yes, slightly	Yes	-
61	United Kingdom 1984: DHSS COMA	GP	C	Reduce total fat, especially saturated	No	-	-
89	British Medical Association 1986	GP	B	30%	Don't reduce	Yes	-

number of statements about which a reasonable consenus of opinion exists
(see also CHAPTER 1); these are:-

(a)   obesity (or overweight) is a predisposing factor in the development
      of many diseases and should be avoided (93);

(b)   since fat is a concentrated energy source and because a significant
      connection betwen fat intake and cancer appears likely (91, 94)
      total fat intake should be decreased and saturated fat should be
      partially replaced by polyunsaturated:

(c)   sugar (sucrose) is another concentrated source of energy which is
      believed to be a causative agent in the development of dental caries
      (95) - its consumption should be reduced (96);

(d)   dietary fibre is present in insufficient amounts in the daily diet
      and because of its demonstrated therapeutic role in certain diseases
      of the gastro-intestinal tract (97) an increased intake would be
      benefical;

(e)   salt has been implicated in circulatory disease development (98);
      intakes are currently in excess of biological requirements and
      should be restricted.

The order in which these points have been listed is not meant to
correspond to any perceived degree of health risk which may result from
their violation but rather to an order of decreasing agreement among
nutritionists as to their overall importance; this listing agrees well with
one produced in 1978 (91) following an opinion survey of world experts in
the field of cardiovascular disease.

In relation to specific levels of intake, suggested targets for fat
consumption range from a low of 25% (43) to a high of 40% (70) of total
energy intake with a figure of 35% appearing frequently; the desirable
ratio of polyunsaturated to saturated fat is another variable with a value
of 1:2 finding considerable support. An optimum level of salt intake has
been suggested to be 5 g daily while simple sugars should not account for
more than 10% of total daily energy consumption (54). It is difficult to
establish the validity or otherwise of any specific figure quoted above

simply because no conclusive scientific evidence exists to defend them. They have generally been arrived at on the basis of their intake at various times during the early part of this century (61) when degenerative diseases were not common causes of death and also, in the case of some nutrients, on a combination of epidemiological and experimental data (38); increased awareness of the weaknesses inherent in such approaches may be responsible for the trend away from specific target intake figures to more general guidelines. (See CHAPTER 1 for a detailed review of the evidence linking individual nutrients and disease).

Implementation of these guidelines may be achieved either by a reduced intake of foods which are high in fat (especially saturated fat) or a decrease in the fat content of foods currently available. Adoption of the former strategy implies a decrease in consumption of meat (dark meat and pork more than poultry), wholemilk, cream, cheese, butter, margarine, eggs, cooking fat, confectionery etc. and an increased intake of cereal products (bread, especially wholegrain, breakfast cereals and rice), pulses, fruit, vegetables and potatoes, vegetable oils rich in polyunsaturated fatty acids and fish. This represents a significant change in national (and, by implication, individual) diets and would appear to represent a major disruption to the food production sector of the EEC. Since meat and dairy products are the major sources of dietary fat (at least in the UK diet (99)) it is they which would bear the brunt of any sudden marked decline in fat consumption - it has been calculated that implementation of dietary advice contained in the COMA and NACNE Reports would represent the removal of 524 $\times 10^3$ and 452×10^3 tonnes of fat respectively from the human food-chain in the UK (99). Given the complex and poorly understood determinants of food choice (see below), it seems unlikely that such severe alterations in diet will occur voluntarily. For this reason, the alternative approach of selectively modifying the fat content of important foods has been advanced as a more practical strategy for change (100). A reduction of some 240×10^3 tonnes has been suggested to be possible by a decrease in animal slaughter weight while an unspecified extra quantity could be removed by butchering, although the latter approach only creates another disposal problem. Bull beef, which is the traditional form of beef production in continental Europe, is leaner than steer beef; replacement of 50% of the UK market by such beef would result in the removal of a further 45×10^3 tonnes (99). Fewer options are open to the dairy industry since alterations in the lipid content and profile in milk by genetic or feeding techniques are long-term or uneconomic or both: a reduction in milk-fat intake without a corresponding decline in milk consumption is only possible through processing and even then, success is dependent on the complete removal of separated milk-fat from the human food supply. The disruptive effects on agriculture and industry of dietary change brought about in such a manner would be considerably less than the alternative approach mentioned above.

2.3.3 Reception of dietary guidelines

The reception of dietary guidelines has not been without controversy; this is especially true in the USA (101) and UK and, although in other countries the amount of heated discussion has been much less, dissenting voices have been heard (102). Why this should be so is difficult to say, but it may have been related to the fact that committees meeting under the auspices of central government were involved in both these countries, leading to the fear that their recommendations would automatically be the basis for wide-ranging intervention in food supply and consumption

145

patterns.   The fears of those in the food processing industry stemmed from problems which they perceived would arise if dietary guidelines were rapidly enacted and many believed their viability to be threatened; these fears were compounded by the articulate presentation by fringe groups of a "back to nature" philosophy as a public health measure which did not foresee any requirement for a food processing industry.   However, evidence does exist (103) to suggest a change in the attitude of that industry now that the imminent nature of the apparent threat has receded and it has begun to produce processed foods which meet the aims of, for example, the McGovern Report in relation to fat, salt and sugar content (104) (see CHAPTER 3).   The retail trade is also becoming anxious to capitalise on the interest of consumers as evidenced by the menu plans of the cooperating restaurants of Steak House Associates in Houston, USA to produce low-cholesterol meals (105).   Food producers have also been vociferous in their resistance to proposed government action; they, indeed, seem likely to be among the worst affected groups since they tend to be specialised, regard themselves as food rather than commodity producers and do not enjoy the flexibility and insulation of a multi-product line food processor or retailer.   Indeed, in an American opinion poll conducted after the publication of the McGovern report, almost three-quarters of farmers polled opposed the recommended decrease in egg, meat and wholemilk consumption (106).

The scientific basis of the recommendations of certain expert groups has also been criticised (28, 37, 107, 108); the criticisms have been related to the mis-interpretation of national food consumption data used to establish changes in national food intake (37, 108) and in alleging causal relationships between average population nutrient intake and degenerative disease incidence (28, 37, 47, 107, 108).   The latter criticism is an illustration of the different degrees of certainty acceptable to scientists working in the experimentally-difficult field of human nutrition and is explored more fully below (see 2.4.1). However, most scientists with a professional interest in this field do not appear to have seriously questioned the conclusions or recommendations of any set of dietary guidelines, leading to their general acceptance by governments as a secure basis for action.

In relation to the expert groups themselves (see also CHAPTER 1), specific criticism has been made of the lack of relevant expertise on the McGovern committee (37, 107) while their motivation for the promulgation of dietary advice has also been queried; in relation to the latter point, it has been suggested that the effect of such advice would be to reduce chronic disease morbidity and mortality resulting in a decrease in the cost of national health insurance, a prominent feature of Senator McGovern's legislative programme (37). In the UK, concern has been expressed (109) about the relative inaction of government following publication of the COMA report (61) and its tardiness in publishing the later NACNE report (110); in this instance, the controversy has related to the perceived dilution of dietary advice by government and its alleged attempts to muzzle groups which recommend significant change. Given the size of the food processing and distribution industry, their fear of imposed radical change in the products they market and the consumer interest in nutrition and related subjects, it appears likely that recommendations by any group will be subject to some heated debate. The function of government in such circumstances should be to ensure the debate is carried out in a calm atmosphere and that all affected groups are permitted an adequate airing of their views (this approach has been particularly favoured in Canada (111)). Only then are the views emerging from such a debate likely to prove acceptable to those directly affected and therefore have much chance of implementation.

2.3.4 Implications for the future

A considerable number of sets of dietary guidelines are now extant; given that relatively little difference exists between those produced initially and latterly, it is doubtful if a convincing case can be made for a European initiative in this area. However, in view of the trend towards more general advice (e.g. reduce fat intake, increase dietary fibre consumption) and the short-comings of specific target intake levels included in certain sets of recommendations, it would be useful to initiate discussions on the concept of safe intake ranges for various nutrients. If such ranges could be successfully defined, they would more readily permit the identification of individuals and population sub-groups who are "at risk" nutritionally.

In order to ensure the maximum support for any public health policy statement in this area, it is essential that the composition of expert groups and the time-scale for their deliberations be planned with great care. Both a representative range in expertise and opinion are necessary for a balanced report while the time taken in accumulating evidence and deliberating on possible requirements for change must be extensive although a balance is obviously necessary in view of the perceived need for action by a considerable section of public opinion and the significance of any measures recommended (See CHAPTER 1). Whatever dietary advice emerges, it is essential that this be publicised in such a way as to explain the possible ramifications (economic and structural) of its implementation on other sectors of the economy and the need for medium to long-term policy measures rather than rapid alterations in agricultural output and food processing operations. Since no food and nutrition policy can be successfully implemented without the support of food producers and processors, it will be necessary to inform them of the reasons for any required changes and assist them in their implementation. Evidence does exist to show the movement of food processors towards the marketing of products with a more desirable nutritional profile and there is every likelihood that farmers will also adapt, if change is judged necessary, once the economic forces directing agricultural production are modified.

2.4 GOVERNMENT POLICY FORMULATION

Having completed the development of a set of dietary guidelines, the level of debate moves onto another plane: should government involve itself in the implementation of such guidelines or is health, in this context, solely the responsibility of the individual?

Debate on this topic is not a recent phenomenon (112) and many groups have campaigned for the adoption of a food and nutrition policy by central governments in order to effect change in national diets. Pressure has been mounting internationally at least since the 1930s . At that time, nutrition problems were of such concern that they were broadly discussed in the League of Nations in terms of the degree of responsibility which attached to official authorities for the adoption and implementation of food and nutrition policy. Shortly after the establishment of FAO in 1945, each member nation was requested to inaugurate a national nutrition council to permit the planning and implementation of a national nutrition policy. Most recently, the World Food Conference held in Rome in 1974 in response to famine in the Sahel region of Africa and worldwide concern over food shortages stated that each nation should have an official, integrated food and nutrition policy (112).

Food and nutrition policy may be defined as a formalised, coherent set of statements by government which set a framework for the control of food production, processing, distribution, retailing and trade so as to encourage the consumption of nutritious food by the population. To be effective, such a policy must be incorporated at a high level into general development plans and its objectives should be fully considered in sectoral policy measures, especially those concerned with agriculture, industry, transport, infrastructure creation, foreign policy, employment, education and health. It is therefore a far-reaching and positive involvement by central government in all aspects of the food sector. One of its key features is a comprehensive rather than an ad hoc or piecemeal approach to intervention; such an integrated approach is now deemed necessary due to a growing awareness among governments and economists of the interdependence of all sectors of both the national and international economies and the increasingly obvious failure of economic measures which address only one aspect of the food sector economy e.g. the Common Agricultural Policy with its embarrassing surpluses and the problem of their disposal without conflicting with the fundamental aims of the policy and severe disruption of the market-place both within and without the EEC.

With one exception, no developed nation has implemented a food and nutrition policy as defined above. Almost all do, however, have an agricultural or farm policy (an essential ingredient) and do intervene from time to time to control food nutrient content and safety (e.g. restoration and fortification of bread in the UK, regulation of additive use in all EEC member states, preventing the sale of margarine in the UK unfortified with vitamin D etc). Reasons for the reluctance of governments to adopt and implement defined food and nutrition policies are many and various but those most frequently advanced may be grouped under the headings scientific or philosophical and political. Turning to the former category initially, these generally include a stated belief in the sufficiency of the market place, a reluctance to interfere with the freedom of choice of the individual, a lack of confidence in the scientific basis of most nutrition theory and a requirement for 'absolute proof' (41).

2.4.1   Scientific/philosophical constraints

By sufficiency of the market place is meant the assumption in economic theory that in operating in the market, the consumer acts so as to maximise his/her welfare any definition of which must include nutritional well-being. This assumes that the consumer is familiar with and understands modern nutritional theory, can determine his/her own nutritional requirements and buys food which will satisfy these needs as well as others fulfilled by food purchase such as status, convenience, flavour, texture, security etc. Food purchasing patterns which do not conform to recommended dietary advice are therefore explained on the basis that nutritional considerations in food selection are subservient to some or all of the other factors influencing choice (41). In the particular case of food, however, evidence does exist to show that most of the general public are poorly informed on nutritional matters (e.g. 113) and even among those who are well or adequately informed, there is little or no connection between the possession of nutritional knowledge and its application when shopping (114, 115). In the UK, a market research survey (116) showed that 19% of housewives polled thought white bread was good for them compared to 86% who thought wholemeal bread was good for them; yet bread consumption data reveal (117) that in 1974, 84% of all bread consumed in the UK was white and only 8% was brown or wholemeal.

'Freedom of choice' as conventionally applied in a free market economy is a misnomer; while commonly interpreted in the literal sense, such freedom of choice does not actually exist. It assumes that individuals make purchases on the basis of their knowledge, preferences and purchasing power to obtain the most satisfaction in the absence of force or fraud and with complete knowledge of the alternatives available (41). In fact, individuals are only free to choose from a limited range of alternatives and then to make choice according to economic and other constraints on the preferred choice. Freedom of choice must therefore be interpreted in the deterministic rather than literal sense in which it is commonly used in the defence of ever-expanding consumption-orientated market economies. On this basis, interference by government in such a manner as to affect the economic or information constraints on choice can be a positive development by improving access to information , education, affecting advertising and marketing practices etc. Indeed, governments already interfere with 'freedom of choice' insofar as they are directly responsible for the regulation of disposable income, prices, subsidies, restrictions on the supply of certain goods and prohibitions on the sale of others. A rational case can therefore be made for an extension of government intervention in the market place which is consistent with current governmental action and which, paradoxically, would increase rather than decrease 'freedom of choice'.

Perhaps a greater difficulty for government relates to the scientific basis of most nutritional theory. This relatively young branch of science lacks an agreed experimental methodology which is based on a rigorously tested theoretical framework, a shortcoming which is heightened by ethical constraints on experimentation involving human subjects. Thus nutritionists use a group of different theoretical frameworks which include different criteria for the acceptance or rejection of knowledge. In practical terms, this gives rise to significant differences of opinion on the validity and interpretation of nutrition experiments by eminent practitioners in the field (see CHAPTER 1). Given the added complication that most of the debates on the implications of experimental data are conducted under the gaze of a public which is eager for information, the hesitance exhibited by government in siding with one opinion or the other is perhaps understandable.

The fourth objection, the 'burden of absolute truth' relates to the observation that none of the experiments designed to identify a role for dietary factors in the causation of degenerative diseases (e.g. coronary heart disease, strokes, cancer etc.) do so unequivocally; thus, conventional diets are assumed to be safe in the absence of conclusive proof to the contrary. Leaving aside the philosophical objection to the requirement for 'absolute proof' for any scientific theory or assertion, a case can be made for less rigorous proofs in the nutritional than in other sciences due to the moral and ethical factors which prevent the execution of the required experimental procedures; thus, it may be that a hypothesis relating to human nutrition may be accepted as false on the basis of a less complete refutation than is required for, say, the physical sciences. An example could be the accumulating evidence which suggests that current dietary practices are causal to the incidence of certain degenerative diseases. In short, therefore, proponents of this view argue that because human nutrition is a difficult experimental field, the criteria for acceptability of experimental evidence should be lower than in other fields; opponents of this position would suggest that because decisions arrived at in such a field will directly affect human welfare, criteria should not be lowered.

Governments which have been slow to act on the implementation of dietary guidelines have tended to use this requirement for absolute proof in their defence; however, many public health measures enforced by the same administrations are justified without this condition being met. Thus, this burden need not be a significant impediment to the implementation of nutritional guidelines for which a consensus exists.

2.4.2   Political constraints

Among political reasons for the lack of formal policy-making in this area, bureaucratic inertia merits a mention; it is a feature of central government in all modern states and results from the size and complexity of administrative structures. Such inertia mitigates against any change in policy-making and especially a formal, coherent, and far-reaching framework such as that proposed.

The sheer size of the agro-industrial complex with which such a policy would deal must make governments wary of embarking on definite action of a strategic nature in this area. Data revealing the employment and turnover in the agro-food sector for selected developed countries are shown in Tables 4 and 5 with more specific information on EEC member states in Table 6. From many points of view, the food processing industry ranks first in Belgium, Denmark, Ireland, Netherlands and the UK (118). Laissez-faire approaches by government are reinforced by the scale of any action which would be deemed necessary although if the problems caused by the lack of

154

TABLE 4: Food Production in the National Economy in OECD Countries, 1968 and 1978 (percentages)

Country(a)	Agriculture, Hunting and Fishing(b) Value Added as a Proportion of GDP		Manufacture of Food, Beverages and Tobacco: Value Added as a Proportion of GDP	
	1968	1978	1968	1978
Canada	3.4(d)	3.2(d)	3.0(c)	2.5(c)
United States	2.4(d)	2.6(d)	3.1	2.4
Japan	6.1(d) (1970)	4.8(d)	3.8 (1970)	3.3
Australia	8.7(d)	4.9(d) (1976)	n.a.	n.a
New Zealand	11.7	9.1 (1977)	6.7 (1971)	4.3 (1977)
Austria	7.0(d)	4.6(d) (1977)	5.8	4.3 (1977)
Belgium	4.3	2.4	6.2	4.8
Denmark	6.4	5.7 (1974)	4.4	3.7 (1974)
Finland	5.6 (1970)	4.1	3.2 (1970)	3.4
France	6.1 (1970)	4.3 (1977)	4.1 (1970)	4.2 (1977)
Germany	3.8	2.4 (1977)	6.0	4.5 (1976)
Greece	16.4	14.7	3.1	3.2
Italy	8.0 (1970)	7.0	4.6 (1970)	4.1
Luxembourg	3.8 (1970)	2.9 (1977)	3.4 (1970)	3.6 (1977)
Netherlands	6.5 (1969)	4.7 (1976)	5.1 (1965)	4.0 (1976)
Norway	5.3	4.7	3.6	2.0
Portugal	15.9	11.7 (1976)	3.6	3.5 (1976)
Spain	12.9	8.7 (1977)	3.5	2.6 (1977)
Sweden	2.7	2.1	2.6	2.4
Turkey	27.6	23.3	n.a.	n.a.
United Kingdom	2.6(d)	2.3(d)	3.6	3.3
Yugoslavia	17.9(d)	11.2(d)	3.2	3.8 (1973)

n.a. Data not available.
a) Data for 1968 and 1978 unless otherwise indicated, calculated in national currencies at current prices.
b) Agriculture, Hunting and Fishing comprises food and non-food products. Hence the proportions tend to overestimate the importance of farm produced food inputs in the national economy.
c) Manufacture of food, beverages and tobacco at 1971 prices converted to current prices with GDP deflator.
d) Agriculture, Hunting, Fishing and Forestry.

Source: OECD, National Accounts of OECD Countries 1961 - 1978, Paris 1980.

TABLE 5: Employment in Agriculture and in Manufacture of Food, Beverages and Tobacco as Share of Civilian Employment in OECD Countries: 1968 and 1978 (percentages)

Country(a)	Agricultural Employment(b)/Civilian Employment		Employment in Manufacture of Food, Beverages and Tobacco(c)/Civilian Employment	
	1968	1978	1968	1978
Canada	8.6	5.7	2.7	2.0
United States	5.1	3.7	2.4	1.8
Japan	19.8	11.7	1.4	1.2
Australia	8.7	6.4	3.4	2.9
New Zealand	13.5	11.7	5.8 (1971)	5.6
Austria	19.9	10.9	3.0 (1969)	2.7
Belgium	5.5	3.2	3.4	2.5
Denmark	12.7	8.7	3.0	2.9
Finland	25.6	12.3	2.5	2.6
France	15.8	9.2	2.5 (1969)	2.3
Germany	9.9	6.5	3.1	2.8
Greece	44.5	27.3	1.4	1.9 (1978)
Iceland	18.8	13.5	9.1	11.4 (1977)
Ireland	29.4	22.2	4.6 (1971)	5.0 (1977)
Italy	23.0	15.5	2.1	1.9
Luxembourg	10.3	5.7	n.a.	n.a.
Netherlands	7.9	6.2	3.8 (1969)	3.1
Norway	15.4	8.7	3.6	2.9
Portugal	34.1	31.3	1.8	1.7 (1977)
Spain	29.3	20.2	2.7	3.2
Sweden	9.1	6.1	2.6 (1969)	2.1
Switzerland	9.5	7.6	2.1	1.8
Turkey	71.4	60.9	0.8 (1960)	1.0 (1976)
United Kingdom	3.5	2.7	3.1	2.7
OECD TOTAL	15.7 (44.9m) (d)	10.7 (33.9m) (d)	2.3 (6.8m) (d)	2.0 (6.7m) (d)

n.a. Data not available.
a) Data for 1968 and 1978 unless otherwise indicated.
b) Employment in Agriculture, Hunting, Forestry and Fishing
c) Wage earners and salaried employees only.
d) Calculated from employment data for the years and countries indicated.
Source: OECD, Labour Force Statistics, 1967 - 1978, Paris, 1980.

TABLE 6: Important parameters of the EEC food Industry (1976)

Country	D	B	DK	F	GB	IRL	I	NL	EEC(1)	Change since 1972
Turnover (2)	39932	6830	5265	31655	33224	2538	15917	6830	152082	+69%
Employment (3)	479.4	85.0	63.5	399.8	740.8	55.2	252.8	152.5	2231.8	-6.3%
Value Added (2)	7999	1355	1044	5912	8058	710	2851	2705	30672	+48%
Enterprises	2824	713	365	2785	2834	326	2125	939	12951	-22%

Footnotes: 1. Includes Luxembourg
             2. In million ECUs
             3. x 1000

From: Food Industry in the EEC. CEC. DG 111/A/2/ Brussels 2/1981 coherent policy are believed to be of sufficient urgency it seems reasonable to expect action and it is here that a serious problem arises which is linked to the question of the scientific basis of nutrition discussed above. Given the disparate views held by authoritative nutritionists on the same topics, it is politically easier and safer not to act. Several examples of such disagreements are as follows; they have been selected mainly from the USA and UK owing to the often bitter and always public nature of debates conducted in these countries. A summary of recent wrangles in the USA may be found in reference 119.

-----the major health problems of the United States and other affluent countries are coronary artery disease, stroke, cancer, diabetes, hypertension and obesity .... All of these diseases are clearly associated with the diet we eat.

> D. Mark Hegsted, U.S.D.A. quoted from "U.S. Dietary Goals", 1978
> Food and Agricultural Outlook Conference, Washington D.C.
> November 17, 1977.

-----The American diet has been referred to as 'pathogenic' by some and as 'disastrous' by others implying that our diet has 'deteriorated' in the past 50 to 75 years .... The American diet today is better than ever before and is one of the best, if not the best, in the world today.

> G.A. Leveille, Chairman, Dept. of Food Science and Human Nutrition,
> Michigan State University quoted from "Establishing and
> Implementing Dietary Goals," 1978 Food and Agricultural Outlook
> Conference, Washington, D.C., November 17, 1977.

"In an unusual move, the National Academy of Sciences announced ....that some of the nation's most eminent scientists were in an irreconcilable conflict over proposals to alter the recommended levels of certain vitamins and minerals in the human diet".

Robert Pear in New York Times, 8 October 1985, p.AI, AI4.

"Although the number of cancer cases is steadily increasing as the population grows, the age-adjusted total cancer incidence and mortality rates for sites other than the respiratory tract have as a whole remained static during the last 30 to 40 years."

Committee on Diet, Nutrition and Cancer of the National Research Council (1982), Nutrition Today, July/August, pp 20-25.

"...... a partial change from saturated to polyunsaturated fatty acids in the diet (is recommended) because this leads to a decrease in blood cholesterol".
Institute for Preventive Medicine of the West German Federal Health Administration, 1975.

"The health advantages of changing from saturated to unsaturated fats are not scientifically well founded".
Institute for Preventive Medicine of the West German Federal Health Administration, 1981.

While all sovereign governments accept a responsibility for the welfare of their citizens, the extent of their response to a given health risk varies with the perceived severity of that risk. As a rule, this response has been direct when the consequences of exposure to a risk were catastrophic and indirect for less serious consequences; examples of the former would include regulations governing the microbiological control of processed foods, the restoration of UK white bread with minerals to prevent the development of rickets and the control exerted over additive incorporation in processed foods in all member states. A perception of the diet-disease issue as of less than catastrophic proportions is likely to induce governments to minimise their involvement to the provision of information and/or educational programmes.

2.4.3 Implications for the future

As outlined above, the promulgation and implementation of a comprehensive food and nutrition policy represents an extension of government intervention rather than a new departure; scientific/philosophical reasons commonly advanced for a reluctance to increase intervention have been shown to be either invalid or misleading. However, limits to action due to conflicting expert interpretations of nutritional data and differing perceptions of the severity of the problem of degenerative diseases are more serious and need clarification; debate on the scientific criteria used in evaluating nutritional experiments needs to be fostered since confusion caused by such disagreements will reduce the enthusiasm in government for far-reaching action. Whatever decisions are made on the basis of expert medical, scientific and administrative opinion, they will, in the final analysis, be political. Politicians in Europe may be expected to be unwilling to be seen to interfere with food availability and choice in the absence of a clear remit from the electorate. A useful contribution to the initiation of debate in this area could therefore be made by holding a Community-wide opinion poll to ascertain the extent of public concern in relation to food, nutrition and health. Such a poll might conveniently be timed to coincide with national population census collections and could include questions designed to uncover the level of nutritional knowledge in the Community's citizens. If public opinion is seen to demand action, the political will necessary to overcome administrative inertia may then appear.

2.5   IMPLEMENTATION OF DIETARY GUIDELINES

While the decisions which need to be made during the development of dietary guidelines are essentially scientific, those involved in the implementation of such guidelines are taken in the world of politics and the realms of political philosophy. The options open to central government in relation to guideline implementation are basically only two in number and are reflections of differing political philosophies rather than degrees of attachment to the value of the guidelines themselves; they are

(a)   that the attainment of nutritional well-being is the responsibility of the individual, with the role of government being confined to the promulgation of dietary guidelines, nutritional information and data on food composition (minimalist approach), or

(b)   that the role of government is not only to alert the individual to the health-risks which may result from malnutrition but also to actively intervene in the economy so as to facilitate the achievement of optimum nutrition for all citizens of the state (planned interventionist approach).

The accusation has been levelled at governments which adopt the former approach that they do so not out of high political motives but from a rather ignoble protection of vested interests in the economy. In addition, it is often pointed out that such administrations sometimes act inconsistently by legally enforcing the addition of selected nutrients to staple foods (e.g. fortification of white bread with vitamins in the UK) or their reduction in others (restriction of salt addition to bread in Belgium). However, such inconsistencies are the inevitable result of ad hoc problem-solving, are a feature of government action in many spheres and do not negate the premise on which the minimalist action programmes are based. It might also be pointed out that the difference between "protecting vested interests" and "minimising disruptive effects in sensitive sectors of the economy" is often one of political perspective rather than incontrovertible fact.

Most countries which have issued dietary guidelines have implemented a minimalist approach; in only one (Norway) has government adopted a formal food and nutrition policy to intervene in all sectors of the economy so as to permit the implementation of nutritional guidelines. What mechanisms have been adopted by these different approaches and what have the results been?

2.5.1   Minimalist approach

Characteristic of this approach is the complete absence of any formal commitment by or extensive involvement of government in actively influencing all sectors of the national economic complex so as to change the type of food being consumed by the general public. This is viewed as its major strength by political theorists who favour the minimisation of government intervention in all spheres of personal activity but, while some degree of success has undoubtedly accompanied minimalist approaches in many countries, it is not without significant weaknesses. In practical terms, this approach holds that while changes in the national dietary are desirable, the role of central government should be to facilitate the individual citizen in the implementation of such changes by providing him or her with the necessary information and decision-making criteria i.e. dietary guidelines, nutritional education and nutritional labelling of food. Market "pull" is the mechanism by which consumer demands in relation to food composition are translated into altered agricultural production and industrial food processing; that such an approach can be at least moderately successful is shown by the recent appearance at retail level of a range of new or modified food products with a more desirable nutrient profile (see CHAPTER 3). Sales of skimmed milk, wholemeal bread, muesli, low-fat yogurt, low-fat cheese and reduced-fat sausages have recently increased in the UK (104, 120, 121) while the previously documented (103, 104, 105, 122) willingness of food manufacturers to produce foods for which there appears to be a consumer demand has again been recently highlighted by the production of preservative-free breads in the UK (123) and Republic of Ireland and a public announcement of the "total elimination from all (our) products of all artifical colours including tartrazine and all other azo dyes and a reduction in the number of other additives including monosodium glutamate and polyphosphate "by Birds Eye, the UK frozen foods market leader (124). The retail trade has also become involved, with Sainsbury's, the UK's largest food retailer announcing (124) an examination of their 3,000 own-label products with a view to removing all non-essential additives following such action by the competing Safeway chain (121).

Nutrition education programmes have been initiated in most developed countries and have used a variety of strategies and techniques (125-127) to adequately inform the general public about nutritional matters. In order to achieve significant results, such educational campaigns must be large, professional and sustained - the financial costs are high. The focus of such campaigns must be specific since the perspective of the problem tends to be different when nutrition education is taught as part of a science or health education course (128). These efforts require the support of government at the highest level in order to ensure the continuous financial support necessary if significant results are to be obtained; if such support is not forthcoming, short-term financial exigencies are likely to severely disrupt the functioning of health education organisations. Difficulties exist in relation to measurements of the effectiveness of nutritional education (129) but it has been stated that it will be ineffective ab initio in the presence of too many constraints on the desired changes people would like to make (129).

As a result of increasing demand for information on the nutrient content of foods, measures have been taken (nationally and internationally) to require more information to be given to consumers in relation to the composition of foodstuffs (130). Regulations to control the format of such nutritional labelling have been implemented in the Federal Republic of Germany, Denmark, the Netherlands and USA while draft regulations are being prepared in others such as the UK. International bodies, such as the Codex Committee on Food Labelling of the FAO/WHO Codex Alimentarius Commission, have also been active in harmonising approaches to this topic. Thus, the consumer is currently being presented with the opportunity to make better informed choices of food in many countries.

Food advertising is acknowledged to be a powerful mechanism for influencing food choice; often such influences act so as to direct consumption towards foods which may not have a desirable nutritional profile (131). However, minimalist action programmes only interfere with advertising when spurious or misleading claims are made for individual food products or if any detrimental effect on the consumer's health may follow their consumption e.g. slimming aids which function by inhibiting the normal activity of digestive enzymes.

School lunch programmes (well-developed in France, Belgium and the UK, absent in the Netherlands and marginal in Greece, Denmark, Ireland, Italy, Luxembourg and the Federal Republic of Germany (132)) have been used by a number of governments with minimalist approaches, as a vehicle for changing part of the daily diet of school-children and raising the consciousness of children and their families in relation to food habits (133). In the USA, an idea of the scale of the intervention may be obtained from the fact that in 1980, 4.4 billion school lunches were served and 57% of all school-children participated in the National School Lunch Program (NSLP); the total cost of these meals was 3.1 billion dollars and 85% of the meals were distributed free or at low cost. The objectives of the NSLP were re-written in 1980 to incorporate nutritional considerations in addition to the original aim of providing market support for food surpluses. The new guidelines contained recommendations to decrease the levels of starch (sic), sugar and fat in prepared lunches and to vary the source of starch by providing alternate servings of wholewheat bread, pasta, rice, macaroni etc; more recently, a reduction in the salt content of lunch foods has been encouraged. The implementation of these guidelines has varied from state to state but in many the changes have been marked. Approaches involved have been different also, with some choosing to introduce novel foods e.g. textured vegetable protein or tofu (a protein supplement made from curdled soy milk) and others altering the formulation of common foodstuffs; those adopting the latter approach (e.g. New York City) have encouraged the use of low-fat milk and cheese and the production of low-fat, low-salt and low-sugar versions of fast food (fried chicken, french fries, hamburgers and cheeseburgers). (Some idea of the 'muscle' exerted by these school-lunch programmes may be gleaned from their ability to obtain supplies of gelatin which was coloured using natural colourants and soup bases free from monosodium glutamate). Many are exceeding specific dietary guideline provisions by excluding from lunches any foods containing preservatives or additives and are forcing the supply, for example, of bread and bakery products free of preservatives (Atlanta, Georgia). While no such action has been undertaken in Europe, individuals within the educational sector in the UK have been attempting to implement nutritional recommendations in a practical manner. Thus, at the behest of a Health Education Officer in the Grampian region of Scotland, the home economics course in a second-level institute of education was altered to bring the recipes used in practical classes into line with the recommendations of the NACNE report (134). Pastry was made with a mixture of white and wholemeal rather than solely white flour while the sugar and fat content of pastries has also been reduced. Dietary fibre content of prepared food has been raised by leaving skin on fruit where appropriate and the avoidance of heavy syrup in connection with canned fruit is being practiced. The reaction to these changes was reported to be generally favourable on the part of pupils and their parents although the teachers found difficulty in obtaining some foods at an economic cost (e.g. fruit canned in light syrup or water) and there was a general dearth of background educational material to support the practical demonstrations.

In Japan also, government has intervened in school-lunch programmes to displace bread as a source of complex carbohydrate by re-introducing rice in line with its policy of encouraging the consumption of foods which are traditional in Japan and which may be readily produced there. Rice is supplied at 35% less than the normal market price and financial incentives are used to encourage the installation in schools of rice-cooking facilities. As is the case in Europe (135), the Japanese government subsidises liquid milk supplied to schools while in 1979, a new scheme to encourage the consumption of a native fruit juice (unshu mandarin) was inaugurated.

Despite the apparent success of minimalist approaches (those mentioned above plus the gradual improvement in public health witnessed in many countries over the last decade due to the decline in death-rates attributed to degenerative diseases) their central weakness is the absence of any formal, high-level commitment to action. This means that the high degree of integration of government policy programmes necessary to maximise action in relation to population nutritional status is almost totally lacking. As already mentioned, educational programmes may have inadequate funding, be disrupted by other fiscal policy measures and be patchy (geographically and temporally) in their implementation. Market "pull" may be expected to exert the strongest effect in centres of high-population density and strong retail competition; the fact that new and/or modified food products tend to be sold at a premium price often limits their availability in sparsely-populated and impoverished areas of a country. Populations in rural areas may be at a further price disadvantage due to the costs (distribution and storage) of servicing such regions unless special measures are taken. The solution of problems such as those identified requires an assimilation of nutritional planning into the policy deliberations of all government departments and some administrative mechanism for integrating government actions which affect all parts of the national economy.

Thus, minimalist approaches to food and nutrition policy can make significant improvements in national food habits; a compromise is, however, made between the maximisation of such improvements and the minimisation of governmental interference in individual decision-making. Dangers inherent in this compromise were expressed by the Australian Minister for Health, Neal Blewett, as follows (136):

"There has been much emphasis in recent conservative rhetoric on the individual's responsibility for his or her own health. There are dangers in the proposition that living a long and healthy life is very much a do-it-yourself proposition. It becomes a splendid ideological justification for user-pay principles. If we are to have effective preventive health programs we need to recognise that our lifestyles are socially conditioned. We face the paradox that while economic development has helped to eliminate certain diseases, it has served to underwrite others. A preventive health program must tackle not only personal lifestyles but the environmental setting of those lifestyles."

Dangers inherent in the assumption that people will change dietary or personal habits, even when highly motivated, were reported in an American study designed to test the hypothesis that if people at high risk for heart disease reduce their exposure to risk factors, they will reduce the incidence of heart disease (137); in a comment on the results of the study, Leonard Syme (an epidemiologist from the University of California at Berkeley) says that "it is not enough to tell people they are at risk and then expect them to make the necessary changes in their lives. We have got to do other things as well such as change the forces in society that are contributing to the high incidence of heart disease."

2.5.2   Planned interventionist approach

The alternative approach to the implementation of dietary guidelines is that of planned intervention. Such a procedure aims to devise an integrated approach to policy—making which attempts to alter food consumption while minimising or removing potential conflicts with various other aspects of government policy. Thus, a food and nutrition policy has inputs into agricultural, industrial, employment, regional, transport, trade and consumer policies among others and recognises the interdependencies of the food system and the national and international economies. By its very existence, it permits a meaningful discussion of national priorities in a range of areas and paves the way for trade-offs to be made between conflicting positions. To this end, an essential characteristic of such policies is transparency i.e. the overall goals, mechanisms for achieving them and procedures for progress assessment should be clearly expounded.

Food and nutrition policy is a complex set of statements which has as its aim the harmonisation of food supply, food demand, and nutritional well-being. Since such a policy impinges on the entire national economy, each of the three headings above needs to be considered in conjunction with other policy objectives.

The achievement of nutritional well-being will be attained, it is assumed, by implementing a set of dietary guidelines. These will broadly direct decisions relating to the desirability or otherwise of various foods and influence policies in relation to food demand and supply.

Policies relating to food demand encompass policies concerning population, prices, income, distribution, employment, subsidies and other socio-economic benefits.

Food supply policies, as well as being consistent with food demand, must be guided by nutritional considerations. In addition they should take account of the level and composition of domestic agricultural output and structural policies related to international trade, marketing, distribution, processing, transport, storage and retailing.

2.5.3   Interactions with food supply policy

2.5.3.1   Agricultural policy: Policies relating to agriculture and fisheries are a feature of all developed countries since one of a government's first duties is to ensure that the nation is fed; in the EEC, policies of individual member states are subsumed in the Common Agricultural Policy (CAP), the basis for which is laid down in Article 39 of the Treaty of Rome.   The relevant section states that the objectives of agricultural policy are:-

    (a)   to increase agricultural productivity

    (b)   to ensure a fair standard of living for the agricultural community

    (c)   to stabilise markets

    (d)   to ensure the availability of food

    (e)   to ensure that food reaches the consumer at reasonable prices

Various structural mechanisms have evolved since the initial ratification of the Treaty in 1957 to assist in the achievement of the stated policy goals e.g. productivity has been improved by measures taken to rationalise farm holdings, improve farmer education, aid drainage and irrigation etc and permit more efficient uptake of technical advances.   As a result of the evolution of European agriculture, a range of ancillary industries have developed to meet its needs; these include the fertiliser, machinery and agricultural chemical industries. Farmers' incomes have been improved and markets for a range of agricultural commodities have been stabilised to some degree by price support mechanisms. Increased farm productivity and the gradual reduction of national barriers to trade have paved the way for the provision of a greatly increased food supply at relatively uniform prices throughout the Community e.g. between 1973 and 1984 the Community's level of self-sufficiency has increased from 90% to 105% for cereals, 90% to 101% for wine, 92% to 102% for meats, 92% to 123% for sugar and 104% to 147% for butter (138). To date, consumer concerns in relation to the type of food produced in Europe have not figured largely in the operation of the Common Agricultural Policy which would seem to many to have been operated mainly with objectives a) and b) in view. However, with 65-75% of the total EEC budget being spent on agriculture and 95% of that on price-support mechanisms (139), the increasing burden of the Guarantee Section of the Agricultural Guidance and Guarantee Fund has approached a point where a change in emphasis is being investigated - witness the recent introduction of a co-responsibility levy on milk production and current discussions on alterations in the marketing arrangements for cereals and beef in the Community. Any change, especially one which may seek to influence the nature of food produced must be reconciled with the provisions of the CAP outlined above; it is apparent that the minimisation of inevitable conflicts will be difficult. For example, as a means of reducing carcass fat contents, any move to reduce slaughter weight of cattle or sheep would directly affect farm income while it is possible that for certain breeds of cattle, conformation at reduced weights would be such as to render them ineligible for Intervention or payment of the variable premium; conflict immediately arises with point b) of the CAP. In relation to dairy products, current payment methods for milk in most EEC member states encourage the production of milk with high fat content; a reduction in the fat content of wholemilk may be deemed desirable as an element of nutrition policy and a change in payment method would therefore be required. Movement in this direction is underway in many European countries with an alteration in payment levels to incorporate protein content as a variable although there appear to be technical limits to the reduction in fat content which is achievable.

For nutritional reasons, an increased output (and consumption) of fruit and vegetables in the Community may be desirable; however family farms producing such commodities are generally not economically viable. Production limits exist in relation to sugar beet and recent Community discussions suggest a decreased return from cereal production. Therefore, while a reduced output of fat from agricultural enterprises may be desirable, sudden change in the type of farm output is probably not possible or perhaps even desirable in view of the sociological considerations which also underlie the CAP. As a result, a food and nutrition policy may not impinge on the agricultural policies in the short-term and the conflicts which undoubtedly exist may go unresolved. This approach has been used in Sweden and the Netherlands, where direct effects on agriculture, following the adoption of a food and nutrition policy, were deliberately avoided with the emphasis on changed food composition being placed on the food processing industry (145).

2.5.3.2 Trade policy: In an EEC context, trade policy will be taken to refer to international trade between the Community and the rest of the world. The EEC is currently the world's largest trading bloc in food, both importing and exporting (140). This trading network has developed out of a need to import foods which cannot be grown in the EEC so as to provide a varied diet for the Community population and as a means of disposing of commodities in surplus within Europe, thereby raising the economic well-being of the Community. These trading links have generally been inherited from individual member states on accession to the Community (e.g. between Britain and Commonwealth countries such as Australia and New Zealand, between France and Mauritius etc.) although more recent arrangements have been developed between the Community as a whole and African, Caribbean and Pacific countries (Lomé Convention) and the wider international community (General Agreement on Tariffs and Trade - GATT). These arrangements are mutually beneficial since in 1979, 36% of Community exports went to developing countries which in turn supplied 40% of EEC imports. Any alteration in EEC trading patterns must take such arrangements into account by re-negotiation of the relevant agreements and minimising the rate of agreed change; sudden shifts in trading policy could have major effects on a number of smaller trading partners e.g. sugar exports from Mauritius to the EEC constitute 60% of that country's total exports (140). While any dramatic reduction in trading concessions currently granted to New Zealand may be somewhat less calamitous, the importance of this country to the foreign policy interests of the EEC makes balanced consideration of the desirability of any change in trading arrangements essential. Due to the general increase in agricultural production in developed countries and a widespread deceleration of consumption growth, more agricultural production is traded internationally. Shrinking markets and the dubious ability of Third World Countries to pay suitable prices for food imports has led to increased strain and competition on world food markets. This strain has led recently to competition between the USA and EEC for important markets previously in the domain of the latter; in 1983, the USA contracted to supply Egypt with 1 million tonnes of wheat flour, thus displacing the EEC (the world's major flour exporter) as its main supplier. Subsequently, the USA agreed to supply Egypt with 18,000 tonnes of butter and 10,000 tonnes of cheese at heavily subsidised prices while more recently (141) the US administration has threatened to apply curbs to the import of EEC products (to the annual value of 500 - 600 million US dollars) as a result of a dispute over tariffs on their exports to Spain and Portugal. These have been widely interpreted as 'warning shots' in a conflict of interests which extends beyond commodity trading into wider aspects of EEC-USA foreign policy relationships. Clearly, alterations in trading practices involving the EEC must take account of such sensitivities; pressure for changes in these practices is also mounting within the Community due to the financial costs involved through export refunds and a number of strategies for change are currently being debated (142).

2.5.3.3   Industrial processing policies:

Due to the exodus from the land and increasing urbanisation of European and other countries, an ever-enlarging proportion of the population is divorced from the process of food production. This group has come to depend on the food processing industry to supply their food needs and in response this industrial sector has expanded steadily throughout this century. For example, the turnover of the food processing industry in W. Germany was DM 123.5 billion in 1979 and in the UK it is the second largest industry in net terms with some 12% of total UK manufacturing net output in 1981 (143); in Japan it accounted for 11.9% of total industrial sales in 1976 (83). A recent additional feature of this industry in most countries has been its centralisation, with an ever-decreasing number of companies exerting an ever-increasing degree of control over the composition of the population's diet. Current policies relating to this sector in general involve food safety issues but any major induced change in the demand for specific foodstuffs could have serious implications for its viability in the short-term with obvious risks to security of food supply. An additional consideration relates to employment in the food processing and ancillary industries; in 1976, they accounted for 10% of manufacturing industry employment in Japan, about 470,000 jobs in W. Germany (83) and approximately 590,000 in the UK (140) in the early 1980s (see also Table 6). Clearly, and especially in view of current Community unemployment levels, extreme caution needs to be used when adjustments affecting this industrial sector are made. Such caution is required even if dietary change were to be encouraged through the increased consumption of non-processed foods.

However, as discussed above (see 2.5.1), the food processing industry has demonstrated a willingness and ability to tailor its finished products in line with consumer demand. Food processors should be encouraged to produce foods with reduced contents of fat, sugar and salt and energy (calories) and where appropriate, increased contents of polyunsaturated fats and dietary fibre. Encouragement may take the form of assistance in modifying established processes to produce altered food formulations or incentives to increase the research and development activity in the area of product innovation. In general, however, provided gradual change is the target, the industrial processing industry seems likely to respond positively to food and nutrition policy goals.

2.5.3.4 Distribution: Policies impinging on food distribution relate to transport, storage and regional aspects of the retail trade. An important feature of this sector has been a process of concentration. Expansion occurred initially through the opening of new stores and/or increases in shop floor space but due to a decline in population growth leading to a static food market and saturation of prime site locations, expansion has increasingly been via merger and/or acquisition although collaboration has recently become popular with the formation of large buying-groups e.g. in France, Contact (Socadip and Paridoc) and Arci Association (Auchan, Carrefour, Sogara, Casino, Promodes, Metro and Comptoirs Modernes) were formed early in 1984. A further trend reflecting concentration is the increasing internationalisation of the retail trade. Numerous mechanisms for such internationalisation exist (subsidiary creation, franchise operation, equity participation etc.) and examples of its occurrence include the acquisition of companies in Austria, the Netherlands and the USA by the German discount food retailer Aldi while French companies, in particular Carrefour, have been investing strongly in hypermarket development outside France (178). In terms of the horizontal relationships between retail outlets, the result of this concentration has been a major reduction in the market share held by unaffiliated independent outlets and an increase in that held by multiples (144, 145) in all European countries except Italy, where legislative restrictions on the opening of large stores have helped to support the small independent retailer, Belgium (146) and Greece (147). The demise of the independent grocer has led to fewer but larger food shops all over the Community (see, for example, UK data (148)) save Italy and Belgium where the independent sector retains about 80% of total sales. Large stores tend to operate on the basis of a high turnover - low margin; this determines to a large extent the product range which they carry. It also accounts for the scarcity of such stores in rural areas with obvious consequences in relation to food availability for people in sparsely-populated regions of the Community. Such areas may also be at a financial disadvantage owing to the haulage and storage requirements necessary for access to a varied food supply.

Food and nutrition policy aims to make nutritious foods available at reasonable cost to all consumers; existing distribution and retail networks must be utilised to these ends. Conflict with current trading practices and patterns will emerge as a result of the divergent aims of policy-makers and retail and distribution companies. Since the latter act so as to maximise profit, the location of retail outlets, the range of foods stocked by them and the prices charged for such foods will be decided on financial considerations. These have resulted in existing imbalances whereby large retail outlets offering the keenest prices and greatest food selection are located in urban centres with sparsely-populated and deprived areas of the Community being less well served. Steps may be required to encourage the siting of supermarkets in regions which could not otherwise support them, to defray the cost of transporting and storing foods with a desirable nutrient profile the long distance from point of production to point of sale, and to encourage the stocking by such retail outlets of a minimum range of desirable foods. Given the recent concentration of purchasing power in the supermarket chains (concentration which is projected to continue (149)), it will be necessary to oversee the range of foodstuffs sold by such groups and perhaps even their pricing strategies. Legislative controls on shop opening hours in a number of member states (e.g. the UK, Norway and Italy) have the effect of restricting food availability at certain times; an examination of such controls needs to be undertaken to achieve a balance between less restricted access to desirable (snack) foods other than sugar confectionery and the social implications of longer trading hours.

2.5.3.5   Food law: Food law is concerned with preventing the sale of foods which are or may be injurious to health, making misleading claims about the nature or quality of a food an offence and with defining compositional standards for particular foodstuffs.   It is the latter activity which may require attention should food and nutrition policy statements require an alteration in the composition of processed foods of an undesirable nutrient profile.   (Such an approach would be less disruptive of both individual diet and the agro-food industry than the alternative removal from the diet of specific foodstuffs (100)).   For example, a minimum concentration of sugar is legally specified in the UK for soft drink and jam (150) as is fat in cream (151), ice-cream (152), chocolate (104), butter (153), margarine (154), and certain cheeses (155). Most of these products have specified compositions in the national legislation of EEC member states.   Therefore, while sugar-reduced jams or fat-reduced butter or margarine may be produced, they may not be described as jam, butter or margarine respectively.   Any movement to the production of modified versions of such foods will need legislative adjustment to permit the use of established generic names as an aid to marketing.

2.5.4   Interactions with food demand policy

Food consumption patterns are subject to influence from a number of sources; these include:-

(a)   social and cultural factors,

(b)   price and income,

(c)   education, and

(d)   advertising.

All these variables may be influenced by policy decisions taken by central government and their impact must be considered in order to predict the likely success of any policy measure which attempts to alter food consumption patterns.

2.5.4.1 Social and cultural factors: The complexity of these factors and their operation in altering food consumption has been indicated by McKenzie (156) who discussed five criteria which determine 'tastes and preferences'. These are that food is an aid to security, a substitute for material creativity, a demonstration of conformity or prestige, an indication of mood or personality or a compensation for denial or during times of crisis. Difficulty in understanding these factors limits the design of any programme to change or differentially reinforce them. It must also be recognised that awareness or understanding of these motivating influences does not necessarily permit accurate prediction of food purchasing behaviour as observed by Bender (157) when he stated that "the British public have very little interest in food values and their knowledge, such as it is, has virtually no influence on what they eat" and by Tremolieres (quoted in ref. 125) in the observation that "human behaviour in matters of food will always be affective behaviour – that is to say, based on pleasure and only in limited degree governed by reason". However, a recent social trend which appears to have influenced food consumption is the desirability of slimness; the desire to avoid obesity and appear fit is a strong motivating factor at least in certain sub-groups of the population and this knowledge may be useful in aspects of the presentation of food and nutrition policies. Indeed, it is already being applied in the advertising material of at least one commodity trading organisation (158). In the "Guide to Food, Exercise, Nutrition and You" published by the US Dairy Council and aimed at teenagers, motivating factors addressed were, in order of priority, appearance, performance and, lastly health.

2.5.4.2 Price and income policies: The adjustment of food prices by aids to production and processing, direct consumer subsidy (and even taxation in certain countries e.g. the Netherlands) and regulation of disposable income by the alteration of personal taxation levels etc. have long been instruments by which the consumption of foods have been affected by central government. The relative price of food in relation to disposable income is arguably the single most important factor influencing food purchasing patterns and while economic parameters such as demand elasticity are useful historical indicators of purchasing response, they do not provide any insight into the mechanisms responsible for a given response pattern. In order to alter food purchasing patterns in line with any particular set of dietary guidelines, it will be necessary to understand the response of individuals in different socio-economic groups to changes in the relative price of selected foods (41).

Most government action in this sphere has been in the area of prices policy - in the CAP, for example, the increased prices paid to producers have resulted in higher food prices for consumers. There is little evidence to suggest that governments have increased food prices so as to reduce consumption although in many countries health protection has been used as a reason for increased taxation of, for example, tobacco and alcohol. Direct consumer subsidy of staple dietary items such as bread and milk has been introduced for socio-economic and political reasons in many countries at the height of the current international recession but such measures tend to be temporary; in Norway, however, the rate of increase in the retail price of skimmed milk has been lower than that of full-fat milk since 1st July 1980 in an attempt to direct consumption (159).

In order to encourage a national dietary pattern which conforms to the consensus guidelines described previously (see 2.3.1), it would be necessary to stimulate the consumption of poultry, fish, cereals and cereal products, fruit and vegetables, reduced-fat dairy products and oils rich in polyunsaturated fats. Consumption of butter and fat spreads should be discouraged while it would be undesirable to increase red meat intake above present levels. A combination of price adjustment mechanisms may be required to thus alter food consumption patterns, depending on the food group involved. Direct subsidy of bread is already practised by a number of member states although differential rates may be necessary to encourage purchase of wholegrain products in addition to or at the expense of white breads; a complication here lies in the practice of below-cost selling of white pan bread in the UK and Republic of Ireland which places wholegrain products at a major price disadvantage. Attempts have been made to alter this retailing practice in Ireland (160) but without any success to date (see 2.5.4.4). Selective subsidy application to low-fat dairy products to increase consumption is already practised in Norway with some degree of success (see 2.6.1.2) but the problem of disposing of the butterfat thus separated will increase as a result. This problem would be exacerbated by price adjustments to butter (and other high-fat spreads) for the purpose of decreasing its attractiveness; conflict will arise here with other Community measures currently utilised to decrease Intervention stocks of this commodity i.e. subsidised disposal within the EEC for domestic consumption (161) or subsidised disposal of butter concentrate to the food processing industry (39) and the consumer (162). Until changes in CAP discussed above (see 2.5.3.1) significantly alter agricultural production, disposal problems for several commodities or fractions of commodities may, in fact, become worse. Any increase in demand for oil-based products which may be desirable on account of their polyunsaturated fat content, may currently be met only by increased importation; levies associated with such imports raise their cost to the consumer and reduce their competitiveness vis-a-vis butter etc. Tariff reduction may be warranted until European supplies of such commodities reach sufficiency levels although the practical difficulties of selective change in such levies may be considerable. With the recent accession of Spain and Portugal to full membership of the EEC, increased availability of fruit and vegetables is inevitable; EEC self-sufficiency in fresh fruit and citrus fruit is forecast to rise from 84-88% and 45-69% respectively (163). The application of direct consumer subsidy for these commodities may not be the most suitable mechanism for price reduction due to their distribution and marketing arrangements. It may be more useful to explore the introduction of freight subsidies and/or grant arrangements (to ensure the provision throughout the Community of improved storage facilities) in order to reduce the cost and improve the quality of fresh produce towards which the consumer is, in general, already favourably disposed (164). Stimulation of poultry consumption (at the expense of dark meats) may be difficult to achieve in the absence of a direct consumer subsidy or a subsidy on feed grain which represents a major element of production costs; a careful balance needs to be struck so as not to overly depress the existing market for beef, lamb and pork due to the importance of these commodities in the agricultural economy. Increased fish consumption is generally regarded as desirable and great scope would appear to exist for improvement in this area; the marketing structures for fish may prevent direct consumer subsidy and, like the case of fruit and vegetables, price reduction and an increase in the quality and availability of fish and fish products may better be achieved by other fiscal mechanisms. Developments in this area may also be appropriate as a result of the accession to the EEC of Spain and Portugal. Exploration of the possibilities of fish-farming would be merited; such activities have recently expanded in the Republic of Ireland in particular and have the major advantage of strengthening employment and infrastructure in disadvantaged areas of the Community e.g. all of the developments in the Republic of Ireland have taken place in the rural west and projected employment levels (7,500 in five years) are of major significance in such areas (165).

Apart from the political opprobrium governments may face should they choose to stimulate or depress consumption of specific foods by direct price intervention, the effect of any measures introduced would need careful monitoring so as to ensure the desired goals were being achieved. Despite these risks, direct intervention has the political attraction of being visible evidence of government concern and of being relatively simple to operate; it therefore would seem to be a likely area of administrative activity should a national food and nutrition policy be implemented.

2.5.4.3 Education: Nutrition education is a prerequisite for the adequate expression of consumer sovereignty and is now actively encouraged to varying degrees in all developed countries. Such education may take place in formal educational establishments at all levels and additionally through the local health authority infrastructure. Efforts along traditional lines need to be reinforced to ensure access to such educational structures in all regions of the Community; the particular needs of rural, sparsely-populated areas require to be met using all the means of communication now available (see, for example, ref. 166) while the establishment of in-service courses to continually up-date the knowledge of practicing nutritionists must be a priority. (Some interesting developments in relation to the latter point are reported to be underway in France (167)). Indeed, the consumer is nowadays subjected to a bewildering array of nutritional information from newspapers, magazines, television, radio, books etc. and usually lacks the competence to sift such information for inaccurate or misleading messages. Even assuming such a level of discernment, the possession of information and the execution of decisions based on that information are two distinct processes and considerable evidence exists which reveals that, in practice, there is a gap between the possession and application of nutritional information (114-116). The reasons for this gap are not understood (168) but before effective nutrition education programmes (129) can be mounted so as to alter food consumption trends, research in this area needs support and intensification.

A major difficulty in information dissemination is the general reluctance of scientists to become directly involved; this reluctance stems from a number of causes including a distaste and suspicion of mass communications media and individual reticence. For their part, media personnel do not understand the scientific method or the need for measured prose in discussions of scientific theory or fact. As a result of this awareness gulf, those who are more confident in their use of the printed word and visual image show no unwillingness to promulgate their own ideas and recommendations in order to fill a perceived need in the public at large. Increasingly, it is essential that practising scientists learn to use all the means at their disposal to ensure that correct nutritional advice gains widespread circulation. To facilitate this, mechanisms need to be found to increase the understanding of each side by the other and it may be that the Commission could become involved in sponsoring and/or organising meetings of media and scientific personnel in each member state with this end in view. It might also consider ways and means of aiding the publication of suitable popular books and magazine articles by the scientific community either through training in the relevant writing techniques or the support of sabbatical arrangements for the production of such educational tools. Support (mainly organisational in nature) for the establishment of a Community-wide Media Resource Service has much to commend it; such a service would operate along the lines of the US-based Scientists' Institute for Scientific Information which was launched in 1977 and maintains a register of 15,000 experts in defined fields of science. Journalists needing expert opinion on a particular matter would be put in touch with one of a number of relevant people available for a rapid response. Such a service would also be of use to parliamentarians in national and European assemblies especially if it was to be expanded to take initiatives and hold, at short notice, briefing sessions for draft legislation which had nutritional implications (7).

In the event of the EEC adopting an integrated food and nutrition policy, conflict would immediately arise between the support for nutrition education which is an essential part of such a policy and existing mechanisms for funding advertising and disposal of, for example, full-fat dairy products through the dairy co-responsibility levy. Perhaps such expenditure could be transferred to the general nutrition education field in an attempt to decrease the colossal discrepancy between the operating budgets of national health education agencies and the sums spent on advertising campaigns by food processors and retail food chains (see

2.5.4.4). As a further means to achieving this end, it may be possible to use some of industry's advertising budgets as educational expenditure for specific products; in 1974 the Potato Board in the USA launched a campaign to better inform the consumer about the nutritional attributes of their product and as a result, per capita potato consumption rose from 114 pounds in 1974 to 124 pounds in 1978 (169). Working in combination with specific groups to such an end could benefit all parties involved. A further example is provided by the co-operation of a food processor, food retailer and central government in the Netherlands which aims to permit consumers to obtain accurate information on the energy and nutrient content of their diets. During a shopping expedition in the particular chain store, consumers record exactly the items purchased using a supplied questionnaire; these are collected at pay-points and taken to the food processor's premises where they are entered into a computer by the company staff. Following analysis of data on individual questionnaires (using software supplied by government), a breakdown of information is posted to each respondent for his/her own information (170). This paves the way for a continual monitoring of nutrient and energy intake and capitalises on the perceived neutrality of the retailer in the food and health area; perhaps major efforts should be made to utilise chain-stores and smaller retail outlets in the dissemination of nutrition information since they appear to be perceived as neutral and reliable by the consumer.

2.5.4.4 Advertising: That food advertising is pervasive is readily apparent; rather less, however, is known about its effects on total food consumption or consumption of specific foods, although in the absence of any definite information to the contrary, it can be argued that a sign of the effectiveness of food advertising is the substantial expenditure on it

by food firms. Details of the total media expenditure on food in ten EEC
member states may be seen in Table 7. These figures should be contrasted
with the current annual operating budgets for national health education
agencies (or their equivalent) in Ireland (IR£1.3m), Scotland (ST£2.8m)
France (33.6m FF), Belgium (112m BF) and the Netherlands (1.5m D.Fl).

TABLE 7: Total media expenditure on food advertising, 1984

Member State	Amount	Member State	Amount
Denmark	10m Dkr	Netherlands	110,025m DFl
France	2,608m FF	Portugal	593,074 Esc 000s
Greece	1,626m Drs	Spain	16,320m Pts
Rep. of Ireland	100m IR£	UK	472m ST£
Italy	824b Lit	FRG	1,053m DM

data taken from ref. 171

Food advertising is of two types - brand and generic advertising. Brand
advertising is competitive within food types and is designed to increase
market share; generic advertising has as its aim the promotion of
commodities such as beef, milk or eggs. The latter is designed to halt a
decline or increase consumption of generic products and, although not
primarily intended to do so, brand advertising has been suggested to result
in an increase in total market size (41). One of the most commonly-
employed advertising techniques is the creation of an assocation between
certain foods and a particular life-style such that foods become purchased
less for their nutritional value or other intrinsic functional values than
for what they convey to other people about the purchaser's life-style.
Almost without exception, nutritional information is absent from
advertising copy. In attempting to manipulate or alter the national diet,
government will need to understand the precise effects of advertising and

187

perhaps move to control it, as it has already done in many states (e.g. Denmark, France, Greece, Ireland, Italy, Spain, UK, FRG, Belgium, Sweden, Switzerland) in relation to tobacco and alcohol (172, 173). Specific control mechanisms are not without precedent in member states; for example, on the recommendation of the Restrictive Practices Commission, the government of the Republic of Ireland introduced in 1980 a ban on advertising of products being sold below-cost (160). Although the ban was later judged to be unconstitutional by the courts, it showed the willingness of government to curtail a specific type of advertising for a particular end (in this case the protection of small retail traders). Similarly, television advertising of toys which is specifically aimed at young children is under threat of curtailment in the UK. In the EEC context, conflict will arise between Community-support for generic advertising compaigns featuring e.g. full-fat dairy products and nutritional policy as already mentioned (see 2.5.4.3).

On a positive note, opportunities should be available to allow the use of the greater financial resources of the food industry for its benefit and that of the consumer. An example of one such arrangement is to be found in the UK where the Health Education Council endorse specific foods which are viewed as having a desirable nutrient profile; the bakery trade has been quick to include this endorsement on their packaging material to their benefit and that of the consumers.

2.6 NATIONAL APPROACHES TO FOOD AND NUTRITION POLICY

Activity in the area of policy concerning food and/or nutrition has become more marked in a number of developed countries over the past two decades; with the exception of Norway, no government in the developed world has implemented a coherent food and nutrition policy along the lines discussed in the preceding section. A number of different approaches have been used reflecting political realities as well as differences in national character; some of these are described below.

2.6.1   Norway

The food and nutrition policy implemented in Norway originated from a Report to the Storting in 1975 (44); in recognition of the interrelationship between food and other policy areas, the aims of the food and nutrition policy were as follows:-

(a)   to produce healthy eating habits in the population;

(b)   to implement the recommendations of the World Food Conference of 1972;

(c)   to maintain the regional development programme i.e. halt the decline in the rural population and increase the area of land devoted to agricultural production, and

(d)   to maximise domestic food production to ensure security of supply.

Specific changes in food intake recommended for the population were;

(a)   to reduce fat intake to 35% of total dietary energy intake through gradual change;

(b)   to replace the fat thus displaced by increased consumption of cereals and potatoes;

(c)   to increase the proportion of polyunsaturated fat in the diet (P/S ratio of 1:2 was the aim);

(d)   to increase fish consumption.

These policy statements must be viewed against the background of Norwegian agriculture and land resources in order to understand the scope for action by government. Because of the climate prevailing in Norway and the topography of the country, the production of sugar and grain is very limited; therefore grain, feed concentrates and sugar are the most substantial food and fodder imports. Norwegian crop production is characterised by the cultivation of grass; thus the production of milk and beef are two major agricultural activities. Another positive aspect of Norwegian agriculture is its fishing industry which is a major exporter of fish and fish products.

Food consumption trends were generally the same as those found in other industrialised countries i.e. a decrease in complex carbohydrate consumption (grain, potatoes, and rice), an increased intake of fruits and berries, sugar and meat while milk consumption had tended to decline slightly. Absolute values for the mean intake of certain foods were, of course, markedly different from other European and American countries; for example, consumption of full-fat milk, fish and margarine were very high while butter intake was higher than in the UK and USA. Skim milk consumption was lower than in other Nordic countries, the Netherlands, the UK and USA.

What were the main measures proposed to change the Norwegian diet in line with nutritional principles while at the same time fulfilling the other three elements of the food and nutrition policy outlined above?

2.6.1.1 Agriculture and fisheries policy measures: Measures of agricultural policy are shaped within the Agriculture Agreement between the state and farm organisations. Since several important agricultural products were protected against competitive imports by government, possibilites existed to influence the production levels of various commodities by direct action.

However, the main concern was to increase the amount of cereals, fruit and vegetables grown nationally to a) minimise the very large import bill for grain in particular and b) facilitate the dietary requirement for increased consumption of these products. Given the topographical limitations to an increase in land area suitable for cultivation of these commodities, the main strategy for their raised national production was to be increased productivity.

Since the land and climate of Norway meant that dairying and beef cattle production were the most successful forms of agricultural enterprise, no significant short-term changes in policies impinging directly on them were foreseen. On a medium to long term basis, changes in relationship between fat and other nutrients in livestock products were to be pursued by breeding and feeding methods. Pricing mechanisms to catalyse this were changes in milk payment-schemes to include protein as well as fat content and premia for leaner beef and pork carcasses.

Fish prices were almost entirely unprotected from world prices since most of the catch was exported; previous government intervention to influence consumption had been through subsidies but this was not easy to administer due to the unstructured marketing arrangements then existing for fish. Policy aims were therefore to increase the proportion of the catch being used as human food and an overhaul of marketing arrangements to permit more effective fiscal intervention.

2.6.1.2 Price policy and consumer subsidies: Policy in relation to prices paid to producers was influenced by trading commitments between Norway and other countries and this limited any scope for using pricing policy as a means of production control. However, the use of consumer subsidies as a means of influencing food consumption was already in widespread use as a vital element of general economic and social policy. In 1976, subsidies were in use for liquid milk, cheese, most types of meat, butter, margarine and fish and food flour and government viewed the modification of these schemes as a tool to stimulate the consumption of nutritionally desirable foods. Therefore it proposed to:-

(a) maintain the subsidies then in force for flour;

(b) adjust the subsidies for meat so that its consumption relative to fish was not increased;

(c) adjust milk subsidies so that low-fat milk consumption was stimulated more than wholemilk (this did not occur until 1 January, 1980);

(d) investigate the introduction of a subsidy for potatoes;

(e) while subsidies in relation to vegetables, fruit and berries were not contemplated, the maintenance of price at a moderate level was to be encouraged by reducing the price ex farm through a system of grants (packaging, quality, production area etc.) and minimising distribution costs by extending the then operative freight grants;

(f) consider removal of the subsidies on butter and margarine

2.6.1.3   Industrial processing: Few specific action plans were drawn up under this heading although, due to the increased intake of processed food and the centralisation of processing operations, it was noted that relatively few processors controlled the nutrient content of the diet to a considerable degree. While specific controls relating mainly to hygiene and food safety (microbiological and toxicological) were in existence, it was stated policy to encourage processors to provide the population with a range of foods in accordance with the aims of the food and nutrition policy. One interesting suggestion was the replacement of certain imported vegetable oils by marine fats produced locally in margarine formulation. This would reduce the import bill and guarantee an outlet for a local commodity. As a means of increasing wholegrain food consumption, the Norwegian Grain Corporation has worked to improve the baking-quality of wholemeal flour at the request of the National Nutrition Council.

2.6.1.4 Marketing and distribution: Advertising and distribution influence food consumption in two ways:

(a)   they influence which foods are available for consumption, and

(b)   they influence purchasing behaviour and food selection.

Norway has experienced the increased concentration of the food distribution chain previously noted (see 2.5.3.4) with the implications in terms of food availability in sparsely-populated areas of the country. To correct these distortions, proposals were made to the Ministry of Trade and Commerce on two different subsidy arrangements to enable shops in outlying areas to provide a complete range of services - these were an investment support and an operational support arrangement and it was proposed that they would be paid provided the store carried a suitable range of foods to permit the consumption of a diet in accordance with dietary goals. Such policies are also in agreement with regional policy goals.

Food advertising in Norway was extensive and it accounted for 9% of total brand name advertising in 1974 at a cost of 32 million Nkr. Most of such advertising was on products with a poor nutritional profile (chocolate, soft drinks, ice-cream etc) and there was seldom any mention of a suitable overall diet. The law current in 1976 forbade misleading advertising but in a proposal to the Ministry of Consumer Affairs and Government Administration, it was suggested that advertising should contain (undefined) mandatory information to better inform the consumer about products promoted in this way.

2.6.1.5 Information and education: The Norwegian government in 1976 had
no specific proposals in relation to information provision and education
but did call for greater coordination of the former under the aegis of the
National Nutrition Council and increased attention to the nutritional
content of school courses at the nursery, primary, secondary and tertiary
levels. Interestingly, they suggested a need for food producers to be
taught about the requirement for high quality foods in the belief that this
would assist in the implementation of dietary guidelines. Adult education
was also singled out for improvement especially in the encouragement of
allotment cultivation. In order to facilitate some of these desired
developments, 1.5 million Nkr has been allocated annually from the
national budget.

2.6.1.6 Legislation: Laws extant in Norway in 1976 which related to food
were concerned with safety, good manufacturing practice and fraud or
deception. The government felt that closer examination of regulations
concerning the declaration of fatty acid content in foods, especially
margarine, would be appropriate as would an extension of this form of
nutritional labelling to other products.

2.6.1.7 Research needs: The implementation of any national policy
implies a certain level of basic information, a knowledge of traditional
practices in the relevant sector, information on ways and means of
effecting change and mechanisms for monitoring the results of any programme
developed. Specifically in relation to a food and nutrition policy, while
data on Norwegian agricultural output and productivity were generally
satisfactory, information on the following other aspects was poor:

(a)   food consumption - this data was generally highly aggregated and
        figures for various social groups within the population were
        either absent or insufficent as were estimates of foods consumed
        outside the home;

(b)   the precise linkage between food and disease and the mechanisms
        involved;

(c)   determinants of purchasing behaviour and the precise effects of
        subsidies and promotional programmes.

No specific recommendations were made in relation to research needs
save that they should be coordinated.

In a further Report to the Storting in 1981 (159), the results of the
policy actions of government on food consumption were examined.   The main
findings of this progress report were as follows:

(a)   overall agricultural production rose as planned;

(b)   fat consumption did not decrease in line with the
        recommendations of the 1975 Report; this was ascribed to a
        failure of meat intake to level-off, the absence of a sustained
        swing from full fat to low-fat milk and no increase in fish
        consumption. The increase in meat consumption took place over
        a period when meat prices were increased substantially in order
        to limit increased consumption and increase farm income, thus
        illustrating the difficulty in accurately predicting
        consumer response to prices. The type of meat consumed was
        influenced by the use of subsidies - these existed for red
        meat but not for poultry since poultry feed was entirely
        imported. Ironically, most European health agencies suggest
        a swing from red meat to poultry for reasons of their
        respective fat contents. Milk, cream, cheese and butter
        between them accounted for about the same proportion of fat
        in 1970 and 1979 - 36%.   Details of changes in food intake
        over the period 1953-1984 are shown in Table 8.

(c)   potato consumption had not increased; this has been blamed on
        an inefficient marketing system and price variations between
        different parts of the country due to the selective imposition
        of freight charges.

Reaction in Norway to this progress report has been to change the
price policies for various products so as to continue the attempt at
altering the national diet.   In particular, all subsidies on butter and

TABLE 8: Food consumption in Norway (kg/head/year)

	1953/55	1970	1975	1984
Butter	4	6	5	5
Margarine, total	24	19	18	14
Other fats	4	4	4	5
Whole milk	193	172	169	146
Skim milk	10	14	27	34
Cream	5	7	7	7
Cheese	8	9	10	12
Meat and offals	35	43	52	51
Fish	40	40	26	38
Cereals, flour equivalent	98	71	75	76
Potatoes	92	81	71	62
Potato products	-	7	8	15
Vegetables	35	40	38	52
Fruits and berries	41	67	74	78
Sugar, syrup, honey	40	42	32	41

margarine were withdrawn from the beginning of 1981, VAT compensation for pork and poultry has been discontinued and subsidies on other types of meat have been reduced.   As an indication of the complexity of this type of intervention, flour subsidies have also had to be reduced despite nutritional considerations so as not to cause an excessive price differential between it and feed concentrates. Budget proposals in 1981 included a duty of 1.0 Nkr per kg of sugar, effective from a date to be determined by the Ministry of Finance. A legislative development which should assist the implementation of food and nutrition policy decisions was the Food Control (Co-ordinating) Act of 17 March 1978 which came into force on 1 January 1980 - this Act established a Food Control Board whose function was to ensure the incorporation of nutritional considerations in the legislation of all government ministries.

2.6.2   Other countries

In __Canada,__ as a preliminary step in formulating proposals for a food and nutrition policy, a National Food Strategy Conference was convened in 1978. All interested parties made presentations to this Conference and, as a result, an inter-departmental committee was convened to develop a framework to allow full consultation with affected parties before any action took place. However, either from bureaucratic inertia or a realisation of the political and financial impediments to a wide-ranging approach to the problem, enthusiasm and activity have declined since 1978 and no further progress is evident.

__Japan__ has a marked national concern with food security due to its population density and low level of self-sufficiency. Basic government policy in relation to food aims to supply "better quality food at stable prices"; this is further clarified under headings which include protection of consumer interests, ensuring food supplies which meet the consumers' needs and the promotion of a diet in harmony with the climate and resources of Japan.   These serve as guidelines for the activities of all government ministers but no special ministerial body has been charged with food and nutrition policy development and surveillance.

The "Quadrifoglio" Act in __Italy__ lays the foundation for that country's agro-food policy.   Policy objectives were based on a wide-ranging analysis of the Italian economy and trade commitments and prescribed targets for agricultural production, a reduction in per capita daily calorie intake (from 3250 to 2880 kcal), a reduction in the agricultural trade deficit and control of the influence of the food component in cost-of-living increases. Interestingly, this Act provided for the creation of an Inter-Ministerial Agricultural and Food Policy Committee to deal with all agro-food matters.

The <u>West German</u> administration has expounded a food policy which has as its twin main objectives the supply of high-quality foods at reasonable cost and an attempt to solve world food problems. Detailed sub-targets and partial objectives are appended to these two broad policy goals which cover the activities of the entire agro-food sector.   One aspect of the German situation which should more readily enable the implementation of food and nutrition policy is that the Federal Minister of Food, Agriculture and Forestry is responsible for the food industry, food trade, international agricultural policy and consumer protection in relation to food.

Food and nutrition policy in <u>The Netherlands,</u> described as a priority item in consumer affairs programmes, has recently been outlined in detail (36).   Its aim is to improve the available range and consumption of foods which are judged capable of bringing about a reduction in the incidence of certain degenerative diseases while maintaining the consumer's own sense of responsibility and freedom.   Food policy is to be implemented by close cooperation between the government Ministries of Welfare, Health and Consumer Affairs, and Agriculture and Fisheries together with relevant sections of the Ministry of Economic Affairs. Measures to improve the diet include an expansion of information gathering in relation to the current dietary practices of a range of population sub-groups, a shift of emphasis in the activities of the Bureau of Nutrition Education towards specific 'at-risk' groups of the population and a commitment to improve nutritional education through adjustments in basic school curricula and adherence to the standard of one dietitian per 50,000 population as a national average. Prohibitions on the attachment of misleading prophylactic claims to foods are to be introduced in addition to standardising nutritional labelling information.   A number of specific controls on the composition of foodstuffs and maximum inclusion levels for additives are planned as is the inauguration of a national food databank. No policy statements in relation to change in agricultural production are contained in the document since "As a general rule, --- it is mainly the stages to which the product is subjected subsequently which call for attention from the point of view of policy on nutritional value". This approach is therefore on the scale of the Norwegian strategy, although it avoids any interference with the problematic food production sector.

In January 1983, the Swedish government appointed a committee (the Food Committee of 1983) to formulate proposals for a national food policy (45). This committee appointed eight sub-committees to facilitate it in its work and the Expert Group for Diet and Health devised a set of dietary guidelines. The main methods for achieving dietary change were to be through information, education and product development within the food industry - no changes in agricultural production methods were felt necessary. Particular attention was to be focused on school-lunch composition, investment in preventive health measures, and a reduction of the minimum fat content of butter and normal margarine from 80% to 75%. Opportunities for the selective stimulation of particular foods in any given food group by consumer subsidy were to be investigated.

Less well-developed mechanisms for the formulation and implementation of policy exist in other countries. Most resemble the USA, where widespread public debate continues in an effort to inform both government and consumer of the issues involved. The French government has recently suggested the creation of a National Food Council as a means of coordinating food policy decisions while the operation in Australia of the Industries Assistance Commission (IAC) - a body charged with conducting public enquiries into government proposals involving financial assistance to industry - at least ensures a reasonable airing of a range of views in relation to specific proposals affecting the food industry. A set of dietary guidelines has also recently been compiled and adopted by government in Australia as a first step in the implementation of a food and nutrition policy (5) while New Zealand has begun the process by setting-up (in October 1985) a committee to advise on policy on the prevention of cardiovascular disease (174). In the Republic of Ireland, the Food Advisory Committee of the Department of Health has recently recommended the formulation of a national food and nutrition policy (175, 176) but no specific recommendations have yet appeared. The UK government has defined current nutritional problems and possible strategies for their minimisation (61, 110); draft regulations for the provision of nutritional labelling of foods (for fat only) are currently being debated by government and industry.

2.7 CONCLUSIONS

(Comprehensive conclusions and recommendations are presented in CHAPTER 4 in addition to those outlined below).

a. As a result of public health policies in developed countries, a change has occurred in the major causes of death during this century. Pre-eminent among those now important are degenerative diseases; medical and public opinion seeks to prevent or delay the onset of such conditions.

b. Diet has been implicated in the genesis of degenerative diseases by many expert groups and dietary guidelines have been compiled in an attempt to control them.

c. Government accepts responsibility for the welfare of citizens. Legislative action is taken when a risk to health/welfare is perceived to be of sufficient magnitude; lesser risks are dealt with by educational measures.

d. Many medical, consumer and political organisations (national and international) have called for the inclusion of nutritional considerations in the formulation of policy affecting the agro-food industry - such a policy framework would take the form of a food and nutrition policy which is coherent, wide-ranging and transparent.

e. Government needs to decide if such a formalised, planned intervention is necessary. In so doing, answers must be sought, through public debate, to a number of questions which include the following:

    -   how serious is the public health risk posed by degenerative diseases?

    -   is the link between diet and degenerative disease adequately demonstrated? Discussion of this question should include the criteria for acceptance of scientific hypotheses specifically in relation to nutritional science.

    -   what would the political response by the electorate be to active and sustained intervention in the market place by government with a view to altering food habits?

Unless the consensus response to all these questions indicates the readiness of the electorate to accept change in the face of a serious public health risk caused by their food choices, government is unlikely to

promulgate a coherent national strategy but may continue to act in an 'ad
hoc' fashion to effect specific changes.

f.   If government judges a food and nutrition policy to be necessary and
     politically acceptable, consideration must be given to the development
     of such a policy and the administrative structures necessary for its
     implementation and monitoring.   Initially, the promulgation of a set
     of dietary guidelines will serve as a touchstone by which food
     production and supply policies can be tailored and their effectiveness
     assessed over time.   To be successful, dietary guideline
     implementation will require action in relation to agriculture,
     processing, distribution, retailing, education, regional, and foreign
     policy objectives to remove conflicts.   Mechanisms which control
     demand such as prices and incomes policies and advertising will also
     require attention.   Consideration needs to be directed to the
     administration of food and nutrition policy, in particular to the
     level at which administrative structures may act e.g. supra-
     ministerial or sub-ministerial.

g.   Given the prevailing political trend in Europe and the USA towards de-
     regulation and reduction in public spending programmes, it seems
     unlikely that many EEC member states will undertake a full food and
     nutrition policy of the type described above.   The most likely course
     is the minimalist approach with education and nutritional labelling
     regulations being increasingly emphasised and encouragement to the
     food industry to market products with a better nutritional profile so
     as to offer a 'real' choice to consumers.

2.8 REFERENCES

1. Tijdschrift voor Sociale Geneeskunde (1980), Vol. 58, part 20.

2. McKenzie, J.C. (1979) Proc. Nutr. Soc. 38, 219-223.

3. Richardson, D.P. (1981) Proc. Int. Fd. Sci. Tech. 14, 87-102.

4. Telser, E. (1978) Food Product Development 12, 82-84.

5. Langsford, W.A. (1979) A food and nutrition policy. Food Nutr. Notes Rev. 36, 100.

6. Chou, Marylin (1979). "The preoccupation with food safety" in Critical Food Issues of the Eighties (eds. M. Chou and D.P. Harmon, Jr.) Pergamon Press, New York, pp 18-42.

7. The public understanding of science (1985). Report of a Royal Society ad hoc Group. The Royal Society, London.

7a. Commission of the European Communities (1975) The agricultural situation in the community. CEC.

8. Walsh, J. (1982) Public attitude toward science is yes, but -.Science 215, 15 January, pp. 270-272.

8a. Hegsted, D.M. (1977) "U.S. Dietary Goals", paper presented at the 1978 Food & Outlook Conference, Washington D.C., Nov. 1973, pp 21-25.

9. Etzioni, A., Nunn, C. (1974) The public appreciation of science in contemporary America. Daedelus 103, 191-205.

10. Commission of the European Communities (1977) Science and European public opinion. CEC

11. Commission of the European Communities (1979) The European public's attitude to scientific and technical achievement. CEC.

12. Commission of the European Communities (1982). Public opinion in the European community: energy. CEC.

13. Commission of the European Communities (1983). The Europeans and their environment. CEC.

14. Anon. (1985). What do people think of science? New Scientist, 21 February, 12-16.

15. Flamand, F.X. (1986) Personnal commun. (Agricultural adviser to French Ambassador, Dublin).

16. Kahn, H. (1979) "The world at a turning point: New class attitudes" in Critical Food Issues of the Eighties (eds. M. Chou and D.P. Harmon, Jr.) Pergamon Press, New York, pp 5-17.

17. Whitehead, R. (1983) quoted by K. T. Walsh in <u>US News and World Report</u>, 16 September 1985 p. 59-63.

18. Truswell, A.S. (1981) Nutrition in Australia. <u>J. Human Nutrit.</u> <u>35</u> (4), 241-242.

19. Central Statistical Office (1982) Social Trends No. 12. London. HMSO.

20. Ford, J.A. <u>et al.</u>, (1976) Clinical and sub-clinical vitamin D deficiency in Bradford children. <u>Archives of Disease in Childhood</u> <u>51</u>, 939-943.

21. Callender, S. (1973) in <u>Nutritional deficiencies in modern society</u> (eds. Howard, A.N. & McLean, B.J.) Newman Books. London.

22. Willoughby, M.C.N. (1967) An investigation of the folic acid requirements of pregnancy. <u>British Journal of Haematology</u> 13, 503-509.

23. DHSS (1972) A nutrition survey of the elderly. Report on Health and Social Subjects No. 3. London. HMSO.

24. Nijhuis, H.G.J., Zoethoud, H.E. & deJong, G.M. (1982) Return of rachitis as an endemic disease. <u>Epidemiologisch Bulletin's - Gravenhage</u> <u>17</u> (3), 7-15.

25. "Turista" is bad joke to travellers, death to locals. <u>New York Times</u>, October 3, 1977.

26. <u>The Economist</u>, May 25, 1985, page 64.

27. Thom, T.J., Epstein, F.H., Feldman, J.J., Leaverton, P.E. (1985) Trends in total mortality and mortality from heart disease in 26 countries from 1950 to 1978. <u>Inter. J. Epidemiology</u> 14(4), 510-520.

28. Leveille, G. A. (1977) "Establishing and Implementing Dietary Goals", paper presented at the 1978 Food and Outlook Conferences, Washington D.C., November 17, 1977.

29. Segi, M., Aoki, K., Kurihara, M. (1981) World cancer mortality. GANN Monograph on Cancer Research <u>26</u>, 121-250.

30. Committee on Nutrition of American Academy of Pediatrics (1983) Toward a prudent diet for children. <u>Pediatrics</u> <u>71</u> (1), 78-80.

31. Dietary Goals for the United States (1977). Select Committee on Nutritional and Human Needs, U.S. Senate. U.S. Govt. Printing Office, Washington D.C.

32. Doll, R. and Peto, R. (1981) The causes of cancer. Oxford University Press.

33. Prevention of coronary heart disease (1982). WHO Technical Report Series 678, Geneva.

34. Medical Viewpoints on the Swedish public diet (1966). Nutrition Section of Swedish Medical Council.

35. Perisse, J., Sizaret, F. and Francoise, P. (1969). The effect of income on the structure of the diet. FAO Nutrition Newsletter 7, 3, 1-9.

36. Food and Nutrition Policy in the Netherlands (English translation) (1985). Information Service of the Ministry of Welfare, Health and Cultural Affairs.

37. Olson, R. E. (1975) The U.S. Quandary: can we formulate a rational nutritional policy? in Critical Food Issues of the Eighties (eds. M. Chou & D.P. Harmon, Jr) Pergamon Press, New York, pp 119-133.

38. National Research Council: Food and Nutrition Board (1980). Towards healthful diets. National Academy of Sciences, Washington D.C.

39. Oliver, M.F. (1985) Strategies for preventing coronary heart disease. Nutrition Reviews 43(9), 257-262.

40. Leitch, I. (1942) The evolution of dietary standards. Nutrition Abstracts and Reviews 11 (4), 509-521.

41. National food policy in the UK (1979) Centre for Agricultural Strategy. Report No. 5. Reading.

42. Payne, P.R. (1976) Nutrition planning and food policy. Food Policy February, 107-115.

43. Anon. (1968) Medicinska synpunkter pa folkkosten i de nordiska landerna. Var foda 20, 3-5.

44. Royal Norwegian Ministry of Agriculture (1975) Norwegian nutrition and food policy (1975-76). Report to the Storting (English translation) Oslo.

45. A summary of the Report of the Expert Group for Diet and Health (1983) Uppsala, Sweden (English translation, 1985).

46. National Nutritional Council (1981) Recommendations concerning the nutritional composition of the diet. Norway.

47. Ministry of Social Affairs and Health (1981) Summary of Report of the Finnish Nutrition Committee. Helsinki, Finland.

48. Inter-society Commission for Heart Disease Resources (1970). Primary prevention of the atherosclerotic diseases. Circulation 42 A55-95.

49. Mayer, J. (1973) Heart disease: plans for action. US nutrition policies in the seventies (ed. Mayer, J.) W.H. Freeman, San Francisco. pp 44-52.

50. Food and Nutrition Board: National Academy of Science – National Research Council and the Council on Foods and Nutrition of the American Medical Association: joint statement (1972) Diet and coronary heart disease. _J. Am Med. Ass._ _222_, 1647.

51. American Health Foundation (1972) Position statement on diet and coronary heart disease. _Prev. Med._ _1_, 255-286.

52. American Heart Association (1973) Diet and coronary heart disease. New York.

53. U.S. Senate Select Committee on Nutrition and Human Needs. (1977a) Dietary Goals for the United States. Washington D.C. U.S. Government Printing Office.

54. U.S. Senate Select Committee on Nutrition and Human Needs (1977b) Dietary goals for the United States. 2nd edition, Washington D.C. U.S. Government Printing Office.

55. American Heart Association (1978) Diet and coronary heart disease. Statement for physicians and other health professionals by the AHA committee on nutrition. Dallas, Texas.

56. US Department of Health, Education and Welfare (1979) Healthy people: the Surgeon-General's report on health promotion and disease prevention. Washington D.C. US Government Printing Office, Publication No. 79 55071.

57. Glueck, C.J. (1979) Appraisal of dietary fat as a causative factor in atherogenesis. _Am. J. Clin. Nutr._ _32_, December Supplement.

58. American Medical Association: Council on Scientific Affairs (1979). Concepts of nutrition and health. _J. Am. Med. Ass._ _242_,2335-2338.

59. US Departments of Agriculture and of Education and Welfare (1980). Nutrition and your health: dietary guidelines for Americans. Washington D.C. US Government Printing Office.

60. National Research Council (1982) Committee on Diet, Nutrition and Cancer. Diet, nutrition and cancer. National Academy Press. Washington D.C.

61. Department of Health and Social Security (1984). Committee of Medical Aspects of Food Policy (COMA). Report of the panel on Diet in Relation to Cardiovascular Disease. London. HMSO.

62. Royal College of Physicians of London and the British Cardiac Society Joint Working Party (1976) Prevention of coronary heart disese. _J. Roy. Coll. Physns._ _10_, 213-275.

63. Truswell, A.S. (1977) The need for change in food habits from a medical viewpoint. _Proc. Nutr. Soc._ _36_, 307-316.

64. Department of Health and Social Security (1978) Prevention and health: eating for health. London. HMSO.

65. Passmore, R., Hollingsworth, D.F. and Robertson, J. (1979) Prescription for a better British diet. Br. Med. J. 1, 527-531.

66. Royal Society of New Zealand (1971) Coronary heart disease. Wellington, New Zealand.

67. National Heart Foundation of New Zealand (1971) Coronary heart disease: a New Zealand report. Dunedin. New Zealand.

68. National Heart Foundation of New Zealand (1976) Coronary heart disease: a progress report. John McIndoe Ltd and National Heart Foundation of NZ, Dunedin.

69. New Zealand Department of Health (1982) Nutrition goals for New Zealanders. Health 34, 11-12.

70. National Heart Foundation of Australia (1971) Dietary fat and coronary heart disease: a review Med. J. Aust. 1, 1155-1160.

71. National Heart Foundation of Australia (1974) Committee on Diet and Heart Disease. Diet and coronary heart disease - a review. Med. J. Aust. 2, 575-9, 616-20, 663-8.

72. Australian Academy of Science (1975) Diet and coronary heart disease: report of a working group. Canberra.

73. Commonwealth Department of Health (1982) Dietary guidelines for Australians. Government Publishing Service, Canberra.

74. National Heart Foundation of Australia (1979) Committee on Diet and Heart Disease. Diet and coronary heart disease: a review. Med. J. Aust. 2, 294-307.

75. Anon. (1979) Eating to live. Med. J. Aust. 2, 467.

76. Simons, L. et al (1982) Heart foundation cookbook: guide to healthy eating. Canberra. National Heart Foundation of Australia.

77. Voedingsraad (1973) Advies over hoeveelheid enlof aard der vetten in de voeding. Ministerie van Voeksgezondheid en Milieuhygiene, Staatsuitgeverij. The Hague.

78. Department of National Health and Welfare (1976) Health and Welfare in Canada. Report of the Committee on Diet and Cardiovascular Disease. Ottawa, Canada.

79. Government du Quebec (1977) Quebec's policy on nutrition. Montreal, Canada.

80. An Foras Taluntais (1977) Prevention of Coronary Heart Disease - diet and the food supply. Health Advisory Committee of An Foras Taluntais, Dublin.

81. Anon. (1975) Dietary fats and degenerative vascular diseases. Nutr. Metab. 18, 113-115.

82. Dupin, H. et al (1981) Apports nutritionnels conseilles pour la population francaise. Paris. Technique et Documentation.

83. Agro-food plan - "Quadrifoglio Act" (1977) quoted in "Food Policy. Country notes on Germany, Canada, Italy, Japan, Norway" OECD, Paris, 1981.

84. Reshef, A. (1985) Personal Communication.

85. FAO/WHO (1977) Dietary fats and oils in human nutrition. Report of an Expert Consultation jointly organised by FAO and WHO, Rome, September 1977. FAO Food and Nutrition Paper No. 2.

86. WHO Expert Committee (1982) Prevention of coronary heart disease: a report. Technical Report Service 678. Geneva.

87. Council on Rehabilitation (1973). International Society of Cardiology. Myocardial infarction: how to prevent, how to rehabilitate. Mannheim. W. Germany. Boehringer.

88. European Society of Cardiology (1978) Preventing coronary heart disease: a guide for the practising physician. Van Gorcum. Assen, The Netherlands.

89. British Medical Association (1986) Diet, Nutrition and Health. BMA, London.

90. Truswell, A.S. (1983) The development of dietary guidelines. Food Technology in Australia 35 (11), 498-502.

91. Norum, K.R. (1978) Some present concepts concerning diet and prevention of coronary heart disease. Nutrition and Metabolism 22, 1-7.

92. Grundy, S.N., Bilheimer, D., Blackburn, H., Brown, W.V., Kwiterovich, P.O., Mattson, F., Schonfield, G., Weidman, W.H. (1982) Rationale of the diet-heart statement of the American Heart Association. Circulation 65, 839A-854A.

93. Royal College of Physicians of London. (1983) Obesity J. R. Coll. Physicians Lond. 17, 5-65.

94. FAO (1978) Dietary fats and oils in human nutrition. FAO Food and Nutrition Paper No. 3. Rome.

95. Newburn, E. (1982) Sugars and dental caries: a review of human studies. Science 217, 418-423.

96. Shaper, A.G. and Marr, J.W. (1977) Dietary recommendations for the community towards postponement of coronary heart disease. Brit. Med. J. 1, 867-878.

97. Royal College of Physicians of London (1980) Medical aspects of dietary fibre. Pitman Medical Ltd. Kent.

98. Proposals for nutritional guidelines for health education in Britain (1983) National Advisory Committee on Nutrition Education. Health Education Council. London.

99. Jones, A.S. (1985) An agricultural approach to a new health policy. Proc. Nutr. Soc. 44, 409-418.

100. Fallows, S.J. and Wheelock, J.V. (1983) The means to dietary change - the example of fat. J.R.S.H. 5, 186-202.

101. "Twenty Commentaries: The McGovern Dietary Goals for the US are examined by Twenty Correspondents". (1977) Nutrition Today 12 (6), 10.

102. Skrabanek, P. (1986) Preventive medicine and morality. The Lancet Jan. 18, 143-144.

103. Scala, J. (1978) Responsibilities of the food industry to ensure an optimum diet. Fd. Technology Sept., 77-78.

104. Richardson, D.P. (1982) Changing public ideas about the wholesomeness of food. BNF Nutrition Bulletin 7, 31-38.

105. See ref. 238 of Chapter 1.

106. Austin, J.E. and Quelch, J.A. (1979) US national dietary goals. Food industry threat or opportunity? Food Policy 4, 115-128.

107. Jukes, T.H. (1979) The predicament of food and nutrition. Fd. Technology 33, 42, 44, 46, 48, 50, 51.

108. Ashton, C.T. (1984) Nutrition - a scientist's view. Food December, 42, 43, 50.

109. Dillon, A. (1985) in "Partnership with responsibility". Milk Industry 87(7), 33-36.

110. National Advisory Committee for Nutrition Education (1983) A discussion paper on proposals for nutritional guidelines for health education. Health Education Council, London.

111. Report on presentation of briefs on "A Food Strategy for Canada" to a panel of Federal Ministers, December 5, 6 and 9, 1977. Health and Welfare, Canada.

112. Norum, K.R. (1985) Ways and means of influencing nutritional behaviour - experiences from the Norwegian nutrition and food policy. Biblthca Nutr. Dicta. 36, pp 29-43 (Karger, Basel, Switzerland).

113. McSweeney, M. and Kevany,J. (1981) Nutrition beliefs and practices in Ireland. Health Education Bureau, Dublin.

114. Den Hartog, G. (1966) Nutrition in the Netherlands. World Review of Nutrition and Dietetics 6, 90-123.

115. Schwartz, N.E. (1975) Nutritional knowledge, attitudes and practices of high-school graduates. Journal of American Dietetics Association 66 (1), 28-31.

116. BRMB (1969) Food facts and fallacies. London.

117. MAFF (1976) Household food consumption and expenditure: 1974. London, HMSO.

118. Kostaropoulos, A.E. (1983) Concentration, Competition and Competitiveness in the Food Industry of the EEC. CEC IV/584/83-EN.

119. Marshall, E. (1986) Diet advice with a grain of salt and a large helping of pepper. Science 231 (4738), 537-539.

120. The banger bursts (1985) Economist, 25 May, p. 30.

121. Hilliam, M.A. (1985) British health food market. Nutrition & Food Science Sept/Oct., 2-4.

122. Leveille,G.A. (1983) Industry's response to problems related to nutritive value of the US diet. Proc. Sixth International Congress of Food Science and Technology, Dublin, Sept. 18-23, Vol. 4, pp 315-318. Boole Press, Dublin.

123. Anon. (1986) New moves from Allied. Milling, March, p. 8.

124. Levy, Paul (1986) "Food zealots" force issue. The Observer, 9th March, p. 53.

125. Buhl, F. (1980) The nutritional education of the public: French experience. J. Human Nutr. 34, 439-444.

126. Nielsen, H. (1983) Nutrition in health promotion programs: a Canadian perspective Human nutrition: Applied nutrition 37A, 165-171.

127. Schurman, M. (1983) Community teamwork in nutrition education: an example in Canada's north. Human nutrition: Applied nutrition 37A, 172-179.

128. Reginster-Haneuse, C. (1981) Nutrition education at school (Comparative analysis of syllabuses in the Community countries). CEC Symposium on nutrition, food technology and nutritional information. London, 19-20 March, 1980. EUR 7085 EN.

129. Oshaug, A., Eide, W. Barth. (1983) The effectiveness of nutrition education. Proc. Sixth International Congress of Food Science and Technology, Dublin, Sept. 18-23. Vol. 4, pp 293-304. Boole Press, Dublin.

130. Kermode, G.O. (1983) Nutrition labelling. Proc. Sixth International Congress of Food Science and Technology, Dublin, Sept. 18-23. Vol. 4, pp 305-314. Boole Press, Dublin.

210

131. McNeil, N.I., McNeil, R. (1985) Healthy eating - 1. Can people really judge whether foods are healthy? Nutrition & Fd Science July/August, 2-3.

132. Bequette, F. (1985) Enquête sur la restauration scolaire dans les états membres de la communité européenne. Situation actuelle et perspectives. CEC. Brussels.

133. Price, C. and Brown, J. (1982) A natural twist to the school lunch program. National Food Review Spring, pp. 20-22.

134. Dewhurst, Y. and Lockie, G. (1984) NACNE into practice. Nutrition and Food Science 91, 7-8, 15.

135. Council Regulation (EEC) No. 1080/77 (1977) on the supply of milk and certain milk products at reduced prices to school-children.

136. English, R.M. (1984) Developing dietary guidelines J. Fd Nutrition 41 (2), 79-86.

137. Kolata, G. (1986) Reducing risk: a change of heart? Science 231 (4739), 669-670.

138. CEC (1986) Europe's common agricultural policy. 2/86.

139. Reid, I.G. (1985) Pressures for change in the Common Agricultural Policy. Proc. Nutr. Soc. 44, 399-408.

140. Turner, M. and Gray, J. (1982) Implementation of dietary guidelines. Obstacles and opportunities. British Nutrition Foundation. London.

141. Boland, C. (1986) EEC threatens retaliation against US The Irish Times, 10 April, p. 12.

142. Commission of the European Communities (1985) Perspectives for the Common Agricultural Policy. COM(85) 333.

143. Business Statistics Office (1981) Business monitor, PQ 1002. London: HMSO.

144. Euromonitor.

145. Anon. (1985) Grocers and supermarkets. Retail Business November, pp 3-12.

146. Anon. (1985) The retail trade in Belgium. Mark. Res. Eur. November, pp 29-37.

147. Anon. (1985) Retail distribution in Greece. Marketing in Europe No. 275 (October), pp. 40-46.

148. Smith, E. (1985) Chains and convenience stores are still growing. Retail World 38 (22), 14.

149. Anon. (1985) Study predicts that super stores wil continue to thrive. Supermarket Business November, p. 11.

150. Food Standards (Preserves) Order 1953 (1953) SI 691. London: HMSO.

151. Cream Regulations 1970 (1970) SI No. 752 London: HMSO.

152. Ice-cream Regulations 1967 (1967) SI No. 1866. London: HMSO.

153. Butter Regulations 1966 (1966) SI No. 1974. London: HMSO.

154. Margarine Regulations 1967 (1967) SI No. 1867 London: HMSO.

155. Cheese Regulations 1965 (1965) SI No. 2199 London: HMSO.

156. McKenzie, J. (1974) The impact of economic and social status on food choice. Proc. Nutr. Soc. 33, 67-73.

157. Bender, A.E. (1976) Food preferences of males and females. Proc. Nutr. Soc. 35., 181-189.

158. National Dairy Council (1984) A Guide to Food, Exercise, Nutrition and You. NDC, Illinois, USA.

159. Report No. 11 to the Storting (1981-82) On the follow-up of Norwegian Nutrition Policy. Royal Ministry of Health and Social Affairs.

160. Anon. (1986) Below cost selling to be outlawed. The Irish Times 10 April 1986, p. 6.

161. Council of the European Community. Regulation No. 2991, 1982.

162. Council of the European Community. Regulation No. 3143 of 1985.

163. CEC. (1985) The agricultural situation in the Community. Luxembourg.

164. Douglas, G. (1985) Balanced diet - the cognitive cop-out. Paper presented (on behalf of Presight Ltd.) at KMS Seminar "Marketing & Nutrition", London.

165. Douthwaite, R. (1986) Salmon farming - more than a sporting chance. Business & Finance 20 March, 22-24.

166. Schurman, M. (1983) Community teamwork in nutrition education: an example in Canada's north. Human nutrition: Applied nutrition 37A, 172-179.

167. Bleyer, R. (1981) A correspondence course for the further education of French dietitians - A pilot experiment run by Nancy University. Human nutrition: Applied nutrition 35(3), 199-203.

168. Oddy, D.J. (1976) Perspectives and strategies for effective nutrition education. Proc. Nutr. Soc. 35, 139-144.

169. Chou, M. (1982) Information gaps to address. Cer. Fds Wld 27(5), 234.

170. vander Heide, R. (1986) Person. commun. (Min. Public Health, Holland).

171. Anon. (1986) Advertising Age's Focus. European Media & Marketing Guide, January.

172. Anon. (1985) Advertising Age's Focus. European Media & Marketing Guide, pp. 25, 35, 41, 44, 47, 68, 77, 82.

173. CEC. (1978) Symposium on Enforcement of Food Law. Rome. ISBN 92-825-1752-7.

174. Egan, Theresa (1986) Personn. commun. (Dept. of Health, New Zealand).

175. Report of the Food Advisory Committee (1979) Recommendations for a Food & Nutrition Policy in Ireland. Department of Health, Dublin.

176. Report of the Food Advisory Committee (1980) Fats and oils in human health. Department of Health, Dublin.

177. World Health Organisation (1980, 1981, 1982). World health statistics annual: vital statistics and causes of death. Geneva: World Health Organisation.

178. Dawson, J.A., Shaw, S., Burt, S. and Rana, J. (1985). Structural change and public policy in the European food industry. Interim Report. Institute for Retail Studies, University of Stirling, Scotland, UK.

CHAPTER 3

REVIEW AND ASSESSMENT OF AGRICULTURAL PRODUCTION AND FOOD
PROCESSING TECHNOLOGIES WITH RESPECT TO THEIR POSSIBLE IMPACT
ON HUMAN HEALTH

D. O'BEIRNE

CHAPTER 3 consists of an assessment of the present and future impact of selected technologies and practices used in agricultural production and by the food industry on consumer health. Consumer attitudes to these technologies are also discussed.

In the case of effects of agricultural production, the issues considered include current and future effects of breeding, husbandry and fertilizers, the significance of natural toxicants, safety and consumer aspects of the use of pesticides, the use of anabolic hormones in animal production, and the use of antibiotics.

In relation to the effects of present and future food processing, chemical changes of nutritional and toxicological significance are considered. The significance of nutrient loss during food processing is discussed and the relative effects of different technologies and of storage considered. The impact of technological change, particularly in relation to the effects of thermal processing on nutritional value and quality are discussed. The toxicological implications of selected chemical changes are assessed as is safety evaluation of current and novel food processes. The functional roles of fat, sugar, salt and refined ingredients in processed and formulated foods and the potential and limitations for modifying levels of these ingredients are discussed.

3.1   INTRODUCTION

This chapter considers some of the implications of technologies used
in agricultural production and by the food industry for consumer health.
Because of advances in nutrition, toxicology, molecular biology, and
related fields, the interaction of diet and basic life processes is now
better understood, and as a result, there are increasing demands for
methods of production, processing, and distribution of foods to better meet
the requirements for maintaining and improving health (1).   The two main
issues addressed here relate to nutrition and toxicology.   In the case of
nutrition, the agricultural and food industries can be judged on how they
assist consumers in meeting current and future dietary guidelines;
developments in this area have been discussed in detail in CHAPTER 1.   The
toxicological risks considered include those from chemicals occurring
naturally (2), from residues of chemicals used in agricultural production
(3-5) and from chemicals added to foods (6) or formed during food
processing.   The emerging needs to distinguish between large and small
risks from chemicals in the diet (7-9) and for methods to evaluate novel
foods (10) and novel food processes are also addressed.

3.2   CONSUMER ATTITUDES

It is useful at this point to consider in some detail a number of
aspects of consumer attitudes to safety and wholesomeness of food,
particularly where these attitudes can be related to practices and
technologies used by agriculture and the food industry.   For some time it
has been apparent that the attitudes of an important minority of consumers
and the content of press comments on the relative risks in the diet have
tended to reverse the generally accepted risk priorities (11 - 13, see also

CHAPTER 1). The actual order of importance of risks has been estimated to be first those due to microbiological contamination and nutritional imbalance, then (one thousandfold less) those due to environmental pollutants, contaminants, and natural toxicants, then (one hundredfold less again) those due to pesticide residues and food additives (12, 13). The more extreme consumer and press comments have tended to make food additives, pesticide residues, and environmental contaminants the top priorities (13). According to Gray (11) the only change since Hall's work in 1971 is perhaps an increasing awareness of the importance of nutrition-related issues.

Studies in a number of developed countries (14 - 18) confirm that consumers are poorly informed and are confused about health-related food issues. A major factor in this appears to be the poor quality and poor credibility of information available to the consumer, particularly when one sets this against a background of either poor or no general nutrition education in schools. For example, a large study (19) carried out for the British Nutrition Foundation (BNF) found that the main sources of information on healthy eating in the UK were television (including commercial advertisements), magazines, and popular books. These sources had low levels of credibility i.e. only 17% would believe information from television on this topic and 18% would believe magazine information. Only 2% and 3% respectively ever acted on information from these sources. Research (16) among consumers from lower socio-economic groups indicated that journalistic features on dieting appearing in womens' magazines were a major source of information and subsequent confusion on nutrition issues. Large changes had taken place in dieting strategies (e.g. changes from high protein intakes to high fibre intakes), and these had led to the feeling that experts were permanently divided on health-related food issues. The importance of this confusion is that it can leave the consumer in a weak position, open to being exploited by sections of the food industry using prevailing fads to promote their products. More important for consumer health, confusion may foster the permissive attitudes to health issues seen in many studies, exemplified by bland statements such as "it's all right as long as we stick to a reasonably varied and balanced diet" (18), and this may be a factor in the low percentage of consumers appearing to take health-related food issues seriously enough to significantly modify their diet e.g. presented as 10% of 'food worriers' in the BNF study; as 20% of consumers, 'The Believers', in the Allen Brady and Marsh study (17).

3.2.1 Consumer attitudes to agricultural and food industry practices

The picture in this area is often one of concern, confusion, and lack of accurate information. A number of studies (14, 15, 18) indicate that the safety and necessity of/for food additives is the largest single area of concern among consumers. A major Canadian study (14) involving 25,000 consumers indicated that, although they were aware that safety testing and control of additives by government existed, 68% thought that controls were inadequate. Typically 80-90% of consumers would prefer a lot more food without additives (20). In the Canadian study, 60% (65% of females) said that they would be prepared to pay more for additive-free foods. This large gap between consumer attitudes and the objective scientific evidence (which considers the risks from additives to be low, although difficult to quantify absolutely, see 3.4.5.2) represents an important issue of credibility for the food industry. One indication that attitudes to additives in general may be exaggerated is found in the BNF study. When questioned about five specific additives (artificial colourings, monosodium glutamate, caffeine, "preservative", and "flavouring"), only 10-18% of respondents were "very" or "quite worried". Again, only some of this concern was health-related, ranging from 1% of consumers in the case of flavourings to 7% in the case of caffeine.

A similar dichotomy may exist in relation to attitudes to the preservation technologies used by the food industry. In an Australian study (15) 40% of consumers (wrongly) agreed that commercial freezing of fruits and vegetables causes major deterioration in their nutritional quality. However, when preservation methods were examined in the BNF study, the percentages of consumers who "ever worried" about canned, frozen, and dried foods were respectively 26%, 16%, and 9%. In addition, although their worries were mostly health-related, virtually no one related the food preservation method per se to health. Instead, the respondents were mainly concerned that either (a) the process had been properly carried out (e.g. that they would not suffer from botulism from eating improperly canned fish) or (b) foods processed in these ways were not stored for excessive periods either prior to or after purchase. Of the five additives and three preservation processes considered by BNF, 18% of consumers worried about more than two, while 45% worried about none.

An area of special difficulty is the prediction of consumer acceptability of new technologies prior to their introduction. This has been attempted in relation to food irradiation (21). The methodology used involved exploring attitudes of consumers to the types of benefits irradiation would bring. Because of the current availability of fresh foods and alternative technologies such as refrigeration, there was no demand for one major benefit of irradiation - shelf-life extension of foods. However, the authors believe that other benefits, such as elimination of <u>Salmonella</u> from poultry products, will eventually enable the technology to gain some acceptance. Provision of full consumer information on toxicological studies and full labelling were considered essential to gain consumers' trust in this area. Given the types of consumer confusion, fears and uncertainty discussed already, an emotive technology such as irradiation can expect some problems. As the UK moves towards legalisation of irradiation in line with WHO/FAO/IAEA recommendations (22) the use of the technology for shelf-life extension has already been made a consumer issue in a consumer publication (23). The issue raised is whether irradiation misleads the consumer into thinking that irradiation-processed food is fresh food, whereas in effect it has lost some of its vitamin content and other attributes of freshness as a result of the irradiation process.

However, Bruhn <u>et al</u>. (24) have shown that such attitudes may only be relevant to "alternative" or fringe consumers. Their work suggests that conventional consumers' attitudes to food irradiation can be positively influenced by an education effort, especially when this is carried out by an expert in the field. By contrast, the level of concern among "alternative" consumers was increased by such educational efforts.

Beyond the work of Hall (13) discussed earlier, attitudes to technologies and practices used in agricultural production have been more difficult to quantify - little work seems to have been done in this area. Indications of concern about pesticide and fertilizer use can be seen from the growth in demand for organically grown foods (25). Other indicators are the attitudes and actions of consumers' associations. The Bureau Europee des Unions de Consummateurs (BEUC) played a leading role in having anabolic hormones banned in animal production. There has also been concern about antibiotic uses and controls (26, 27).

3.2.2   Education of consumers

As Gray (11) has said there is an urgent need for issues relating to food safety to be put in perspective in the consumer arena. On a wide range of issues there is evidence of lack of information, misinformation and confusion - culminating in a crisis of confidence among a minority of consumers in aspects of food production and processing. Responsibilty for consumer education in this area lies with a number of sectors including governments, the agricultural and food industries, and academics involved in the study of food hazard assessment.

The nutrition education dimension of food and nutrition policies is discussed in CHAPTER 2. As a component of their role as nutrition educators, governments individually or on a Community-wide basis, must seriously consider accepting more responsibilty for the provision of information, guidance, and opportunities for discussion of issues relating to safety of the food supply. Both the relative significance of different potential hazards and the safety of technologies and practices used by agriculture and the food industry should be addressed. As part of the latter process, governments should be seen to be implementing adequate surveillance and control measures to ensure that technologies are used safely. Consumer confidence could also be improved through involvement of consumer representatives in the process of regulating some technology applications (see 3.4.5.3). Farmers' representatives and the food industry could do considerably more in the areas of informing consumers, and of explaining and justifying the use of some technologies. Academic researchers can be an important source of impartial information for the consumer on safety issues. Consumer education is an essential component of the efficient application of safe technologies in food production. In the absence of information and education, there will be risks of further political pressures to restrict some technology applications along the lines that the apparently safe anabolic hormones have been restricted (see 3.3.4).

3.3 EFFECTS OF AGRICULTURAL PRACTICES AND TECHNOLOGIES

Over the past forty years there has been extensive technological change in agriculture. This has occurred through advances in farm mechanisation and through applications of advances in genetics, biology, and chemistry and has resulted in more intensive agricultural production. Yields have increased for most crops by 100-400% through a combination of plant breeding, improved use of fertilizer, better agricultural chemicals, etc. More than 50% of yield increases have generally been attributed to genetic improvement. In fact, plant breeding may account for all of the yield improvement in wheat in the UK since 1970 (28, 29) and applications of advances in biotechnology will probably make a major contribution in the foreseeable future. It can be expected that most European countries will continue to adopt new high-yield crops and animal species, more advanced agricultural machinery and equipment, more fertilizers and other agro-chemicals. These, in combination with structural change will continue to improve output and productivity. This report examines some of the implications of this continued intensive agricultural production for consumer health. It does this mainly by considering the effects of technologies currently used and examines the prospects for the future. The focus of the report is not the effects of intensive agriculture on food quality per se. These have been extensively reviewed, for example in beef production by Harrington (30) in pork production by Naudé (31) and in plant foods by Gormley (32). In addition, the Agro-Food Programme of the EEC (DG Vl) has evaluated the effects of modern production methods on the quality of tomatoes and apples (33) and of pigs (34, 35) and further studies on the effects of production methods are proceeding. Some of these effects on quality are relevant to nutritional aspects and are discussed below. Similarly, the effects of intensive (as opposed to extensive) production systems are mainly relevant in relation to fat deposition in farm animals. One example of this has been discussed by Robbins (36) using data of Crawford and Ledger, showing carcasses of extensively produced cattle with 69-79% lean meat compared with 50-52% lean in those intensively produced. Triglyceride fat, adipose carcass fat and the ratios of triglycerides to phosphoglycerides were all higher in intensively produced animals. The fat gains in the intensively produced domesticated animals were the result of a combination of over-feeding with high energy feeds, lack of exercise, and genetic selection.

Based on the consensus among scientists as to where hazards may lie and on issues raised by consumers, the implications of a number of aspects of agricultural production will be considered in detail. These are human nutrition considerations, natural toxicants, use of pesticides, anabolic growth promoters, antibiotics and fertilizers.

3.3.1 Agricultural production and human nutrition

The nutritional value of agricultural products is determined by their chemical composition which is a function of their genetic potential and the effects of husbandry. In plant products post-harvest factors can also be important. Up to now, however, the objectives of breeding and husbandry have mainly been high productivity, evenness of maturity, suitability for processing, storeability, expression of specific attributes demanded by consumers, minimising levels of natural toxicants, etc. (37, 38, 2). Nutritional value has been a significant consideration in only a few crops, notably in relation to protein quality of grains particularly in the context of malnutrition (37).

Increasingly however, as part of an overall food policy, agriculture may have to contribute to the solution of nutritional problems as these are perceived now and in the future in developed countries. In the immediate future, a major focus of attention will be on reducing saturated and total fat intake. As a result, there will be increasing pressure to mobilise agriculture to produce animal products, notably meats, with lower fat content. In the longer term, the more general potential of both plant and animal agriculture to contribute to the nutritional requirements of the population will be important.

3.3.1.1 Leaner meat: Since the fat content of muscle meats ranges from 15-20% and up to 35% in sausages (36), meat consumption is an important factor in fat intake. In the UK 25% of fat and saturated fatty acids are obtained from meat and meat products (39). Animal breeding for leanness and the use of lean breeds in theory makes economic sense, because the energy required to synthesise protein is less than that required to synthesise fat (40). Of the cattle breeds currently available, increased use of limousines would result in leaner beef production (41). On the other hand in poultry breeding, selection of birds which grow rapidly appears to have selected for compulsive eaters, and resulted in meat of higher fat content. In pigs, British breeders selecting for increased feed conversion and improved carcass traits, including low back fat, have found that selected lines have decreased food intakes. This is somewhat discouraging for efficient lean production (40). The meat quality problem PSE (pale soft exudative muscle) and DFD (dark firm dry) have increased in highly selected lines. However, some have claimed that this is related to other factors such as changes in pre-slaughter handling (42).

Having selected the leanest breed available, a number of husbandry practices can further affect fat levels. "Intact" males grow faster and produce leaner meat. The use of bulls can present management problems in semi-intensive or extensive production systems where animals are kept beyond sexual maturity (30). Their use ranges from 4% in the UK to 17% in France and 70% in Italy. In pigs, use of boars is becoming more popular, now at 20% in the UK. Initial fears of acceptability problems associated with "boar taint" have subsided, but there are still some trade concerns about other aspects of carcass and meat quality (42).

Use of anabolic agents in castrated (steer) cattle restores some, but not all, of the growth rate and lean carcass characteristics of bulls. These agents can allow steers to grow to relatively heavy weights without becoming over-fat (43). The removal of anabolic agents from the market will therefore make the production of lean beef more difficult.

Type of feed used can affect fat levels. For example the American feedlot production system involving more than 100 days of intensive feeding on grain increases intra-muscular fat and produces meat considered to be of superior palatability (30). It is a practice not used in Europe and given current nutrition thinking, unlikely to be considered in the future. However, animals are often fed past the point at which lean meat is produced most efficiently, and excess fat is deposited. For example, in 1976 50,000 tonnes of fat are estimated to have been produced in this way in the UK (39). Attempts to make meat fat more unsaturated by feeding diets high in polyunsaturates have resulted in off-flavours (44).

In summary, cattle production in the immediate future may involve increasing use of "intact" males, slaughter of animals at a younger age before the depot fats have accumulated, and the use of bulls from larger, leaner, later maturing breeds (36). Developments may occur in the use of compounds such as Clenbuterol which are β-adrenergic agonists and affect repartitioning of nutrients, resulting in reduced fat deposition and increased muscle formation (45). These compounds have been shown to both increase feed efficiency and leanness. According to Wood (42) the ideal red meat carcass would contain about 60% lean meat and 20% fat i.e. a bacon carcass with 13 mm P2 fat thickness, a beef carcass in EEC fat class 3 or 4L and a lamb carcass in MCL fat class 2. There are currently price advantages for producing lean pigs but not beef and lamb and this will have to be faced up to.

One of the reasons why the meat trade is slow to pay more for lean animals is the belief that fatter animals have superior flavour, juiciness and tenderness. However, several large studies carried out both within and between breeds have shown this to be untrue (46 - 48). For example, Smith and Carpenter (46) reviewed in detail the effects of fat on flavour, tenderness, and juiciness in beef, pork, lamb and processed meat products. Overall, in muscle meats a minimum of only 3-5% intra-muscular fat was required for acceptable palatability to the majority of consumers. Ground or comminuted meat products may require 20-25% fat. They suggest that minimum fat levels be used as an index of acceptability (at grading or in quality assessment), instead of attempting to relate acceptability to different fat levels. However, many meat traders continue to set their minimum acceptable limits at levels higher than those determined scientifically to be adequate (30).

Implementation of advances in post-slaughter technologies may be an important adjunct to the effects of breeding and husbandry. Among technologies used by the meat plants of the future will be electrical stimulation, hot boning, vacuum packaging, controlled cooling and ageing, and portioning and freezing within an hour of slaughter (30). As a result, many of the effects of changes in breed and husbandry in reducing fat content should have even less impact on eating quality. Instead, the new technologies will tend to produce uniform meat cuts of good acceptability.

3.3.1.2 Plant foods: In the case of plant foods, dietary guidelines have for some time urged increased consumption of fruit, vegetables, and cereal products. The basis of this has included their composition - low fat, high fibre, high complex carbohydrate - and their displacement of animal products in the diet. Plant foods are also important sources of some vitamins (e.g ascorbic acid, provitamin A) and minerals such as potassium and magnesium (see CHAPTER 1). Although major improvements in the nutritional contribution of plant foods are possible in the long-term they do not present the urgent problems posed by animal products. Although there can be large differences between cultivars in the content of specific nutrients (e.g. different levels of ascorbic acid in blackcurrants (49) or different levels of β- carotene in carrots), usually only a small number of cultivars are used commercially and selected on the non-nutritional criteria discussed earlier. Nutrient content can be affected by methods of production. For example, nitrogen fertilizer generally increases protein content of wheat and baking quality of bread (50, 51). In field beans (52) increased potassium fertilizer levels lead to higher levels of potassium in the pods. In greenhouse tomatoes, changing growing medium from peat-based compost to nutrient film reduced ascorbic acid levels in fruit (14.4 mg/100 ml juice compared with 17.8 mg); β-carotene levels in carrots were lower when grown in peat compared with mineral soil (8.4 mg/100 g compared with 17.7 mg/100 g) (53). In general, the effects of herbicides (54), fungicides (55) and insecticides on nutrient content were either that they had no effect or that they improved composition (probably due to improved plant growth), although there are some reports of nutrient reduction due to use of specific pesticides. For example, Decallonne and Meyer (56) in work carried out under the Agro-Food Programme (DGV1), found that although most fungicides and insecticides tested had little effect on the composition of tomatoes, the soil disinfectant methyl bromide reduced ascorbic acid levels by 15%. There are limited data available on the nutritional quality of crops grown using non-conventional "organic" methods of production. Some workers (57) report higher protein and vitamin C levels in vegetables. However, according to Barker (58) surveys have shown no difference in nutritive quality of horticultural crops grown organically versus those grown conventionally. Overall, for most crops, differences in nutrient content due to small differences in methods of production are small and the significance for the diet as a whole is probably negligible.

However, in the case of important staple foods, changes over time in cultivar used or in production or storage methods should be monitored. For example, potato cultivars currently used in the UK (59) had levels of some nutrients considerably below values in the Food Composition Tables – riboflavin and niacin (50%), potassium (40%) iron, copper and zinc (20-30%)

228

and ascorbic acid levels declined more rapidly in storage. On the other hand, levels of thiamine and folic acid were 2-3 times higher and chips contained 40% less fat. There were varietal, locational and seasonal effects. The study indicated an erosion of some of the nutritional content of an important staple food due to technological change in agriculture.

Another area worth attention in the short-term is the nutritional implications of storage and handling of fresh produce. In fresh fruits and vegetables, losses of ascorbic acid and folic acid can be substantial where produce is not chilled or protected from wilting (60). For example, up to 50% of folic acid was lost from a range of vegetables stored for 3 days at ambient temperatures (61). β- Carotene (provitamin A) is relatively stable in some vegetables but leafy vegetables subjected to wilting can lose > 50% after 4 days at ambient temperature (61).

3.3.1.3 Assessment of longer-term prospects: A recent series of workshops in the USA (62) have tried to identify priority objectives for long-range research to improve the nutritional quality and safety of the food supply. Some of the draft recommendations of relevance to agricultural production were as follows:-

(a) Within the context of a broad programme of fundamental research, more information is needed on the biochemical pathways by which plants and animals synthesise, accumulate and break down compounds of nutritional significance, the nature of the controls over these, and ways to manipulate these controls.

(b) In animal products, in order to reduce the fat content of meat there is a need for more research on mechanisms of lipid and protein synthesis and deposition. To improve the nutritional composition of meat, poultry and dairy products, more research on the effects of life-cycle of animals, feeding regimes, and management systems is required. Cholesterol metabolism in chickens and its transfer to eggs should be studied.

(c)   In relation to plant foods, attention should be directed to the factors affecting the concentration of minerals, specific unsaturated fatty acids, antioxidants such as vitamin E and ascorbic acid, and some carotenoids.

Work on bioavailability, and more work on the effects of husbandry was also urged as well as greater co-ordination between agronomists, researchers in plant and animal sciences, food technologists and nutritionists.

In many of these priority areas, once the molecular biology and control mechanisms have been understood, the task of implementation will rest with the plant and animal breeder. According to Swaminathan (63) intelligent use of classical genetics in combination with recombinant DNA technology will greatly accelerate developments. Gene transfer at molecular level helps to broaden the variability available to breeders, and assists in the introduction of specific characteristics controlled by one or a few genes. The possibilities for exploiting some of the new biotechnological techniques in plant and animal production have been discussed by Cunningham (29). Considerable progress has been made in applying recombinant DNA techniques in animals. Mammalian embryos can now be manipulated, cultured and grown to adult stage. Provided that specific useful genes can be identified, commercial application of interspecific gene transfer in cattle may be possible by the end of the decade. In theory some of the priority objectives could be met using such techniques. Theoretical examples of the useful application of interspecific gene transfer would be in the areas of growth hormones or promoters of protein synthesis in milk (29). It seems reasonable to speculate that such developments may substantially improve the impact of agriculture on human nutrition by contributing to fat reduction in animal products, improved specific mineral and vitamin accumulation, bioavailability, etc.

3.3.2   Natural toxicants in plant foods

Many plants used as food synthesise toxic chemicals, apparently as part of their defence against pests and diseases. The significance of these toxins in human health is largely unknown, but the consensus among toxicologists is that they are substantially underrated as a food hazard (2, 13). Two recent major review articles (2, 8) have dealt with this subject in detail and are used here to provide background information and develop some of the current issues. According to Curtis (2) a major reason for the underrating of natural toxins is a "gut feeling" among breeders, food scientists, toxicologists and consumers that natural is synonymous with safe and wholesome. As a result, there has been limited economic incentive to investigate these materials. Exceptions to this occur when there is a consumer scare about specific toxins, as occurred in the UK over glycoalkaloids in potatoes. The result was a survey of levels in potatoes and potato products (64). The data were reassuring in that only 2 of 133 samples exceeded the maximum recommended "safe" level of 20 mg/100 g fresh weight. However, this is a somewhat arbitrary safe level related to bitterness as well as toxicity, and there may well be unanswered questions about long-term effects at even these levels.

In fact, toxicological studies have been completed on only a small percentage of natural toxicants. However, there is evidence of increased interest among regulatory agencies, and in recent years mutagenicity testing and some increase in carcinogenicity testing have identified many natural mutagens, teratogens and carcinogens in the human diet (8). These include the glycoalkaloids in potato, vicine and convicine in broad bean, psoralen derivatives in the Umbelliferae (celery, parsnip etc.), a hydrazine derivative in mushrooms, conavanine in alfalfa sprouts, lupine in some legumes, theobromine in cocoa, safrole and related compounds in black pepper and oil of sassifras. In addition, there are some ubiquitous toxins (quercitin and similar flavonoids such as chlorogenic acid; quinones; pyrrolizidine alkaloids) found in a range of plant foods.

Plant toxins are a heterogeneous group of chemical compounds (65) and have different biological effects. For example, potato glycoalkaloids are strong cholinesterase inhibitors and possibly teratogens (66); psoralens, when activated by sunlight, can cause direct damage to DNA or can produce oxygen radicals; quinones act through generating products which can react with DNA or participate in a redox cycle generating H_2O_2. The potential of H_2O_2 as a source of harmful hydroxyl radicals has been noted in CHAPTER 1.

3.3.2.1 Current and future change: Of special relevance to technical change in agriculture are possible risks (from toxicants) introduced through breeding programmes. The implications of the rapid changes which occur in the genetic makeup of common fruits and vegetables have never been assessed (2). Introduction of qualities such as disease resistance from wild types may result in introduction of, or increased levels of toxins. The pace of change is likely to increase as breeding programmes combine biotechnological and conventional breeding methods (63) and the increasing potential of interspecific crossing introduces the possibility of transferring toxins from one species to another. Curtis (2) discussed several examples of problems associated with high levels of glycoalkaloids in potatoes which occurred in conventional breeding programmes. In one instance, a new cultivar "Lenape" had completed most of its trials in the U.S.A. The high levels of glycoalkaloids were observed only when it was grown under the day-length and temperature conditions found in north-eastern states. Because of such experiences, breeders are now sensitised to the possible problem of introducing or increasing toxins, and routine screening is carried out. Awareness will need to keep pace with more general efforts required on hazard assessment and reduction in this area.

As discussed above, there is not sufficient information on the chemistry and biological potency in animals and man to assess the risk that natural toxins may pose to human health. Curtis (2) has proposed criteria for deciding on which toxins should get priority attention. These criteria include use of epidemiological data such as hemolytic syndromes associated with legume (vicine) consumption in the Mediterranean (67); reported physiological disturbances in man; performance data in farm animals; known chemical and physical properties of toxins; areas of plant breeding where dramatic changes have occurred in important food crops by extensive use of genes from wild species. Once the target species were identified, research would focus on methods of isolating the toxins, on toxicity studies, and finally on rational methods to reduce levels where the toxin was considered hazardous. According to Ames (8) quantifying risk after this work has been done is still a major challenge. Because of the impracticality of eliminating all natural toxins from the diet, efforts will have to be made, perhaps for the first time, to distinguish between important and unimportant hazards in food. Some of the conclusions of the American Council on Science and Health (7) on the hazards of natural carcinogens in food outline the regulatory dilemma:

233

"the increasing body of evidence documenting the carcinogenicity of common, everyday substances in nature (at least under laboratory conditions) points up the contradiction that we have created in our past regulatory approach to carcinogens. The contradiction consists of the huge discrepancy in the weight we have hitherto placed on man-made carcinogens - trying to purge our land of them - and natural carcinogens - which we have simply ignored, even though our means of assessing cancer hazards indicate that the latter hazard is far greater than the former. Our new regulatory emphasis should be on the potency of a chemical carcinogen and the level of human exposure to it rather than on the chemical's natural vs artificial origin. Regulatory priorities must be set on the basis of clearly distinguishing the risks that matter from the multitude of tiny ones. We must gain a renewed appreciation for the scientifically sound and time-honoured principle, the most basic tenet of toxicology, that "only the dose makes the poison".

Our conclusion is that more research and regulatory attention to natural toxins is required. The regulatory dilemmas introduced must be faced and solved.

3.3.3 Pesticides

A pesticide is a chemical or mixture of chemicals used in agriculture for prevention/elimination/control of unwanted species of plants or animals, and includes plant growth regulators, defoliants and desiccants (68). The world market for pesticides in 1984 was 13.8 billion US dollars of which 43% was for herbicides, 32% for insecticides and 18% for fungicides. Of these 19% were used in Western Europe. In the UK sales were £168M (herbicides), £31M (insecticides) and £90M (fungicides). UK sales showed a steady rise from 1980 to 1984 with 1984 sales 50% higher than in 1980 (68). Growth of pesticide use in developed countries is not as rapid as it was in the 1960s, but many feel it is stabilising at levels above those maximising economic return (3) perhaps due to excessively cosmetic standards used in grading high-value fruit and vegetable crops. In any event, pesticides are an important input in modern intensive agriculture. Chemically they comprise a diverse group including organophosphorus esters, carbamates, substituted ureas, acids (benzoic, phenoxy, picolinic), nitriles, nitro compounds, phenols, triazines, organometallics and others (69).

The benefits from pesticide use are very large. Pesticide industry sources (70) have estimated that without pesticides the yield of cereals in the UK would be reduced by 24% in the first year and by 45% in the third; the potato crop reduced by 27% in the first year and 42% in the third, the yield of sugar reduced 37% and 67% respectively. German work on apples showed that without any pesticides, yield was reduced by 40% and the percentage of marketable fruit fell from 80% to 30% compared with a normal pesticide programme. Large losses in yield and marketability were also recorded when an incomplete pest control programme was used. Another way to consider the benefits, potential and actual, of pesticides is that 30% of total food production is lost annually to pests in the post-harvest phase.

Pesticides are generally toxic chemicals and are subject to a number of regulatory controls. These vary from country to country but may include product registration, certification of effectiveness, maximum residue levels and use restrictions of some products. To register a pesticide, the manufacturer must supply sufficient scientific data to convince government that it is safe to use as recommended. From a consumer safety standpoint these are data on properties, persistence, breakdown products and the results of a range of toxicology studies. The toxicology data required include acute toxicity studies; evaluation of neurotoxicity, teratology, mutagenicity, metabolic studies, toxicology of plant metabolites, and long-term toxicology and carcinogenicity studies. These tests are usually done in consultation with the registering authority, take 6-10 years to complete, and cost about UK£10 M (1981) for each new product (68, 71). National and international committees of experts advise/provide guidelines for national registration authorities. For example, in the UK there is an Advisory Committee on Pesticides which reviews the risks of pesticide use. The FAO prepares "specifications" for each pesticide, specifying permissible levels of impurities, and analytical methods. The Codex Alimentarius Commission (FAO/WHO) establishes maximum limits for pesticide residues in food. EEC directives and regulations require member states' regulations to be harmonised. An important way in which advisory committees contribute to greater safety is through restricting the use of more toxic pesticides.

As a result of such regulatory controls, the risk to consumer health from pesticide residues in foods is generally considered to be low (11, 13). According to Ames (8) the human dietary intake of "nature's pesticides" (natural toxicants) is likely to be several grams per day — probably at least 10,000 times higher than the dietary intake of man-made pesticides. In addition, data from the UK and Germany indicate that the level of exposure of consumers to pesticide residues is low, well below limits of acceptable intake set by WHO, and steadily falling. In fact, in a major assessment and comparison of the effectiveness of regulatory controls used in Germany and the UK in the late 1970s (72), it was concluded that both systems adequately protected the consumer. At that time both countries used effective pesticide registration schemes. In the UK "good agricultural practice" was relied on to keep residues within acceptable limits. In Germany, in response to greater consumer fears, there were legally enforced maximum limits for residues. The German system is far more expensive than that in the UK and involves analysis of large numbers of food samples annually. Oddly enough, very little domestically produced food is monitored, because German farmers are considered to be "responsible". Instead, the focus of attention is on those imported foods considered to present residue risks. At present EEC directives are moving European legislation towards the strict residue control approach.

3.3.3.1 Pesticide abuse: In spite of the fact that these legislative frameworks appear to work well, there are some potential gaps in consumer protection. One area of concern is the potential problem of abuses (or errors) in pesticide use at farm level. In a survey of pest control decision making, Tait (3) found that although most farmers carefully observed recommended intervals between pesticide applications and harvest, a minority (15%) appeared to feel that such intervals represented excessive caution. The surveyors got the subjective impression that failure to observe harvest intervals was a frequent occurrence. To overcome this,Tait and Russell (4) have suggested that regulatory controls should involve substantially more monitoring of pesticide usage to ensure that codes of good agricultural practice are observed. They suggest that there is need for improved user training especially in such areas as problem diagnosis as well as safe and humane use of pesticides. A continuing problem in the area of minimising pesticide use is the reliance by many farmers on pesticide distribution personnel for advice on pest control. According to Tait and Russell (4) the objective should be to provide impartial advice from the agricultural advisory service. At the very least there should be a system for certifying pesticide distributors who advise farmers, to ensure that they are competent in diagnosis and in decision making on pesticide use.

3.3.3.2 Pesticide monitoring: A second and somewhat related issue in consumer safety is that of adequate monitoring of foodstuffs for residues. The level of monitoring appears to vary from country to country and often depends on adequate funding from central government to be effective. Perhaps because of the confidence that some countries have in their regulatory controls, there may be a slowness to fund extensive sampling and analysis of foods. For example, in the UK many public analysts were unable to participate in a survey of pesticide residues carried out in 1981 due to restrictions in local authority financing (73). The London Food Commission, a vocal if radical consumerist group, complain that only two food samples are analysed in the UK per £1,000,000 spent by consumers on food. Although pesticide residue levels are, overall, low and falling, monitoring has at least two important functions. Firstly, by punishing offenders it should reduce abuses at farm level and tend to reduce the future risk of individuals being exposed to excessively high residue levels. Secondly, in an era of consumer concerns about the safety of food in general, and exaggerated fears about pesticide residues in particular, extensive monitoring may reassure the consumer. Reassurance here and elsewhere could be an important basis for increased confidence in the agricultural and food industries, and more rational attitudes to technologies used and technical advances in these sectors. Tait and Russell (4) note that in the consultative document on 'Implementing Part 111 of the Food and Environment Protection Act 1985', the UK government proposed to levy companies at 0.4% of their UK turnover to contribute towards information collection and monitoring. Since this would only cover the continuance of current levels of monitoring, the authors feel that it is totally inadequate. The figure required for adequate monitoring according to these authors is 5% of turnover. They claim that such a move would not be unreasonable at this time because, even when passed onto the farmer, it would leave pesticides still cheaper in real terms than in 1980. Whoever pays, government or industry, or both, it appears that a standardised, comprehensive Community-wide monitoring procedure is essential in the years ahead.

3.3.3.3 Technological change and future challenges: Trends in pesticide development and use have been considered by the British Agrochemicals Association (BAA) (70). Up to now the major trends have been in improved specificity for individual pests, reduced persistence, better formulation, better application (to reduce drift), better labelling, etc. In the immediate future the heavy dependence of intensive agriculture on pesticides will continue for economic reasons, and because alternatives do not exist. Ecological pressures will result in pesticides being used more carefully and result in further improvements in formulation and application technology and increase the opportunities for pesticide use as part of integrated control strategies. Integrated pest control involves the use of both chemical and non-chemical control measures together. Typically, optimal methods of husbandry (crop rotation, use of resistant cultivars, careful timing of sowing, etc.) and biological methods (if available) are combined with minimal use of pesticides - often pesticides of high specificity. The objectives are both to reduce pesticide use and to delay the development of resistance to some pesticides. Advances in novel chemical control methods such as the use of juvenile hormones, insect attractants, chemosterilants, etc. can be expected. They felt that experience to date with biological control methods suggested that these were unlikely to compete in any significant way with conventional/integrated pesticide use. However, we can expect improvements resulting from closer liaison between pesticide and sprayer applicator manufacturers on the one hand, and between pesticide manufacturers and plant breeders on the other. Taken together, it would seem that such developments will tend to minimise the use of pesticides in specific applications and thereby tend to reduce the risks from excessive residues.

Predicting further into the future is more difficult. The BAA feel that the current high-cost/high-risk nature of new pesticide development will result in less innovative research and fewer new materials. This may mean safer or more effective pesticides will be slower to appear. For economic reasons new products may cover a range of pests and be more potent. Such developments could have negative safety and environmental implications. Perhaps manufacturers and controlling agencies should explore ways in which these latter trends can be modified in the interest of consumer safety.

Many of the other long-term trends should make pesticide use safer than it is today. These trends include on-going evaluation of exisitng pesticides using more powerful evaluation methodologies and restricting more hazardous types. The opportunities for improved user training, improved surveillance of both application procedures and residue levels discussed earlier could both allay fears and make a contribution to reducing risks particularly from abuse of pesticides. In relation to surveillance of pesticide residues, the FDA Surveillance Index which evaluates the potential health risks of pesticides via dietary exposure is a development worth following (74). Pesticides are assigned to one of five risk classes indicating priority for attention. Gaps in monitoring and analytical methods can be identified and rapidly rectified.

Finally, uncertainties relating to the possible effects of long-term exposure to permitted residue levels, and to possible synergistic effects of combinations of residues, or of combinations of residues and other chemicals foreign to the body, require more research attention.

3.3.4   Anabolic hormones in animal production

Anabolic agents with hormonal action are used worldwide to increase the efficiency of meat production; they are administered as implants in the ears of cattle and increase growth rate and carcass weight (75). The implants provide castrated bulls (steers) with a combination of androgen and oestrogen, bulls with oestrogen alone and heifers with androgen alone (76). In steers, implants containing a single hormone increase growth rate by 10-20% and increase final weight by 6-15 kg. With a combined androgenic and oestrogenic implant, the growth rate increase is 20-35% and the increased final weight 12-25 kg. The increase in carcass weight is in the form of lean meat (77).   This extra weight gained is worth £35 M in the UK annually.

The commercial preparations used either contain endogenous (natural) hormones e.g. oestradiol, testosterone and progesterone, or exogenous (synthetic) anabolic compounds such as trenbolone and zeranol.   Stilbene oestrogens are a further group of potential anabolic agents but because diethyl-stilbestrol (DES) is a known carcinogen, and because these compounds are orally active and persistent, their use has been prohibited (Council Directive 81/602/EEC).   The implications for consumer health arising out of the use of the hormones present in permitted commercial preparations have recently been evaluated in detail by the EEC (78) and WHO (79).   The EEC study was prepared by a specific Scientific Group on anabolic agents in animal production and commented on by the Scientific Veterinary Committee, the Scientific Committee for Animal Nutrition and the Scientific Committee for Food.   In the case of natural hormones (and products readily yielding these) it was concluded that, when properly used they did not constitute any risk to consumer health.   The reasoning behind this decision was that studies have shown that normal use of these preparations results in no qualitative or quantitative differences in hormone levels present in edible tissues compared with untreated cattle. In fact, these levels are orders of magnitude lower than can occur in mature males, mature females and pregnant females.   In man, these low levels are too low to elicit hormonal responses at receptor sites; the compounds have low bioavailability and are rapidly metabolised, mainly by the liver.   Thus, the Scientific Group felt that no question of safety arose.

In the case of trenbolone and zeranol, the Scientific Group felt that, although the metabolism and toxicology of both of these compounds had been extensively studied, there was insufficient data on "hormonal-non-effect" levels and on aspects of their toxicology. More information was required before a final conclusion on their safety could be made. The need for such caution is underlined by Metzler (80). Using DES as an example, he illustrated the need to look beyond hormonal activity when evaluating the risks from use of hormones which are not identical to natural compounds. The risks from carcinogenicity or mutagenicity may be greater than those from hormonal effects. The Scientific Group also concluded that proper programmes to control and monitor the use of anabolic agents were essential and the three committees commenting on the document all underlined the need for attention to methods of use and monitoring (including analytical methods) to prevent abuses. Abuses mainly involve incorrect use or failure to observe the required withholding time before slaughter (from time of implanting). The resulting hormone levels may be a serious threat to consumer health particularly if exposure occurs over long periods of time (81).

The WHO Working Group (79) came to largely the same conclusions as the EEC study but made some additional points worth noting. The importance of providing adequate manpower, expertise and facilities to enforce regulatory controls was highlighted. They felt that a total ban on the use of anabolic agents might precipitate dangerous and illegal practices. It was recommended that legal and safe use of licensed anabolic agents be allowed under appropriate control. The WHO group felt that the first priority should be to prevent the illegal use of banned products (e.g. stilbene oestrogens).

Consumer fears about the safety of anabolic hormones have been an important factor in the setting up of these studies, particularly the EEC study, and these fears have subsequently resulted in a complete ban on the use of all anabolic hormones both natural and synthetic, within the European Community (76). Thus the politicians have rejected the advice of the Scientific Group, and have apparently ignored the risk of a black market developing in anabolic agents, which could include the previously banned stilbenes. The developments leading to this decision have been traced by O'Driscoll (77). Consumer interest was first aroused when several Italian baby boys developed abnormal swelling of the mammary glands in 1980 as a result of consuming veal-based baby food. As a result of subsequent consumer pressure through BEUC, the Council of Ministers stated on 30/9/80 that is was "favourably disposed towards a ban on the use of oestrogens whether natural or artificial" and also agreed on the desirability of greater harmonisation of legislation on veterinary medicines and a more efficient monitoring system. In 1981, a directive banning stilbenes was introduced but due to disagreements in the Council a decision on the other preparations was deferred until the Scientific Group reported. When the Group reported, a draft directive was proposed which would amend Directive 81/602 to allow the use of natural hormones. However, in spite of the recommendations of the Scientific Group, it did not specify conditions of use, or include legislation covering manufacture, sale, distribution or importantly monitoring. Finally, under consumer pressure, the commitment to ban all anabolic agents was honoured.

A number of implications arise from this situation. The banning of natural hormones is another reflection of a substantial lack of confidence among an important minority of consumers in some agricultural and food technologies, even though these technologies are regarded as "safe" by the scientific community (see CHAPTER 2). Part of this lack of confidence is related to ineffective policing of the minority of abuses which take place and the punishing of offenders. As a result, it raises questions as to whether technological developments and their implementation will be evaluated in a calm and scientific way. For example, the Chairman of the Scientific Group has said "I never thought that scientific evidence would be disregarded in favour of misinformed consumer pressure". One result of such action may be that industry will be slow to invest in developing and licensing new products for use in agriculture when political decisions can suddenly prevent these products from being used. The decision has also implications for agriculture's efforts to produce foods which conform to current nutritional guidelines. Steers produced with hormones give leaner beef than untreated steers (see 3.3.1.1).

3.3.5   Antibiotics in animal production

Antibiotics are important tools in intensive animal production. They are used (a) therapeutically to treat (or sometimes prevent) disease and (b) sub-therapeutically as an aid to growth promotion. An example of therapeutic use is the treatment of mastitis in cattle an antibiotic such as penicillin is released into the cow's udder and passed in the milk over five days. The incidence of this disease is higher at some times of the year than at others - in Ireland it is highest at the beginning and end of the main milk producing season (February/March and October/November) - and antibiotic use is highest at these times (82). Prophylactic dosing of antibiotics in young calves is sometimes practised (83). Sub-therapeutic use of antibiotics involves their use in the feeds of intensively produced animals (particularly pigs) at levels < 100 g/tonne to increase growth rate and efficiency of feed conversion. About 40% of antibiotics sold annually in the US are being used as animal feed additives; the annual savings in the pork industry from non-therapeutic use of antibiotics in 1982 has been put at 200 million dollars (84). The addition of antibiotics to animal feeds began in the early 1950s, at a time when many other changes were being made in animal husbandry. Production facilities for animals were becoming larger and more centralised, and advances in the understanding of animal nutrition had made it possible to raise animals year-round in concentrated, enclosed production facilities. The use of antibiotics has helped to make modern production methods possible by allowing large numbers of animals to be housed together without the major infectious disease problems that might otherwise be expected (85).

The mechanism whereby antibiotics increase growth rate and efficiency of feed conversion is not fully understood. A disease control effect is probably most important but other mechanisms such as a "nutrient sparing effect" (due to changes in gut microflora and reduced thickness of intestinal wall) or possible metabolic effects (in the case of some antibiotics) have been suggested (85). In the USA, 21 antibiotics and other anti-microbials, including the tetracyclines and penicillin are approved for animal feed use. Under EEC Feed Additives Directive 70/524 only seven antibiotics, none of which is used in human medicine, are permitted for use as growth promoters in animal feed.

3.3.5.1 Hazards to human health: There are important potential hazards to human health resulting from antibiotic use in agriculture. They arise through (a) antibiotic residues and (b) antibiotic resistant organisms. The main sources of antibiotic residues in food are milk and meat. They arise through abuses (marketing of products before the required withdrawal period), mistakes (e.g. failure to mark treated cows in a large herd) or due to lack of information on withdrawal periods (82). Reported occurrence of residues in milk in Europe are generally low, typically in <1.0% of samples tested, but problems have occurred. For example, in Ireland a high incidence of residues was recorded - in up to 18.7% of samples tested in an 1981-82 investigation. This appeared to have been due to inadequate monitoring and enforcement in the liquid milk trade (86). The significance of antibiotic residues for human health relates to allergic or hypersensitive responses, to toxic effects, and to a lesser extent, to possible induction of bacterial resistance or disturbance of normal gut flora. Certain antibiotics, notably penicillin but also streptomycin, chloramphenicol and novobiocin are strongly allergenic compounds. Sensitisation of consumers usually has occurred during therapeutic treatments, but once sensitised, as little as 0.024 mg of penicillin can elicit an allergic reaction. Most food-related incidents of allergy reported in the literature have involved penicillin in milk, but the problem could occur with residues in other foods. Although the levels of antibiotic residues are too low to cause acute toxic reactions, there is a possibility of long-term toxicity problems (87). To control allergy effects and possible chronic toxicity of antibiotic residues in foods there are now WHO/FAO guidelines for maximum levels in milk, meat and eggs. Because of its toxicity, residues of chloramphenicol must be absent from foods.

The second risk is due to antibiotic resistant organisms arising from antibiotic use in agricultural production, and interference by this antibiotic resistance with the treatment of human illness. This can occur through contamination of food with an antibiotic resistant organism which causes disease in both animals and man e.g. <u>Salmonella</u> species. More seriously, it may occur through resistance being transferred from harmless bacteria to pathogens. Resistance to a number of antibiotics, notably tetracyclines and penicillin, is carried on plasmids called R-factors, which readily move from harmless organisms to pathogens, transferring the resistance in the process (85). A fixed sequence of events must occur to make this a health hazard. It is generally agreed that the early and late steps in this sequence do occur i.e. that antibiotic resistance develops in farm animals, that antibiotic resistant bacteria get into the food supply and that human infections caused by antibiotic resistant bacteria are more difficult to treat. There is considerable controversy, however, over the extent to which R-factors are transferred in practice and about the extent of the impact of such an R-factor mediated sequence on human health (85). Antibiotic resistance is certainly increasing in <u>Salmonella</u> species isolated from humans. Friend and Shahani (84) quote data showing that from 1969 to 1974 resistance in <u>S</u>. <u>typhimurium</u> to ampicillin increased from 23.4% to 39.9%, resistance to streptomycin from 27.3% to 45.6% and resistance to tetracycline from 12.5% to 44.8%; and they point out that a high level of antibiotic resistant coliforms resulting from antibiotics in animal feeds is well documented.

<u>3.3.5.2 Antibiotics and growth promotion</u>: While it has seemed reasonable to use antibiotics to cure animal disease, the use of sub-therapeutic levels of antibiotics for growth promotion has aroused controversy. The potential problems are greatest where antibiotics used in growth promotion are the same or similar to those used to treat human illness. The subject has been recently reviewed by the National Academy of Sciences (NAS) in Washington (5) and by the American Council on Science and Health (85). Both agree

that despite these theoretical possibilities, there is no hard evidence that a substantial risk exists. Among the conclusions of the NAS report is a passage illustrating their attitude to the evidence available:

"Because the literature provides only isolated fragments of information relating to various components of the meat production system, it is insufficient for assessing the direct relationship between the use of sub-therapeutic levels of antimicrobials in animal feeds and the health of humans. A major deficiency in much of the literature is the lack of a clear differentiation between the consequences of sub-therapeutic and therapeutic uses of antimicrobials in animals. Moreover, data gathered in the United Kingdom, the Federal Republic of Germany, and the Netherlands do not indicate clearly whether restrictive regulations have actually reduced or averted the postulated hazards to human health. Restrictions on the use of antimicrobials in the United Kingdom may well have altered the patterns of their use without significant alteration in the total amounts used or their consequences. Therefore, it is not possible to conclude from the literature that restricting only the sub-therapeutic use of antimicrobials will cause a decrease in the overall prevalence of antibiotic resistant organisms in humans or animals".

They go on to point out that such lack of evidence does not mean that hazards don't exist. They considered, however, that a comprehensive study of the issue was impossible for technical reasons. They make the suggestion that the mechanism of action whereby sub-therapeutic dosing produces beneficial effects should be investigated with a view to replacing this with vaccines (if the effect is mainly one of controlling infections) or with nutrient supplements (if the effect is a nutrient sparing one).

3.3.5.3 Consumer protection: Consumer protection from antibiotic residues can be achieved by a comprehensive regulatory system which should include (26):

(a) High standards of control over the manufacture and distribution of all drugs intended for use in animals to ensure their quality and safety.

(b) Provision that the availability of antibiotics be restricted, with veterinary practitioners having responsibility for their sale through prescriptions and for ensuring that the instructions for use are followed.

(c) An effective residue monitoring programme in operation at both national and local level for all produce, whether for foreign or home consumption.

(d) Impartial information and education for farmers on the risks and dangers of all farm and animal drugs.

The US experience is that residues are not likely to pose a human health hazard as long as adequate surveillance and enforcement exists. Procedures used in the US are claimed to have reduced residues in food to negligible levels. In Europe there are directives on safety, quality, efficiency, and on standardisation of evaluation, approval and registration of veterinary medicines (81/851/EEC and 81/852/EEC). The surveillance situation in the past has been uneven with some countries having scarcely any effective regulations while others had quite comprehensive ones (86). In some cases policing by industry (such as the dairy processors) has been important while in others monitoring for residues was a condition of trade. In 1981 the EEC proposed a directive on "health problems relating to residues of antibiotics in fresh meat of Community origin". This will standardise methods for sampling and testing; at least 2 pigs and 5 calves/100 slaughtered will have to be tested. It provides for identifying the supplier and having his herd marked and slaughter or sale prohibited until cleared by local veterinary authorities (at the farmer's expense) (82). Parallel proposals for other foods are in the pipeline.

The hazard due to antibiotic resistant organisms could be reduced by (a) keeping antibiotic use to the absolute minimum (b) ensuring that the antibiotics used in agriculture continue to be different from those important in human medicine.

3.3.5.4 Future developments: In the longer term, the consumer is best protected by minimum use of antibiotics in agriculture. There are at least two opportunities to achieve this. Firstly the need for therapeutic and prophylactic dosing could be reduced by better animal management practices. For example, separation of calves and dams should be delayed until calves are sufficiently robust to withstand the practices associated with intensive production; animals should be purchased from reliable sources; policies of disposing of all old stock before new animals are introduced should be followed. In intensive production, units should be better designed for better warmth, ventilation and lower population density (82, 83). A second opportunity is that suggested by NAS, i.e. to investigate the mechanism whereby sub-therapeutic dosing aids in growth promotion. As previously discussed this could result in antibiotics being replaced by vaccines or nutrient supplements.

In the future, the use of antibiotics must be kept under constant review with continuing examination of resistance patterns in antibiotic resistant bacteria found in foods and appearing in human disease. As mentioned above, there is Community legislation standardising the evaluation, approval and registration of veterinary medicines, and directives on sampling and testing for antibiotic residues are in the pipeline. Such quality control and surveillance measures are essential to protect consumers, and should be fully implemented without delay. Any remaining problems relating to sampling and test methodology should be solved as a matter of urgency. Consideration should also be given by the Community to the possibility of funding research on animal husbandry methods which minimise antibiotic use.

3.3.6 Fertilizers

Fertilizers provide major benefits in intensive agriculture and are the basis of increased food production, providing an adequate, secure and varied food supply and, as such, making a major contribution to human nutrition. By improving the efficiency of production they have contributed to the living standards of farmers. Estimation of the total economic benefit from fertilizers is complex particularly in an era of surplus production. However, it has been estimated that 9.3 - 10.5 M tonnes of cereal grain per annum (1980-1983) can be attributed to fertilizer use in the UK. The value of this is about £600M and the fertilizer cost £2-300 M (88).

Besides providing opportunities for consumers to over-eat, the major potential hazard to consumer health from fertilizers arises from the contribution of nitrogen fertilizer to nitrate levels in the food supply. In the longer term, cadmium levels in soils could approach toxic levels due to cadmium in phosphate fertilizers, and it may become necessary to extract cadmium from fertilizers in the future (88).

Nitrate per se in the food and water supply is not a hazard as it is rapidly excreted in the urine. The potential problems arise when it is reduced to nitrite by bacterial contamination of food, or by bacteria particularly in the mouth, but also in the stomach and bladder. Extreme bacterial contamination of food high in nitrate can cause sufficient nitrite production to produce methaemoglobinaemia in young children (89). The main potential hazard however relates to the reduction of nitrate to nitrite, and the subsequent reaction of nitrite with secondary amines to produce carcinogenic nitrosamines, a reaction which is favoured by the high acid conditions found in the stomach (90). The main sources of nitrate in the diet are leafy vegetables, drinking water, and processed meats. While the levels permitted in processed meats have been progressively reduced (see 3.4.5.2), the overall levels of nitrate in the diet have been increasing due to increased amounts in vegetables and water (88).

3.3.6.1 Nitrate in vegetables: Large amounts of nitrate can accumulate in plants, particularly leafy plants (91, 92). Levels collated by Jollans (88) from various authors show values in lettuce ranging from 127 to 3547 ppm (the latter value for winter greenhouse production), in spinach from 536 to 2321 ppm, in cabbage from 204 to 917 ppm, in celery from 1001 to 2829 ppm, in beet from 1218 to 2657 ppm, in carrot from 66 to 337 ppm, and in radish from 1519 to 2019 ppm. High levels of nitrogen fertilizer, particularly when applied as a top dressing during growth contribute to these high nitrate levels (93). However, the level of fertilizer use is not the only factor in nitrate accumulation. The combination of high nitrogen fertilizer and the poor light conditions under which winter lettuce production takes place in greenhouses may account for some of the very high levels (94). Normally nitrate is absorbed by plants, rapidly reduced and used in the synthesis of amino acids, proteins, and other nitrogen containing products. Plants accumulate nitrate when the rate of uptake is greater than that of reduction. When it accumulates to high levels, it is believed to do so in a storage pool in cell vacuoles which is not readily available for reduction. Blom-Zandra and Lampe (94) have suggested that nitrate may have an important role in these vacuoles in the control of osmotic pressure, particularly under low-light conditions, when it may compensate for the shortage of organic compounds due to lowered photosynthesis. Thus, the basis for some of the variability in nitrate levels in vegetable samples may be explained by this and other advances in understanding of how plants absorb and utilise nitrate ions. Related work by Blom-Zandra and Lampe (95) indicates that nitrate levels can be dramatically reduced (to well below acceptable levels) in lettuce crops grown in suitable media i.e. sand, rockwool or hydroponically. This is achieved by removing nitrate fertilizer for the last week or so of production, and replacing it with either sulphate or chloride ions. Using this procedure, the benefits of high growth rates can be obtained for most of the crop's life, and excess nitrate removed before harvest.

3.3.6.2 Nitrate in drinking water: The problem of high nitrate levels in drinking water has been discussed by Jollans (88). The extent to which nitrogen fertilizer contributes to nitrate in water courses is incompletely understood - studies show that only 10% of labelled nitrogen applied in a given season ends up in rivers and lakes. However, both nitrogen fertilizer use and nitrate levels in some rivers and aquifers are steadily

rising.   Leaching of nitrate occurs mostly in winter when nitrate use by
plants is low.

The relative contribution of fertilizer applied to arable and pasture
land requires more research.   In pastures, the opportunities for nitrate
uptake by plants continue late into the autumn, so leaching should be
reduced. However, the significance of the contribution of the nitrate from
the urine of grazing animals is unclear.   Leaching from arable land is
better understood, and the amounts lost can be reduced by reducing autumn
cultivation and autumn/early spring nitrogen applications.   An EEC
Directive on the quality of water for human consumption (96) issued in 1980
includes a guide level of 25 mg NO_3/litre and a maximum limit of 50 mg
NO_3/litre.   Some water courses already exceed these limits, and levels are
increasing.   Irrespective of any immediate changes in nitrogen fertilizer
use, the levels in water will continue to rise because the nitrate can take
30-40 years to percolate to groundwater (89).   As a result, it is expected
that water authorities may have to spend substantial sums of money on
blending or treatment of water for human consumption to meet acceptable
nitrate levels.

3.3.6.3 Future developments: Some   doubt as to the seriousness of the
threat posed to human health by high levels of nitrate in the diet has been
introduced by a recent major epidemiological study (89).   It showed that
inhabitants of areas with high rates of gastric cancer had significantly
lower levels of nitrate intake than inhabitants of areas with low rates of
gastric cancer - the reverse of what would be expected.   As a result, more
information on the significance of nitrate in the diet is required.

The problem of nitrate levels in leafy vegetables is being addressed
through selection of low nitrate accumulating cultivars and through
modifications to crop husbandry. Further progress and practical
applications of this work in combination with adequate monitoring should
contribute to lower nitrate intake from vegetables.

The problem of high nitrate levels in drinking water is more serious,
particularly because an immediate reduction in nitrogen fertilizer use would
only affect water nitrate levels in the relatively distant future. Given
the current problems of food surpluses, it may be opportune to consider
restricting nitrogen fertilizer use, at least in some areas. In any event,
there is an urgent need to assess the extent of the hazard posed by nitrate
in the food and water supply and, if necessary, develop a rational strategy
for its control.

3.4   EFFECTS OF PROCESSES AND PRACTICES USED BY THE FOOD INDUSTRY

3.4.1   Effects of food processing

Food processing may involve a single main step as in canning,
freezing, dehydration, etc., or it may involve both primary and secondary
processing (milling of flour followed by baking of bread;
refining/modification of oils followed by incorporation into formulated
foods). The effects of food processes on consumer health and safety
considered here are directly related to chemical changes relating to loss
of nutrients and formation of potentially toxic compounds. Many reactions
occur in food systems, the types and rates depend on (a) the
characteristics of the food - composition, pH, Aw, catalysts present,
oxygen concentration, etc. (b) processing and storage conditions - time x
temperature, chemical treatments, exposure to radiant energy, atmosphere

composition, etc. (97). Some processes cause more severe changes than others. The greatest degree of change occurs in thermal processing and prolonged storage.

The types of reactions and interactions which involve proteins, fats and sugars, have been reviewed by Fennema (98). Depending on conditions, proteins can undergo cross-linking, racemisation, carbonyl amine (Maillard) reactions, and oxidative destruction of amino acids. Unsaturated fats undergo oxidative reactions forming hydroperoxides, dimers and polymers; some of the oxidative products interact with proteins, causing cross-linking and promoting Maillard browning, and can also interact with vitamins A, C, D, E and folic acid. Carbohydrates become involved in caramelisation reactions. Vitamins and provitamins are mostly involved in oxidative reactions (vitamins A, C, D, E, folic acid) and isomerisation (β- carotene). There are also important separation (in milling) and leaching (in blanching and canning) effects of food processes which affect chemical composition, of particular relevance to vitamins and minerals.

3.4.2   Nutritional implications of food processing

"There is no simple statement that can summarise the effect of processing on the vitamin and nutrient content of processed foods" (99). Nutritional losses which occur can be balanced against nutritional benefits - conserving the food and prevention of post-harvest/slaughter losses (100) and increasing the availability and variety of foods. The issue addressed in this section is the effect of processing on nutrients and the practical significance of this for consumers. Fennema (98) summarised the effects of different food processes on nutrient loss as:

Substantial	-	Milling of wheat
Moderate	-	Heat Sterilisation, Irradiation
Insignificant to Moderate	-	Dehydration
Slight	-	Processing of fats and oils, proteins
Insignificant	-	Freezing

Actual effects depend on food composition and factors such as time, temperature, dose etc. within the process. The worst losses occur in separatory processes or with severe thermal processing, depending on time and temperature conditions; foods resulting from these processes can incur 'moderate' nutrient losses during storage (60, 98). In general, the nutritional consequences of chemical changes in proteins, fats, and carbohydrates are of no significance for the majority of consumers (60). However, damage to the nutritional value of proteins could be important for sub-groups such as infants consuming a limited range of foods. Important reactions (which increase in significance with the severity of the process) include:

(a)   early and advanced Maillard reactions: blockage/destruction of lysine and other essential amino acids

(b)   cross-linking due to final Maillard reactions, and interactions of proteins with oxidised lipids, resulting in reduced bioavailability of essential amino acids (101).

In the future, greater use of alkaline treatments may result in higher levels of racemisation; D-amino acids are utilised either poorly (methionine) or not at all (101).

For most European consumers, the effects of food processing on vitamins and minerals present more of a potential problem. However, the experience in practice has been that most food processes currently used

258

(freezing, canning, drying, etc.) do not present significant problems. This appears to be due to a number of factors (after Bender (99) and others):

(a)   many of the losses which occur during food processing are in place of (not in addition to) losses at final preparation. For example, retentions of vitamin C in peas cooked from fresh, frozen, canned, air-dried, and freeze-dried were respectively 44%, 39%, 36%, 25%, and 35% (102). In line with this, a USDA study (103) on vitamin retention in fruits and vegetables which were either canned, frozen, or prepared from fresh, showed that differences were small except that 30-40% of water-soluble vitamins (ascorbic acid, B_6) were lost in the cooking liquid of canned vegetables and that there were substantial losses of thiamine in thermal processes. Similar data have been reported for processed meats and seafoods (60).

(b)   losses have been balanced to some extent by the benefits of food processing. These mostly relate to greater availability and variety of foods, though there are actual nutritional benefits also (vitamin production in fermentations; antinutrient destruction in thermal processing).

(c)   really large losses (due to milling, etc.) are now usually recognised and are often compensated for by restitution/fortification. For example, fortification of ready-to-eat (RTE) cereals have contributed substantially to vitamin and mineral intakes of children (104).

(d)   items which are key sources of some nutrients have had their processing and storage conditions optimised for nutrient retention. For example, in orange juice a range of processing and storage measures have been used to retain vitamin C - oxygen exclusion at processing and packaging, frozen or chilled storage, opaque packaging,etc. (e.g. 105, 106).

When processed foods are stored, they incur nutrient losses in addition to those lost in processing. With the possible exception of ascorbic acid, there are insufficient data available to predict the exact behaviour of individual nutrients under different storage conditions (107), though data are available on nutrient losses from specific stored foods. In addition to time, temperature of storage is a major factor in nutrient loss, though packaging, atmosphere composition within packages, exposure to light, moisture content, pH, and other factors can also be important. Losses in fresh fruits and vegetables after harvest are discussed in 3.3.1.2. In frozen foods quality loss is strongly affected by storage temperature, but the effects of temperature on nutrients have not been studied in detail. Temperatures below $-18\,^{\circ}C$ to $-20\,^{\circ}C$ retain most ascorbic acid for prolonged periods in some frozen foods but not in others (107). Data are available for a number of frozen products which specify maximum storage temperatures for retention of a specified percent of key nutrients for different storage times. In canned foods, legumes lose about 15% ascorbic acid and 25% thiamine during storage for one year at ambient temperatures (107). In canned meats, both leaching and thermal degradation lead to losses of niacin and riboflavin. At $21\,^{\circ}C$ canned meat products lost 15% of thiamine after 6 months and 45% after 24 months (108). In general, the use of chill temperatures would substantially reduce nutrient losses in canned foods. As in the case of food processing, these nutrient losses do not appear to represent a serious nutritional hazard for most consumers. The use of 'sell by' dating of processed foods helps protect the consumer against excessive nutrient losses. In the future, nutrient losses during storage of novel foods or losses due to novel storage methods will require assessment.

3.4.2.1 Technological change: Changes in technology are occurring on a number of levels. Of these the introduction of new food processes, changes in existing processes, and advances in nutrition science, are probably the most important. If food processed in a new way became an important part of the diet as a whole, or an important supplier of essential nutrients, its nutritional effects would need to be evaluated in detail (101). At least three new methods of processing/semi-processing may become important/expand in the next decade. These are irradiation, food chilling and extrusion processing.

The effects of irradiation on nutrient content of foods have been evaluated in detail by the FAO/IAEA/WHO Expert Committee on wholesomeness of irradiated foods (22). They concluded that the process gave no cause for particular concern:

"Evidence from most studies suggests that in the low-dose range (up to 1 kGy) used for the irradiation of food, nutrient losses are insignificant. In the medium-dose range (1-10 kGy), losses of some vitamins may occur, if air is not excluded during irradiation and storage. In the high-dose range (10-50 kGy), the technology used to avoid effects on organoleptic quality (i.e. irradiation at temperatures below freezing and in the absence of air) also partially protects nutrients, so that losses may actually be lower than in the medium-dose range if such precautions have not been taken.

Conflicting results have been reported concerning the effect of irradiation on vitamin C levels in foods. Some authors have determined only ascorbic acid, without taking into consideration that irradiation converts some of this acid to dehydro-ascorbic acid, which is also biologically active. In future studies, both ascorbic and dehydro-ascorbic acid should therefore be determined.

The extent of losses of nutrients due to the irradiation of foods depends on many factors, such as the composition of the food, the irradiation dose, the temperature, and the presence or absence of air during irradiation and storage.

Whether or not the loss of a nutrient in an irradiated food is of importance depends on circumstances, such as the contribution that this food makes to the total diet. For instance, a partial loss of thiamine in fish would be of concern if that was the key source of thiamine to a particular population. Other relevant factors include the nutritional status and requirements of the population for which that food is intended. Some other areas of uncertainty (i.e. folic acid losses) require further investigation.

In 1976 the Joint Expert Committee suggested that the

reduction of nutritional value produced by irradiation alone should be compared with that produced by other processes and during storage, and by combinations of irradiation with other processes. A considerable body of evidence is now available in this regard and the results give no cause for particular concern".

Wilkinson (109) reiterated this position in a scientific and technical survey carried out by Leatherhead Food R. A. in the UK. In summary:

"Proteins are essentially unchanged (by irradiation) although slight decomposition of the sulphur amino acids can occur. The minor changes in carbohydrates have no nutritional consequences but fats are susceptible to oxidation. Most vitamins are reasonably stable although some, e.g. thiamine and vitamin E, are labile. Any changes are comparable with those occurring in other food processes. In some cases the nutritional value of the food as consumed may be increased because of the reduced cooking time required".

3.4.2.2 The COST 91 Programme: The European COST 91 Programme has provided, and continues to provide, extensive information on the effects of heat processing, freezing and chilling on nutritive value and quality of foods. A workshop held in Dublin at the beginning of the programme resulted in a major state-of-the-art review and inventory of on-going European research on the effects of thermal processing on nutritional value of foods (110). A four-year programme followed on the effects of extrusion, freezing and cooking on quality and nutritional value, culminating in a large symposium held in Athens in late 1984 (111). The work has now been extended in COST 91 bis to include HTST (high-temperature-short-time) processing including extrusion, food chilling and food biotechnology. In relation to chilled foods, very little is known about their nutrient composition (112). There are well known benefits from chilling fresh fruits and vegetables but there is little readily available data on chilled foods after the long shelf-lives possible with modified atmosphere packaging or irradiation. As a result, the COST 91 bis Sub-Group dealing with chilling plan to assemble data on nutritional value of chilled foods.

3.4.2.3 Extrusion and HTST: In addition to the activity noted above in the COST 91 programme on extrusion and HTST, the effects of extrusion cooking on nutrients have been reviewed by Bjorck and Asp (113). Though similar to HTST processes, extrusion also involves high pressure and high shear. Because it is being increasingly used for weaning foods and RTE cereals, etc., a thorough knowledge of its nutritional effects is essential. The usefulness of the data available is reduced by the fact that published work has been carried out using different extruders, and conditions are not always well defined. Proteins and fats are involved in the same types of nutritional losses discussed earlier due to Maillard reactions, cross-linking etc., the extent depending on the severity of operating conditions. Starch is gelatinised and antinutritional factors destroyed. Dietary fibre of cereal products may be reduced due to increased solubilisation. Thermostable B vitamins such as riboflavin were found to be stable while losses of thiamine depended on the process variables used. Losses of vitamin C can be lower than in conventional boiling in water. Due to possible interference by other compounds in the analysis of fat-soluble vitamins, the effects of the process on these vitamins need further evaluation.

In relation to changes in existing technology, important developments are taking place aimed at minimising the effects of thermal processes. The thermal processes used by the food industry range from relatively mild blanching treatments through pasteurisation to the rigorous commercial sterilisation of the canning process. Commercial sterilisation involves exposure of the foods to a time x temperature treatment sufficient to reduce the number of $\underline{C. \ botulinum}$ spores by a factor of 10^{12} (114). Most heat of all is required to achieve this in non-acid foods (vegetables, meats, prepared foods, etc.). Besides affecting nutrients more than other processes, these heat treatments alter the natural colour, flavour and texture of foods (115) and may produce hazardous by-products (115, 116). It is these effects on sensory quality that have stimulated the food industry most to modify traditional thermal processing. Fortunately, by minimising quality changes nutrient losses are also minimised.

One important development has been the introduction of the retortable pouch - a flexible laminated food package that can withstand thermal processing (117). Because of its thin profile it takes 30-50% less time to reach sterilising temperature at its coldest point compared with cans or jars. The final quality lies somewhere between the quality associated with canned and frozen food. Though hailed as a major breakthrough in 1978, uptake by industry has not been as rapid as expected. Problems with costs of packaging material, labour intensive packing lines, lack of familiarity by consumers with the packages, and strong competition from the frozen food industry are being overcome but have retarded this important development (118).

A second important trend has been one towards HTST processing. HTST processing exploits the fact that micro-organisms are more sensitive to high temperature than are the rates of chemical reactions affecting vitamin retention and quality generally (114). Thus, commercial sterilisation can be achieved with less chemical change. HTST has the additional benefit for industry of increased output per hour and can be applied to acid fruits in metal cans in the high vacuum flame sterilisation process (119). However, because of slow heat transfer in cans, HTST works best in combination with aseptic packaging. Aseptic packaging involves independent sterilisation of product and packaging, and assembly of the two in a sterile environment (120); the food is heat treated and cooked using sophisticated heat exchangers (scraped surface heat exchangers with particulate/viscous foods). This aseptic technology has resulted in substantial benefits in the dairy, fruit juice, and acid particulate product sectors (121, 122). However, it remains to be efficiently applied in low-acid viscous/particulate foods. The high temperatures required in these applications (ca. 140°C) lead to flow and thermal conduction phenomena which are incompletely understood (123). In practice, this makes it difficult to achieve commercial sterility without over-cooking and/or fouling heat exchange surfaces (123, 124). Because of the potential benefits of this technology, it is the object of intensive research in the areas of process control, food rheology, microbiology, and nutrient retention at laboratory and pilot plant level (see COST 91 bis Programme, 3.4.2.2).

A separate approach to HTST processing of low-acid foods is being pursued by Alfa-Laval in their research and development on the "Multitherm" system (125). Here the food is first vacuum packaged in a flat pack. It is then "microclaved" at 127°C using microwaves and steam pressure. Uneven product temperature distribution is minimised using a layer of cooling water over the surface of the packages. The resulting quality and vitamin retention in some products is claimed to be comparable with frozen food, and commercial applications are expected in a few years time. Besides maintaining the vitamin content and minimising potentially toxic chemical changes in foods, these developments in thermal processing may enable high quality long-life products to be produced without the colour and in some cases flavour additives currently used in thermal processing, and without the preservatives used in some chilled foods. In fact, in the early 1990s the consumer will be faced with a series of novel high quality HTST foods, finding their niche in the marketplace among the products of the other emerging food preservation systems - chilled foods, foods under modified atmospheres, irradiated foods, etc.

Finally, advances relevant to nutritional science in such areas as analytical chemistry and evaluation of bioavailability are an important area of technological change (99). It will be a continuing responsibility to apply state-of-the-art technology particularly in the evaluation of key sources of vitamins and minerals, and in the evaluation of novel food processes. An area of particular importance is infant nutrition where not only losses in vitamin content are important, but also losses of amino acids and protein availability (101).

3.4.3 Toxicological implications of food processing

Many conventional food processes have not been subjected to detailed toxicological evaluation. They pre-dated the development of the science of toxicology, and current toxicological procedures cannot readily be applied to such a complex effect as a process (135, see below). Instead, evidence of their safety is supplied by decades of human experience, and the knowledge that most chemical changes caused by these processes do not pose a hazard to human health. However, some of the chemical reactions which take place are known to result in toxic products or in products which require further safety assessment. Examples of these include products of browning and pyrolysis reactions; lysinoalanine formation due to heating of proteins, particularly under alkaline conditions (126); and production of trans fatty acids during hydrogenation (127). (The toxicological implications of curing are mentioned in 3.4.5.2).

Browning reactions either involve amino acids and reducing sugars (Maillard reactions) or sugars alone (caramelisation reactions). Maillard reactions can occur at relatively low temperatures (128) but both types of browning reactions become important in processes where the surface of food is dried and heated to temperatures > 100 $^{\circ}$C (116). Such conditions prevail in baking, frying, roasting, broiling, etc. Pyrolysis occurs at much higher temperatures (ca. 220 $^{\circ}$C) in the absence of free water; amino acids and sugars are decomposed. These conditions prevail in baking, broiling, charring, etc.

Products of model systems in which Maillard browning reactions had proceeded for an hour at 121 $^{\circ}$C were found to be mutagenic (129), as were commercial caramel powder and caramel-containing foods, dried fruits and cooked meats. In animal studies, long-term feeding of products of moderate to extensive browning reactions in foods and model systems produced liver and kidney damage resembling the cumulative effects of toxic compounds (128). Mutagenic N-heterocyclic compounds produced in advanced Maillard reactions occur during boiling-down of beef stock and frying of hamburgers

(101). The mutagenic compounds in charred beef and fish have been shown to be pyrolysis products of amino acids (notably tryptophan) and proteins (130).

The significance of these mutagenic or toxic compounds is difficult to assess. As far as food processing is concerned, they are clearly more associated with severe cooking conditions than with food processing itself though some mutagens are undoubtedly formed during processing and storage. Since many of these mutagens have been discovered relatively recently (since 1972) we may be only scratching the surface of an important factor in cancer epidemiology (130). Their possible hazard must be seen in the context of the complexity of the food system (with promutagens, desmutagens) and the different physiological states of individuals (levels of liver and other enzymes, etc.). Many mutagens are carcinogens, many are not, and some have been found to be weaker carcinogens than expected (131). There is insufficient information available to estimate human risk (116) and even small amounts may be significant over long periods. There is also a need for more systematic studies of the effects of these mutagens using mammalian test systems and an evaluation of available information on effects in humans (116). In the meantime, it would be prudent to reduce the level of mutagens ingested. According to Sugimura and Sato (130), the full elucidation of the chemical entities of mutagens in coffee is important, since there are two epidemiological studies linking coffee and pancreatic cancer.

Lysinoalanine (LAL) is a non-natural amino acid formed by cross-linkage of lysine and alanine, which occurs in protein foods subjected to severe heat or alkaline conditions. Its formation results in a small loss of protein digestibility, but alkaline treated soy protein and pure LAL have produced reversible renal lesions in rats (101, 126). The levels formed in milk depend on the severity of heat treatment e.g. UHT, HTST and in-can sterilisation had respectively 300, 540 and 710 mg/kg protein. These levels are not considered to be of any significance except in the heat treatment of liquid infant formulae, where the least severe sterilisation should be used (101). However, LAL is relevant to protein isolates (from soya, milk etc.) where alkaline treatments can be used to improve texture or flavour, to promote solubilisation, destroy toxins or inhibit enzymes (132). For example, levels collected by Pfaender (126) for simulated cheese, sodium caseinate and a whipping agent were respectively 1.1, 6.9 and 50g LAL/kg protein, and he considered the latter level a threatening one. In summary, the problem of LAL formation is not considered to be serious up to now. However, with increasing interest in improving the functional properties of proteins by novel processing, careful control and assessment of processes (132) is essential to prevent LAL becoming a human health hazard in the future.

Trans fatty acids are geometric isomers of natural unsaturated fatty acids which are formed by stereoisomerisation occurring during the (partial) hydrogenation process (133). Studies in the US showed that shortenings, margarines, and salad oils made from partially hydrogenated oils contained 14-60%, 16-70% and 8-17% trans fatty acids respectively; most Americans consume 5% of fat as trans isomers of oleic and linoleic acid, though intake can be as high as 10% (134). Trans fatty acids are apparently absorbed and metabolised in the same way as saturated fatty acids and it is generally believed that their consumption exerts no deleterious effects on growth or well-being. However, some questions remain. During the hydrogenation process a complex mixture of positional and geometric isomers is formed, and significant differences have been found in the metabolism of the different isomers in such reactions as lipolysis, catabolism and incorporation into phospholipids (127). For example, Kinsella et al. (134) have found that a trace trans isomer inhibited arachidonic acid synthesis in rats, resulting in low levels of prostaglandins. Recent advances in analytical techniques (133) have enabled the range of trans fatty acids present in common foods to be identified and quantified. In general, there appears to be a need for further evaluation of trans fatty acids in the light of the more precise information now becoming available. In particular, this information will help with the design of more realistic feeding studies.

3.4.3.1 Technological change and safety evaluation: Major changes in current food processing methods or the introduction of novel food processes pose special problems for safety evaluation. As mentioned at the outset, a food process cannot readily be subjected to conventional toxicological evaluation. The major stumbling block arises in relation to the use of a one hundred-fold margin of safety. A recent MAFF document "Memorandum on the testing of novel foods" (10) outlines the problem for novel foods, though an analogous situation would apply in relation to a novel process:

> "The traditional method of assessing the safety of a food
> additive, i.e. allowing a one hundred-fold margin between
> the maximum amount of the additive likely to be consumed
> in the human diet and the maximum amount which has no
> toxic effect when fed to animals, clearly cannot be
> applied to a novel food which would constitute more than
> one per cent of the human diet. In any case, there are
> practical limits to the amounts of certain foods which can

be added to animal diets without adversely affecting the animals' nutritional status and health."

It states that the higher level used in testing must be substantially in excess of anticipated exposure level in man, which in some cases may mean feeding up to the maximum practicable level. According to Hall (135) failure to recognise this issue resulted in a lot of unnecessary toxicological testing of the process of food irradiation over the past 30 year period. Instead of depending solely on animal feeding studies, the more appropriate focus of attention should be on the nature and extent of chemical changes. In the case of food irradiation, the focus of attention finally became the production of unique radiolytic products, which were in due course considered not to constitute a human health hazard. Such focusing on important chemical effects, in combinations with animal testing at these more moderate levels of ingestion, could form the basis of efficient safety evaluation of novel food processes in the future.

3.4.4 Nutritional implications of food formulation

It is useful to classify processed foods into three broad categories based on the degree to which they have been formulated:

(a)   relatively non-formulated foods, examples: frozen vegetables, some chilled foods, fruit juices, some canned foods, etc.

(b)   partially formulated foods, i.e. although formulated, unrefined ingredients make up the bulk of the product, examples: processed entrees, canned vegetables, etc.

(c)   highly formulated foods, i.e. where refined ingredients make up more than 50% of product, examples: some desserts, drinks, soups, many RTE cereals, confectionery items and snack foods.

This classification shows that convenience food need not be synonymous with highly formulated food. Although convenience snacks are generally highly formulated, convenience meals are only partially formulated and with the increasing availability of chilled foods there will be more opportunity for consumers to choose convenient, yet relatively unformulated and minimally processed meals.

3.4.4.1   Ingredients of nutritional significance: The issues dealt with here relate to how food formulation can better help consumers meet dietary guidelines in terms of fat, refined sugar, dietary fibre and salt content of foods, while at the same time taking into account effects on levels of important vitamins and minerals. Fat, sugar, salt, and refined ingredients generally, perform important functional roles in formulated foods. These relate mainly to product acceptability, uniformity, processability, and storeability (136). Depending on the product, fat can make an important contribution to texture, mouthfeel, lubrication, juiciness and flavour. Sugar has important roles in flavour, preservation by controlling water activity (Aw), and texture through control of viscosity and gelation (137). Salt has important roles in taste and flavour enhancement. It is an important processing aid; for example it can improve the water holding capacity of meats (138) has a range of functions in baking (139) and cheese processing (140), and is also an important preservative - here it is more effectve in reducing Aw than sugar because of its lower molecular weight.

The functional value of refined ingredients (i.e. fat, sugar, but also milled wheat and maize flours, etc.) in food processing is due to the fact that they are uniform and easily specified, they are usually stable, their behaviour during the process is predictable, and the final product more uniform and controllable. Because a relatively small number of refined ingredients are used, they are mass produced and available cheaply to industry. Gordon (127) has outlined the steps in producing refined fat for the food processor. When extracted from plants, animals and fish, fats and oils are highly coloured and often unpleasant tasting. They are refined to pale yellow materials with bland flavour, and good chemical stability during food processing. The nutritional consequences of producing this refined fat include considerable loss of β-carotene and vitamin E, while toxicological consequences of fat modification can include synthesis of trans fatty acids (see 3.4.3). Other refined ingredients such as milled wheat and maize flours, white sugar, etc. are similarly stripped of much or all of the vitamins, minerals, and complex carbohydrates which accompanied them in nature.

3.4.4.2 Response of the food industry: Although some sectors will dispute the evidence on which the need for some of the dietary changes is based (104), the food industry can be expected to continue to help consumers meet dietary goals through improved formulation in two main ways: (a) developing "healthier" formulations of existing products (b) developing completely new formulation/product concepts. They could also help by being wholeheartedly involved in labelling and nutrition education programmes (39, 141). It is important to recognise at the outset, however, that dietary changes will only occur if consumers purchase and consume these new products. The weighting of health and nutrition factors in consumer choice of products has, and may continue to increase, but final choice is based on a number of factors of which appearance, flavour, convenience and value are also important (142). Thus, industry must produce improved formulations which are commercially successful; it must meet consumers' needs in the nutritional area without compromising excessively on meeting their other needs. However, there is already evidence of major market-led trends in "healthier" formulations, for example in <u>reduced-fat</u> sausages, milk, yoghurt and spreads; in <u>high-fibre</u> RTE cereals, breads and other products; in <u>low-sodium</u> soups, processed meats, canned vegetables and bakery goods; in <u>reduced calorie</u> entrees, soft drinks and beer; in <u>low-sugar</u> preserves and other products.

Some of these new products offer substantial opportunities for diet modification, notably low-fat milk and processed meats, high-fibre RTE cereals, and reduced calorie entrees. For example, by reducing the fat content of milk from 3.8% to 2.0% in the UK, the national consumption of fat would be cut by <u>7%</u> (the total required cut in fat intake is about 25%) (36). In 1985 low-fat milk, low-fat cheese and low-fat spreads accounted for 12%, 12% and 9% respectively of the total milk, cheese and spread markets in the UK (143).

It is difficult to predict developments in the area of completely new formulations and product concepts. However, as an example, formulations based on a new versatile ingredient, mycoprotein, may become important. This material is rich in fungal protein, contains dietary fibre, and has little fat or cholesterol. It is functionally useful to the food processor in that it has a bland taste, the capability to produce a range of textures and to absorb and retain flavour and colour. The mycoprotein manufacturers see it having applications in products with "healthier" formulations but also in the area of a completely new nutritionally-balanced range of products (144). A non-meat savoury "meat" pie based on mycoprotein is currently being successfully test-marketed in the UK by Sainsburys. A comparison between the composition of 100 g of the mycoprotein pie and 100 g of a conventional meat pie is as follows: 4 g versus 19 g fat, 14 g versus 19 g protein, 425 kJ versus 1010 kJ energy, 7 g versus 0 g dietary fibre , 0 versus 20 mg cholesterol. While this is an application in a conventional product, it shows the potential for nutritionally modified new concepts. Although soya protein has been unsuccessful in these types of application in the past, manufacturers may also look again at applications for fermented soyfoods such as tempeh, tofu and miso and developments along these lines are already apparent in the USA (145).

Another possible area of development is that of formulating products by the use of complementary food types. For example, processed meats are excellent sources of protein but may contain excess fat. By combining meats with plant foods (146), nutritionally valuable foods with low or medium fat levels may be attainable. Similarly, combinations of dairy fats and plant products may yield new products of more acceptable nutritional composition. Research along these lines has in fact been funded by the EEC Co-Responsibility Levy Fund (DG VI). Projects already completed have involved the development of novel products using combinations of dairy and fruit ingredients (147) and the use of milk constituents in confectionery and bakery products (148). Funding of further work on combining dairy and meat ingredients with plant foods could both facilitate the use of commodities in surplus, and contribute to improved consumer nutrition.

3.4.4.3 Limitations to change: There are some technical and organoleptic limitations to how far industry can go. These relate mostly to (a) product identity (b) acceptability (c) processability and storeability. Some foods are what they are because of their composition/formulation. The fat levels in cream, ice cream, whole milk, different cheeses, shortbread, etc. and the sugar levels in confectionery can be an inevitable part of their identity (136). In some cases deviations from these formulations are impossible while in others legal definitions may be a barrier to change.

"Healthier" formulations and new formulations can affect organoleptic qualities and reduce acceptability to consumers. The multifaceted role of fats in texture and flavour probably presents the most difficult problems. For example, evidence of consumer resistance to low-fat and skim milk is apparent in industry's efforts to compensate for loss in mouthfeel and body by adding extra milk solids to some new products e.g. Sainsbury's Vitapint and Kerry Co Op's Hi and Lo milk. In the important area of processed meats there is consumer interest in low-fat sausages of good acceptability. Industry has responded in different ways (141), some substituting unsaturated fat for some of the fat content, but most reducing fat levels. Fat level can be reduced in sausages by increasing the lean meat content or by replacing some of the fat with rusk, and perhaps by greater use of connective tissue. In general, sausages with high levels of lean meat produce a rubbery textured matrix on cooking (149). Substituting rusk can also result in problems of acceptablity, though specially formulated rusk products such as "Lean Fat Filler" from Lucas (UK) are claimed to give acceptable results (141). In general, sausages with a range of different characteristics appear to be acceptable to groups of consumers. For example, sausages with 15% fat (regular level 30-35%) have been successfully marketed in Ireland (150).

In the case of salt intake reduction, gravies, soups, and soup mixes have traditionally contained high salt levels and consumers expect this salty taste as part of the flavour profile. According to Nolan (151) the objective must be to change the sodium level, not the flavour. National Starch and Chemical Corp. have developed a low-sodium soup formulation containing 28 mg sodium per serving, well below the 35 mg limit in the FDA's proposed guidelines for low-sodium labelling. Because straight substitution of sodium chloride with potassium chloride is not feasible due to a bitter after-taste, the formulation was achieved using some potassium chloride in combination with other unspecified ingredients. The formulation was tailor-made for different soup types because other ingredients can affect the salt taste produced. Although National Starch have made palatable soups with very low sodium levels, they have very different flavour profiles to those of traditional soups, and analysts (in the USA at least) believe that this would not be organoleptically acceptable. Therefore, levels of 28 mg of sodium per soup serving may represent the limits of acceptability of low-sodium soups, at least in the short-term. In bread, particularly wholemeal bread, there seems to be scope for sodium reduction without much loss of acceptability. According to Chamberlain (152) tests in the UK indicated that reduction of salt level in wholemeal bread (typically 2.1%) by 25% was barely noticeable. However, a 12.5% drop was just distinguishable in white bread. Low-sodium cheeses have been marketed in the US but have been found unacceptable by consumers because of their bland atypical flavour (140).

The need to maintain adequate levels of fat, sugar or salt to enable current processing and storage procedures to be carried out may become a significant technical barrier to formulation modification in some products. For example, in cheese manufacture adequate salt is essential for the growth of the correct organisms, to expel moisture, and for the development of characteristic body, texture, and flavour (140). In breads and bakery products salt is important in fermentation control, gluten strength, water control, colour development and as a preservative (139). In processed meats salt serves as a seasoning, enhances water retention, texture and colour, dissolves proteins for producing emulsions, and acts as a preservative. This latter function is particularly important with limits on the use of nitrites (153). As mentioned earlier, reducing salt level in cheeses has resulted in acceptability problems, but some processors claim that they can reformulate baked and cured goods to reduce sodium by 50% without loss of processability (153).

Replacement of sugar by non-nutritive sweeteners will affect a range of processing characteristics including development of colour and flavours due to caramelisation and Maillard reactions (154). In the case of storage, Aw control by the use of sugar and salt is essential for shelf-life of fruit preserves and processed meats. The minimum percent soluble solids level (mostly due to sucrose in the formulation) required to prevent microbial spoilage in fruit preserves is generally regarded to be 65% (137, 155, 156). Although low-sugar formulations have been developed, they require the addition of a preservative or to be stored in a refrigerator after opening.

3.4.4.4 Fast foods: The fast service food industry is large and growing rapidly in developed countries worldwide; in the USA it was worth 44.8 billion dollars in 1985, having increased in size by 400% since the mid-seventies (157). According to Shannon and Parks (158), the nutritional implications of fast foods for consumers depend mainly on (a) their composition (b) the extent to which fast foods are consumed and (c) the specific selections made from menus.

In general, fast foods contain excessive levels of calories, fat, and sodium, and insufficient levels of dietary fibre, calcium and vitamin A. Levels of protein are generally high, some B vitamins are present in adequate amounts, while vitamin C levels depend on the menu items (particularly salads) selected (157, 158). Fast foods, however, can readily be accommodated in a varied healthy diet, when appropriate selections are made for other meals. They only present a nutritional hazard when they are used excessively or when they are consumed by individuals who must restrict their fat, cholesterol, or sodium intakes (157). A number of surveys in the USA and UK (158, 159) have shown that most consumers of fast foods consume them no more than 1-3 times per week, a use level which is not a cause for concern. However, some aspects of trends in consumption patterns are less reassuring - a minority consume far more fast food meals than this 1-3 average figure, and some school and college catering is tending towards greater dependence on fast food-type menus (158).

It appears that fast service food will become an increasing part of the European diet in the years ahead. There are at least two important ways in which their nutritional impact can be improved. The variety of menu items available should be increased by making available more salad items including fruits and fruit juices, low-fat milk drinks, and more chicken, fish, and potato dishes in forms other than fried (157). Secondly, consumers should be facilitated in making nutritionally informed fast food selections. This can be assisted by provision of nutritional information on fast food items to the population generally, but particularly by displaying this information in fast food outlets. Fast food promotions, especially those aimed at children should feature nutritionally balanced meals by replacing, for example, soft drinks with milk based drinks and by including salad items in these promotions (157).

3.4.4.5 Future developments: The food industry can make a contribution to good nutrition by providing the consumer with a choice of modified/"healthier" foods which better meet nutritional guidelines than conventional products. Although important developments in formulation have occurred, significant problems remain to be solved. A fundamental one is that of consumer acceptability of existing and future new products. Perhaps a major research programme aimed at investigating and imitating some of the functional properties of important ingredients such as fat in foods should be undertaken. This could provide useful support for industry research and development on "healthier" modifications and novel products. Novel ingredients such as the new modified starch produced by Laing National, " N-OIL", which simulates the mouthfeel of fat may become important. After acceptability, research to solve problems in processing and during shelf-life introduced by formulation modifications may also be appropriate. Other barriers to new product development include legal definitions of some products such as cream, ice-cream etc. Community subsidies on production and disposal of dairy fats may be inhibiting some development in the low-fat product area. Government/Community action in the areas of labelling, information, and education can be an important element in the changeover to products with "healthier" formulations. In addition, opportunities for co-operation between industry and health educators in the area of improved formulations should not be ignored.

In the future, the EEC can be expected to be further involved in research and administrative activities relating to the nutritive value and safety of processed foods. It will become necessary to ensure a high degree of co-ordination between the activities of the different Directorates General (DsG) responsible for this field. Areas worth considering for Community action include consumer education on nutritional aspects of processed foods, a unified approach to nutritional labelling and 'sell by' dating, action to ensure that good manufacturing practices are carried out during processing and storage, and evaluation of the nutritional implications of new food processes. As discussed previously, the existing SCAR Agro-Food Programme (DG Vl) deals with the effects of agricultural production on the composition and quality of fresh foods and some foods for further processing. The COST 91/COST 91 bis Programme (DG 111) deals more specifically with the effects of processing on the nutritional value and quality of foods. These research activities should be fully co-ordinated with administrative and research activity in the fields of human nutrition and toxicology.

3.4.5   Food Additives

Food additives are a diverse group of substances added to food to achieve a range of technological and organoleptic objectives. They are important tools in food processing and their use has been steadily rising; in the UK it is currently estimated to be 200,000 tonnes, worth £235 M per annum (160). A number of classification systems have been proposed for food additives. Within the EEC it is proposed that there should be 23 categories of food additives and the proposal recognises that few have a unique function. Some have proposed the following classification (e.g. 160, 161, and others):

(a) Preservatives and antioxidants. Preservatives are used to prevent or retard microbial growth; they include sulphur dioxide and sulphites, sodium nitrite and nitrate; acetic, propionic, sorbic, and benzoic acids, and some of their salts.

Antioxidants are used to inhibit oxidation of unsaturated fat, to reduce enzymatic and non-enzymatic browning, etc. They include ascorbic acid, the gallates, butylated hydroxyanisole (BHA) butylated hydroxytoluene (BHT). Sulphur dioxide and sulphites have secondary roles as antioxidants.

(b) Colouring and flavouring agents. The majority of colouring agents are synthetic and include the azo dyes (tartrazine, amaranth, orange yellow S, etc.). Natural colours include caramel, cochineal, annatto, chlorophyll, anthocyanins, betacyanins, and carotenoids. Compared with synthetic colours, natural colours have less stability in processing and storage, can be more variable in composition, and do not cover the full range of colours required by industry. In the EEC, 20 colours are currently permitted.

Flavouring agents are either natural or chemically synthesised. Synthetic flavours can be nature identical or consist of chemicals unknown in nature. Flavour boosters are mixtures of natural and synthetic flavours. Flavour enhancers include sodium glutamate, and inosinic acid salts. Added sweeteners are either natural sugars or artificial sweeteners such as saccharine. The major acidulant is citric acid and its salts.

(c)   Texture modifiers (emulsifiers, stabilisers, thickeners and gelling agents):   Emulsifiers and stabilisers are used mostly to stabilise oil and water emulsions but also affect other aspects of texture. They include lecithins, monoglycerides, diglycerides, stearoyl-2-lactates, phosphates and pyrophosphates. Thickeners and gelling agents include carbohydrates and modified carbohydrates (starches, celluloses, pectins, etc.), extracts of plants and seaweeds (carob gum, guar gum, alginates, carrageenans, etc.) and compounds produced by fermentation (xanthan gum).

(d)   Processing aids. These compounds facilitate food manufacture; they are not considered to be food additives by the EEC but they are added to foods or contaminate food in small amounts by contact. They include enzymes (e.g. pectolytic enzymes) clarifying agents (bentonite, clays, gelatin, etc.) and a range of miscellaneous agents for bleaching, acidifying, neutralising, and moulding (release agents); agents to prevent caking, foaming, etc.

3.4.5.1   Regulatory aspects: Besides the general requirements for not adding harmful substances to foods, many non-nutritive food additives are specifically regulated. In the EEC, regulation of food additives involves listing the substances which may be added to foods, in some cases specifying the foods in which they can be used and/or maximum levels of use. There are EEC Directives harmonising permitted lists between Member States and work has commenced on a comprehensive Directive on food additives. Regulated additives must satisfy regulating authorities of their technical justification, their chemical purity, and their toxicological safety (161). Some additives in use before toxicological testing was required (mid 1950s) and which appear safe, have not been subjected to detailed toxicological evaluation (162). Flavourings have generally not been subjected to regulation and the EEC is working on a separate Directive to cover flavourings. National regulating authorities draw on advice from the EEC Scientific Committee for Food and the Joint FAO/WHO Expert Committee on Food Additives to supplement that from national experts on aspects of safety, acceptable daily intakes, and related issues.

3.4.5.2   Benefits and risks: In recent years it has been regularly claimed (e.g. Millstone, 163) that industry derives most benefit from the use of food additives, while most of the risks are borne by consumers. It is clear that industry does benefit from the use of food additives. For example, some processes (e.g. curing) and products (e.g. many snack foods) depend heavily on the use of food additives; considerable value is added to processed foods through the use of added colours and flavourings; and major cost savings are made by replacing "real" ingredients with synthetic substitutes. The proponents of this viewpoint argue that the only clear benefits of additive use which apply to consumers relate to reduced microbial contamination and growth as a result of the use of preservatives, and that other benefits (particularly organoleptic improvements) do not apply as they cannot be described as risk-free. However, this perspective seems to ignore the really substantial nutritional (but also organoleptic) benefits derived from the availability and low price of a wide range of very palatable processed foods. On balance, the consumer does substantially share in the benefits of food additive use.

The possible risks to consumers from food additives can be divided into acute and chronic hazards. No additive causes obvious severe acute toxicity in most consumers, but a minority susceptible to allergy reactions can suffer severely from the acute effects of allergenic additives such as tartrazine and other azo dyes (161, 163). Allergy symptoms include asthma, urticaria, eczema and migraine. The EEC Scientific Committee for Food estimate the percent of susceptible consumers to be in the range of 0.03 - 0.15%, however some workers (163) expect this estimate to be revised upwards. Hyperactivity in children is a serious acute problem which has now been linked to food additives (as well as to other food components) in carefully controlled experiments (164).

The risks from chronic injestion of additives are unknown in absolute terms. Absolute safety even of authorised food additives cannot be assured because of the limitations of animal experiments for predicting chronic effects in man, although animal testing protocols remain very useful tools for detecting whether the use of particular chemicals could involve hazard. In fact, it is often argued that the results of animal testing are interpreted with an excess of prudence, using safety factors which can cause safe chemicals to be rejected in a high percentage of cases (165). More important perhaps than the limitations of animal experiments, is the lack of information on possible chronic "cocktail effects" i.e. effects due to interactions between food additives themselves or between food additives and other chemicals foreign to man (natural toxicants, pesticide residues, contaminants, medication, etc.) (161).

The issue of risk from some specific additives such as tartrazine and the azo dyes, saccharine, and nitrates/nitrites continues to be the subject of controversy. Permission for their continued use is based on the balance of risks and benefits, and on the availability of alternatives. For example, in 1971 problems were discovered in relation to nitrate/nitrite use in bacon curing. Volatile nitrosamines, which are potent carcinogens formed when nitrite reacts with secondary amines, were detected in fried bacon (166). Since then, nitrite levels have been reduced and other reformulation steps carried out, so that growth of C. botulinum is inhibited in bacon and related products, with minimal risk of nitrosamine production during cooking. Levels of volatile nitrosamines in fried bacon in the USA are now < 10 ppb (167).

3.4.5.3   Assessment and future developments: The use of food additives cannot be made absolutely safe- there are known acute and possible chronic risks associated with their use. Is it feasible to reduce these risks? Among the issues worth scrutiny are the technical justification for the use of some additives, the control of additives found to cause allergy reactions in sensitive persons, and the regulation of controversial additives. The food industry is required to provide a technical justification for the use of each additive. Some additives from each of the categories outlined above are clearly essential for the efficient operation of a modern food industry. However, the justification for the use of certain types of additives (e.g. some preservatives) is greater than for others (161). Within the large group of additive applications for improvement of organoleptic and aesthetic qualities in foods, many may be used largely for sales appeal and to add value to low-cost inputs, and are less easily justified. Consumer concern in this area could be addressed by broadening their representation on bodies adjudicating on technical justification requests, so that a substantial, technically informed consumer perspective could be brought to bear on decisions. If this resulted in reductions in the number of additives used, or in the levels and range of products in which they were used, it would be a positive (but perhaps non-significant) move towards risk reduction.

In the case of additives known to be allergenic, it appears necessary to either provide the consumer with clear information on the food label, or to remove these additives from use. The use of labelling in this context is an imperfect solution since the consumer may not read the label or may not be aware of his sensitivity (163).

The regulation of controversial food additives raises complex issues. Where the balance of benefit is shared by industry and the consumer (as is arguably the case in the use of nitrite in processed meats) current review processes appear adequate. However, the involvement of consumers' representatives in the manner already suggested may increasingly be necessary to establish more objectively the degree of benefit derived by the consumer.

Current and future trends suggest that additive use will continue to be important in the food industry and that their use will expand in some sectors such as in snack foods, in some novel foods, in complex foods, etc. and as the patterns of trade change and develop (168). At the same time, consumer concerns about food additives have been transmitted to industry, particularly through the involvement of supermarket chains in product development (169). Purchasing managers are increasingly demanding information on the technical justification of additives, and modifications of many products are being marketed with minimal or no food additives. The food additive industry is also responding, for example with research and development efforts to produce natural colours to replace the azo dyes (168). New technologies such as HTST processing (see 3.4.2.3) minimise damage to colour and flavour of foods and should facilitate reduced use of colours and other additives. The expanding chilled food sector is greatly improving the availability of semi-processed products which contain minimal levels of food additives. Thus, the consumer will increasingly be faced with choices between conventional foods and foods with reduced additive contents or without additives. This trend towards freedom of choice may be an important one in helping to meet consumers' concerns. Consideration should be given to consumer education about additive-free foods to help dispel the uncertainty generated by unfamiliar colours and flavours (170).

Considerably more research is needed on the "cocktail effect" i.e. on possible risks from interactions among additives or between additives and other chemicals foreign to the body. In the longer term, it would be prudent to encourage the food industry to use its resources of innovation and development to modify processing and distribution methods in ways which minimise food additive use.

3.5 REFERENCES

1. Miller, S.A., 1985. Food safety and health: a scientific and legislative perspective. Presented 13th Int. Cong. Nut. Brighton, UK (not published in proceedings).

2. Curtis, R.F. 1986. Diet as a source of natural toxicants. Proc. 13th Int. Cong. Nut: 822-826.

3. Tait, E.J., 1983. Pest control decision making on brassica crops. Adv. Appl. Biol. 8: 121-188.

4. Tait, E.J. and Russell, F.J., 1985. Response to MAFF consultative document: "Implementing part 3 of the food and environment protection act, 1985". Technology Group, Open University, Milton Keynes, UK.

5. National Academy of Sciences, 1980. The effects on human health of subtherapeutic use of antimicrobials in animal feeds. NAS, Washington, 376 pp.

6. Schaffner, R.M., Burke, J.A. and Fazio, T., 1984. Food additives and contaminants. Proc. 6th Int. Cong. Fd. Sci. Technol. 4: 271-282.

7. American Council on Science and Health, 1985a. Does nature know best? Natural carcinogens in American food. ACSH, New York, 33 pp.

8. Ames, B.N. 1983. Dietary carcinogens and anticarcinogens. Science 221: 1256-1264.

9. American Council on Science and Health, 1984. Of mice and men: the benefits and limitations of animal cancer tests. ACSH, New York, 22 pp.

10. MAFF, 1984. Memorandum on the testing of novel foods. Ministry of Agriculture, Fisheries and Food/Dept. of Health and Social Security, UK, 18 pp.

11. Gray, J., 1985. How safe is your diet: general review. Chemy Ind. (Mar 4): 146-148.

12. Wodicka, V.O. (1971): Remarks before the national agricultural outlooks conference sponsored by the USDA Feb. 23, Food Chemical News, 1st March: 130-2.

13. Hall, R.L., 1971. Information, confidence and sanity in the food sciences. Opening address IFT annual meeting New York, reprinted in Flav. Ind. (Aug): 455-459.

14. Ministry of National Health and Welfare, Canada, 1980. Food additives: what do you think? Report on opinion survey conducted in summer 1979, 57 pp.

15. Crawford, D., Worsley, A. and Peters, M., 1984. Is food a health
     hazard? Australians' beliefs about the quality of food.
     Fd. Technol. in Aust. 36 (9) 414-417.

16. Murcott, A. 1984. Developmental research for the Health Education
     Council guide to healthy eating. HEC, London.

17. Allen, Brady and Marsh, 1985. Healthy eating: a red herring? A study of
     the impact of healthy eating on the food and drink markets. Allen
     Brady and Marsh, London, 58pp.

18. Douglas, G., 1985. Balanced diet: the cognitive cop-out. Paper
     presented (on behalf of Presight Ltd) at KMS Seminar: "Marketing
     Nutrition", London.

19. British Nutrition Foundation, 1985. Eating in the early 1980s.
     Attitudes and behaviour: main findings. (survey by MRBI), The
     British Nutrition Foundation, London, 73 pp.

20. Fallows, S., and Godsen, H., 1985. Does the consumer really care.
     Food Policy Research, University of Bradford, UK, 59 pp.

21. Titlebaum, L.F., Dubin, E.Z., and Doyle, M., 1983. Will consumers
     accept irradiated foods? J. Food Safety 5: 219-228.

22. World Health Organisation, 1981. Wholesomeness of irradiated foods,
     WHO, Geneva, 34 pp.

23. London Food Commission, 1985. Irradiation: government to drop ban?
     London Food News 2: 2.

24. Bruhn, C.M., Schutz, H.G. and Sommer, R. 1986. Attitude change
     toward food irradiation among conventional and alternative
     consumers. Food Technol. 40: 86-91.

25. Anon., 1985. Good enough to eat? New Health, June: 28-31.

26. Anon., 1984. Axe farm antibiotics. Inform (Feb) p. 5.

27. BEUC, 1981. Black file on hormones and antibiotics. BEUC,
     Brussels, 101 pp.

28. OECD, 1984. Issues and challenges for OECD agriculture in the 1980s.
     OECD, Paris, 159 pp.

29. Cunningham, E.P. 1984. Agriculture, raw materials and the Irish
     context. Proc. Biotechnology '84 : 3-21 (J.P. Arbutnott, Ed.),
     RIA, Dublin.

30. Harrington, G., 1984. Production factors influencing the quality of
     beef and lamb. Proc. 6th Int. Cong Fd Sci. Technol., 5:
     49-59.

31. Naudé, R.T., 1984. Pork production and the quality of meat. Proc
     6th Int. Cong. Fd. Sci. Technol., 5: 33-48.

32. Gormley, T.R., 1984. Quality of intensively produced crops. <u>Proc 6th Int. Cong. Fd. Sci. Technol</u>., <u>5</u>: 111-132.

33. Gormley, T.R., Sharples, R.O. and Dehandtschutter, J. 1985. The effects of modern production methods on the quality of tomatoes and apples. EEC, Luxembourg, 176 pp.

34. Jul, M. and Zeuthen, P. 1981. Quality of pig meat for fresh consumption; report to the Commission of European Communities, <u>Prog. Food Nut. Sci</u>. <u>4</u>: 6, 133 pp.

35. Jul, M. and Rankin, M. (Eds.) 1986. The quality of poultry meat: effects of agricultural practices. Report of an EEC collaborative research project. CEC Brussels, 108 pp.

36. Robbins, C.J., 1978. Food, health and farming: reports of panels on the implications for UK agriculture. Centre for Agric. Strategy, Reading, UK, 119 pp.

37. Bielig, H.J., 1980. The nutritional implications of the development of agricultural techniques, food processing, and distribution methods. <u>Symp. on Nut., Fd. Technol. and Nut. Inform</u>., London 1980: 71-78. CEC, Brussels.

38. Hughes, J.C., 1983. Potato production and processing. <u>Chemy. Ind</u>. (Aug): 598-603.

39. Fallows, S.J., 1985. Implementing dietary guidelines: a task for all involved in food supply. <u>J. Consum. Studies and Home Ec</u>. <u>9</u>: 101-112.

40. McCarthy, J.C., 1984. The nature of genetic improvement in the efficiency of meat and milk production. <u>Proc. 6th Int. Cong. Fd. Sci. Technol</u>., <u>5</u>: 23-32.

41. Kempster, A.J., Cook, G.L. and Southgate, J.R., 1982. A comparison of different breeds and crosses from the suckler herd. 2. Carcass characteristics. <u>Animal Prod</u>. <u>35</u>: 99-111.

42. Wood, J.D., 1984. Encouraging the production of leaner meat. <u>Res. Dev. in Agric. 1</u> (3): 129-140 (abstract).

43. Wood, J.D. and Fisher, A.V., 1983. Effects of growth promoters on body composition in steers and bulls. <u>Proc. 34th Ann. Mting. Eur. Assoc. An. Prodn</u>. <u>2</u>: 500.

44. Ford, A.L., Harris, P.V., MacFarlane, J.J., Park, R.J., and Shorthose, W.R. 1974. Effect of a protected lipid supplement on organoleptic and other properties of bovine muscle. CSIRO Meat Research Report No. 2/74.

45. Baker, P.K., Dalrymple, R.H. Ingle, D.L., Ricks, C.A. 1984. Use of a β-adrenergic agonist to alter muscle and fat deposition in lambs. <u>J. Animal Sci</u>. <u>59</u>: 1256-1261.

46. Smith, G.C. and Carpenter, Z.L., 1976. Eating quality of meat
     animal products and their fat content. Proc. Symp. Fat Content
     and Composition of Animal Products. Nat. Acad. Sciences,
     Washington: 147-182.

47. Liboriussen, T., Bech Andersen, B., Buchter, L., Kousgaard, K. and
     Moller, A.J., 1977: Crossbreeding experiment with beef and dual-
     purpose breeds on Danish dairy cows IV. Physical, chemical and
     paletability characteristics of longissimus dorsi and semitendinosus
     muscles from crossbred young bulls. Livest. Prod. Sci. 4:
     31-43.

48. Moore, V.J. and Bass, J.J., 1978. Palatability of cross-bred beef.
     J. Agr. Sci. 90: 93-5.

49. Mapson, L.W., 1970. Vitamins in fruits, Chap. 13. In "The
     Biochemistry of Fruits and their Products", Vol. 2. (A.C. Hulme
     Ed.): 369-384. Academic Press, London and New York.

50. Pushman, F.M. and Bingham, J., 1976. The effects of granular
     nitrogen fertilizer and a foliar spray of urea on the yield and
     bread-making quality of ten winter wheats. J. Agr. Sci. 87:
     281-292.

51. Stewart, B.A., 1977. The effects of fertiliser and other
     agricultural inputs on quality criteria of wheat needed for milling
     and baking. In "Fertiliser Use and Production of Carbohydrates
     and Lipids" p. 243.

52. Peck, N.H. and Van Buren, J.P. 1975. Plant response to concentrated
     superphosphate and potassium chloride fertilisers. 5. Snap beans.
     Search 5 (2): 1-32

53. Gormley, T.R., 1980. Quality and nutritive value of horticultural
     food crops as influenced by growing medium and methods of husbandry.
     In "Agricultural Practices and Food Quality" Sem. Proc. 29-34,
     RIA, Dublin.

54. Koslowska, A., 1976. Effect of herbicides on yield, vitamin content
     and germination capacity of beans. Howdowla Roslin, Aklimatyzacja i
     Nasinmictwo 20: 517-534.

55. Engst, R., Noske, R. and Voigt, J., 1969. The effects of pesticide
     and insecticide residues on certain constituents of fruits and
     vegetables. 1. Influence on apples and strawberries, Nahrung 13:
     249-255.

56. Decallonne, J.R. and Meyer, J.A. 1985. A survey of a three years
     study on the effects of agrochemicals on the quality and composition
     of tomatoes. In "The Effects of Modern Production Methods on the
     Quality of Tomatoes and Apples" (Gormley et al. Eds): 5-18, EEC,
     Luxembourg.

57. Schuphan, W., 1974. Nutritional value of crops as influenced by
     organic and inorganic fertiliser treatments. Qualitas Plant. 23:
     333-358.

58.   Barker, A.V., 1975. Organic vs inorganic nutrition and horticultural crop quality. Hort. sci. 10: 50-53.

59.   Finglas, P.M. and Faulks, R.M., 1984. Nutritional composition of UK retail potatoes both raw and cooked. J. Sci. Food Agric. 35: 1347-1356.

60.   Hagen, R.E. and Schweigert, B.S., 1983. Nutrient contents of table-ready foods: cooked, processed and stored. Comtemp. Nut. 8: No. 2. General Mills, Minneapolis, 3 pp.

61.   Heinze, P.H. 1973. Effects of storage, transportation, and marketing conditions on the composition and nutritional values of fresh fruits and vegetables. USDA Eastern Res. Lab. Publ. 3786: 29-34.

62.   Neisheim, M.C., 1985. Personal Communication on workshops held Cornell University re co-operative agreement with Agricultural Research Service, USDA.

63.   Swaminathan, M.S., 1984. DNA in medicine: agricultural production. Lancet: 1329-1332.

64.   Davies, A.M.C. and Blincow, P.J. 1984. Glycoalkaloid content of potatoes and potato products sold in the UK. J. Sci. Food Agric. 35: 553-557.

65.   Watson, D.H., 1985. Natural toxicants. Chemy. Ind. (4 Mar): 153-155.

66.   Maga, J.J., (1980): Potato glycoalkaloids. CRC Crit. Rev. Food Sci. Nutr., 12: 371-405.

67.   Chevion, M., Mager, J. and Glaser, G. (1983). Naturally occurring food toxicants, favism-producing agents. In "Handbook of Naturally Occurring Food Toxicants". (M. Rechcigl Jr. Ed.), 63-69. CRC Press, Florida.

68.   British Agrochemicals Association, 1985. Annual Report and Handbook 1984-1985, British Agrochemicals Association, London, 36 pp.

69.   Lisk, D.J., 1970. Pesticides: benefits problems and future. N.Y. State J. Med. 70(11): 1306-1313.

70.   British Agrochemicals Association, 1977. Pesticides in agriculture. British Agrochemicals Association, London, 25 pp.

71.   British Agrochemicals Association, 1982. The fight for food. British Agrochemicals Association, London, 16 pp.

72.   Consumers' Association, 1980. Pesticide residues and food. Consumers' Association, London, 115 pp.

73.   Hatfull, L.S., 1981. Survey of pesticide residues in food-stuffs, 1981. A report on behalf of the association of public analysts. J. Assoc. Publ. Analysts. 21: 19-24.

74. Reed, D.V., 1985. The FDA surveillance index for pesticides: establishing food monitoring priorities based on potential health risk. J. Asoc. Off. Anal. Chem. 68 (1): 122-124.

75. Keane, M.G., 1983. Evaluating compudose 365 - a new growth promoter for beef cattle, Farm and Food Research 14 (2): 61-63.

76. Wright, R., 1986. EEC bans 'safe' animal hormones. New Scientist 109: (1489): 9.

77. O'Driscoll, K.M., 1984. The use of hormonal growth promoters in animal production - the present situation. Consumers' Association of Ireland, 32 pp.

78. EEC, 1984. Report of the scientific veterinary committee, the scientific committee on animal nutrition and the scientific committee for food on the basis of the report of the scientific group on anabolic agents in animal production. EEC Publications, Luxembourg, 31 pp.

79. World Health Organisation, 1982. Health aspects of residues of anabolics in meat: Report of a WHO working group (Bilthoven, 1981), WHO, Copenhagen, 36 pp.

80. Metzler, M. 1982. Residues of anabolics in meat: risks for consumers. Annex 2 In "Health Aspects of Residues of Anabolics in Meat" p. 28-35. WHO, Copenhagen.

81. Anon., 1985. Hormones in beef production. Inform (January): 6-7.

82. O'Toole, F., 1983. Antibiotics in your food. Technol. Ireland (Jan): 33-36.

83. Anderson, E.S. 1968. Drug resistance in Salmonella typhimurium and its implications. Brit. med. J. 3: 333-339.

84. Friend, B.A. and Shahani, K.M., 1983. Antibiotics in foods. In "Xenobiotics in Foods and Feeds": 47-61. American Chemical Society Symposium Series.

85. American Council on Science and Health, 1985. Antibiotics in animal feed: a threat to human health? ACSH, New York, 27 pp.

86. Anon., 1984. Antibiotics: the present health and legislation situation in Ireland. Consumers' Association of Ireland, 15 pp.

87. Mol, H., 1975. Antibiotics in milk. A.A. Balkema, Rotterdam.

88. Jollans, J.L. 1985. Fertilizers in UK farming. Centre for Agricultural Strategy Report 9. Reading, UK, 215 pp.

89. Forman, D., Al-Dabbagh, S. and Doll, R. 1985. Nitrates, nitrites and gastric cancer in Great Britain. Nature 313: 620-625.

90. Craddock, V.M. 1983. Nitrosamines and human cancer: proof of an association? Nature 306: 638.

294

91. Lee, C-Y., Stoewsand, G.S. and Downing, D.L. 1972. Nitrate problems in foods N.Y. Food and Life Sci. 5: 8.

92. Catliffe, D.J. and Phatak, S.C. 1974. Nitrate accumulation in greenhouse vegetable crops. Can. J. Plant Sci. 54: 783-788.

93. Miyasaki, M., Kunisato, S. and Miya, S. 1972. Accumulation of nitrate in horticultural products. VII and VIII. Effects of nitrogen fertilizer on the accumulation of nitrate in tomato fruits. J. Food Sci. Technol. (Japan) 19: 16.

94. Blom-Zandra, M. and Lampe, J.E.M. 1985. The role of nitrate in the osmoregulation of lettuce (Lactuca sativa L.) grown at different light intensities. J. Expt. Bot. 36 1043-1052.

95. Blom-Zandra, M. and Lampe, J.E.M. 1983. The effect of chloride and sulphate salts on the nitrate content of lettuce plants (Lactuca Sativa L.). J. Plant. Nut. 6: 611-628.

96. EEC, 1980. Council directive on the quality of water for human consumption. Official Journal 23 No. 80/778 EEC L229.

97. Fennema, O.R., 1985. Overview. Ch 1. In "Role of Chemistry in the Quality of Processed Food" p. 1-21 (O.R. Fennema, W-H. Chang, C-Y. Lii Eds.). Food and Nutrition Press, Connecticut.

98. Fennema, O.R., 1986. Food processing and nutrition: an overview. Proc. 13th Int. Cong. Nut.: 762-766.

99. Bender, A.E., 1986. Effects of processing on vitamins. Proc. 13th Int. Cong. Nut.: 786-790.

100. Jul, M., 1985. The quality of frozen foods, p. 4. Academic Press, London.

101. Mauron, J., 1984. Interaction between food constituents during processing. Proc. 6th Int. Cong. Fd. Sci. Technol. 5: 301-322.

102. Harris, R.S. and Karmas, E., 1975. Nutritional Evaluation of Food Processing. AVI, Connecticut, 670 pp.

103. Dudek, J. et al, 1982. Investigations to determine nutrient content of selected fruits and vegetables: raw, processed, and prepared. Final Report, USDA Contract, Cited by Hagen and Schweigert, 1983.

104. Leveille, G.A., 1984. Industry's response to problems related to nutritive value of the U.S. diet. Proc. 6th Int. Cong Fd. Sci. Technol. 4: 315-318.

105. Johnson, R.L. and Toledo, R.T., 1975. Storage stability of 55 Brix orange juice concentrate aseptically packaged in plastic and glass containers. J. Food Sci. 40: 433 - 4.

106. Varsel, C., 1980. Citrus juice processing as related to quality and nutrition. In "Citrus Nutrition and Quality : A symposium" (Nagy, S. and Attaway, J.A. Eds): 225-271. American Chemical Society, Washington, DC.

107. Kramer, A. 1982. Effect of storage on nutritive value of food. In "Handbook of Nutritive Value of Processed Foods" (Rechcigl, M. Jr., Ed.): 275-299. CRC Press, Connecticut.

108. Cecil, S.R. and Woodroof, J.G. 1963. The stability of canned foods in long-term storage. Food Technol 17 (5): 131-138.

109. Wilkinson, V.M., 1985. Effect of irradiation on the nutrient composition of food. Sci. Tech. Survey, Leatherhead Food R.A., UK, 15 pp.

110. Downey, W.K. (Ed.) 1977. Food Quality and Nutrition-Research Priorities for Thermal Processing. Applied Science Publishers, London, 712 pp.

111. Zeuthen, P., Cheftel, J.C., Eriksson, C., Jul, M., Leniger, H., Linko, P., Varela, G. and Vos, G. (Eds.) 1984. Thermal Processing and Quality of Foods. Elsevier, London, 933 pp.

112. Jul, M., 1985. From minutes COST 91 bis Sub-Group 3 Chilling meeting at Leatherhead Food R.A. UK, May 20, 1985.

113. Bjorck, I. and Asp, N.G. 1983. The effects of extrusion cooking on nutritional value - a literature review. J. Food Eng. 2: 281-308.

114. Lund, D.B., 1984. Impact of industrial cooking of food on its nutritional and quality characteristics. In "Thermal Processing and Quality of Foods" (Zeuthen, P. et al. Eds.): 291-300. Elsevier Press, London and New York.

115. Fennema, O., 1984. Chemical changes in food during processing - an overview. Food Technol. 38 (3) 48.

116. Anderson, D. 1985. Genetic toxicology in the food industry. Food Chem. Toxicol. 23 (1): 11-18.

117. Mermelstein, N.H., 1978. Retort pouch earns 1978 IFT food industrial achievement award. Food Technol 32: 22-33.

118. Copley, D.I., 1978. The retort pouch - the way ahead with aluminium foil. IFFA (Jan/Feb): 28-29.

119. Carroad, P.A., Leonard, S.J., Heil, J.R., Wolcott, T.A. and Mersen, R.L., 1980. High vacuum flame sterilisation : process concept and energy use analysis. J. Food Sci. 45 696-699.

120. Goddard, R., 1985. Update on aseptic technology. Food Manuf. Int. (July/Aug): 20, 21, 25.

121. Guise, B., 1985. Aseptics set to clean up the market. Food Proc. (July): 33-36.

122. Kivi, G., 1980. Why process fruits aseptically. <u>Cult. Dairy Prod.</u> <u>J.</u>: 24-26.

123. Wagner, J.N., 1984. Breaking the low-acid barrier. <u>Food Engin.</u> (Oct): 106, 109-110.

124. Burton, H. 1985. Thirty-five years on - a story of UHT research and development. <u>Chemy. Ind.</u> (Aug) : 546-553.

125. Darrington,H. 1985. Multitherm unveiled. <u>Food Manuf. Int.</u> (July/Aug): 22-23.

126. Pfaender, P., 1983. Lysinoalanine - a toxic compound in processed proteinaceous foods. <u>Wld. Rev. Nutr. Diet</u> 41: 97-109.

127. Gordon, M.H., 1986. Effects of processing on fats. <u>Proc. 13th</u> <u>Int. Cong. Nut.</u>: 775-780.

128. Chichester, C.O. and Lee, T-C, 1981. Effect of food processing in the formation and destruction of toxic constituents of food. Chap 5. In "Impact of Toxicology on Food Processing". (J.C. Ayers and J.C. Kirschman Eds.) p. 35-56. AVI, Connecticut.

129. Stich, H.F., Roisin, M.P., Wu, C.H. and Powrie, W.D., 1982. The use of mutagenicity testing to evaluate food products. In "Mutagenicity - New Horizons in Genetic Toxicology" (Heddle, J.A. Ed.): 117, Academic Press, New York.

130. Sugimura, T. and Sato, S., 1983. Mutagens-carcinogens in foods. <u>Cancer Research (suppl.)</u> 43: 2415s-2421s.

131. Barnes, W., Spingarn, N.E., Garvie-Gould, C., Vuolo, L.L., Wang, Y.Y. and Weisburger, J.H., 1983. Mutagens in cooked foods: possible consequences of the Maillard reaction. <u>American Chemical Soc.</u> <u>Sympos. Series</u> 215: 485-506.

132. Finley, J.W., 1983. Lysinoalanine formation in severely treated proteins. <u>American Chemical Soc. Symp. Series</u> 234: 203-220.

133. Anon., 1984. Trans fatty acids in foods. <u>Nutr. Rev.</u> 42 (8): 278-279.

134. Kinsella, J.E., Brucker, G., Mai, J. and Shimp, J., 1981. Metabolism of trans fatty acids with emphasis on the effects of trans-octadecadienoate on lipid composition, essential fatty acid, and prostaglandins: an overview. <u>Am. J. Clin. Nut.</u> 34: 2307-2318.

135. Hall, R.L., 1985. Personal Communication. McCormick and Co. Inc., Maryland.

136. Farrer, K.I.H., 1983. Effects of the dietary guidelines on the food industry. <u>Food Technol. in Aust.</u> 35(11): 515-517.

137. Rauch, G.H., 1965. Jam Manufacture. Leonard Hill, London, 191 pp.

138. Shults, G.W., Russell, D.R., and Wierbicki, E., 1972. Effect of condensed phosphates on pH, swelling and water-holding capacity of beef. J. Food Sci. 37: 860-864.

139. Kroskey, C.M., 1985. Taste too sweet? Colour too pallid? add some salt! Bakery (March): 198.

140. Andres, C. and La Belle, F. 1982. Flavouring low-sodium foods. Food Proc. (Nov): 60.

141. Norris, R., 1985. Health, diet and the ingredients industry. Food (May) 41-42.

142. Wood, J.M., 1985. Product development In "Nutrition and Health" (abstracts of symposium): p. 9, Leatherhead Food R.A., November.

143. Anon., 1985. Boots adds its weight to low-fat sausage drive. Grocer (Feb. 23): 26.

144. Hemsley, J., 1985. Looks like beef ...... tastes like beef ...... comes from a fungus. Meat Ind. (March): 29-30.

145. Byrne, M. 1985. The future for soyfoods. Food Manuf. (March): 49-53.

146. Briedenstein, B.C. and Carpenter, Z.L., 1983. The red meat industry: product and consumerism (review). J. Animal Sci. 57: 119-132.

147. O'Beirne, D., McGlinchey-Kelly, G., Brennan, C. and Connors, B. 1983. Studies on products comprised of dairy powders mixed with fruit including dairy/jams and dairy/fruit frozen products. Final Report to CEC, Contract 2935/79 - 41.8, 89 pp.

148. Kelly, P.M., Mallottee, N., Dwyer, E. and Connors, B. 1985. Evaluation of milk constituents in confectionery/bakery products. Final Report to CEC, Contract 271/82 - 34.4, 113 pp.

149. Griffiths, T., 1986. Personal Communication. An Foras Talúntais, Dunsinea, Dublin.

150. Reid, S.N., 1986. Personal Communication. An Foras Talúntais, Dunsinea, Dublin.

151. Nolan, A.L., 1983. Low sodium soup. Food Eng (May): 70.

152. Chamberlain, N. 1984. Salt levels in bread made by CBP. Ann. Rept. FMBRA: 9.

153. Nolan, A.L., 1983. Low sodium foods: where are we headed? Food Eng. (May): 95-104.

154. Shallenberger, R.S. and Birch, G.G., 1975. Sugar Chemistry. AVI, Connecticut, 221 pp.

155. Anon., 1978. Genu Pectin, p. 37. The Copenhagen Pectin Factory Ltd.

156. Baird-Parker, A.C. and Kooiman, W.J., 1980. Soft drinks, fruit juices, concentrates and fruit preserves. In "Microbial Ecology of Foods, Vol. 2: Food Commodities": 642-668 International Commission on Microbial Specifications for Foods. Academic Press, London.

157. American Council on Science and Health, 1985. Fast food and the American diet. ACSH, New York, 29 pp.

158. Shannon, B.M. and Parks, S.C. 1980. Fast foods: a perspective on their nutritional impact. J. Am. Dietet. 76: 242-247.

159. Ryley, J. 1981. Nutritional aspects of fast foods. Chemy Ind. (18 July): 497-500.

160. Anon., 1975. Good enought to eat. Thames Television publication, London, 8 pp.

161. Anon., 1980. Food additives and the consumer. EEC, Brussels, 54 pp.

162. McQuillan, D. 1985. Additives anonymous. New Health (April): 30-35.

163. Millstone, E. 1985. Food additives: the balance of risks and benefits. Chemy. Ind. (Nov. 4): 730-733.

164. Egger, J., Graham, P.J., Carter, C.M., Gumley, D. and Soothill, J.F. 1985. Controlled trial of oligoantigenic treatment in the hyperkinetic syndrome. Lancet (March 9): 540-545.

165. Kirschman, J.C. 1983. Evaluating the safety of food additives. Food Technol. 37(3): 75-79.

166. Fazio, T., White, R.H. and Howard, J.W. 1971. Analysis of nitrite - and/or nitrate processed meats for N-nitrosodimethylamine. J. Assoc. Offic. Anal. Chem. 54: 1157-1159.

167. Havery, D.C. and Fazio, T. 1985. Human exposure to nitrosamines from foods. Food Technol. 39 (1): 80-83.

168. Miller, M. 1985. Danger! additives at work. A report on food additives - their use and control. London Food Commission, 172 pp.

169. Connolly, M. 1985. Healthy eating through the eyes of a retailer. Paper presented at KMS seminar "Marketing Nutrition", London.

170. Grose, D. 1982. The consumer viewpoint. Proc. Conf. "Food for thought", London. Cited by Miller (161).

CHAPTER 4

4.1   CONCLUSIONS   AND   RECOMMENDATIONS

This report is issued at a time when popular interest in diet and health is exceptionally high. Concern at the quality and safety of the food supply is widespread in Europe and consumer groups in certain countries view the policy instrument of the EEC in this area, i.e. the CAP, as a contributory factor, albeit indirectly, in the development of some of the so-called degenerative diseases. Although such reasoning may be simplistic, it is a fact that the influence of the CAP on food production lacks any balancing European policy instrument concerned with the quality and safety of the food supply in human nutrition terms. The establishment of such a parallel policy is seen as a major requirement by the authors. Its conception and implementation will undoubtedly provide a considerable challenge to the FAST team in DG Xll and also to policy makers and planners in the Commission.

Effective integration between the current, or a modified, CAP and a new downstream policy on food and health matters will require the spanning of different Directorates General (DsG) within the Commission. Unfortunately because of a range of constraints such collaboration between DsG happens too infrequently. However, we feel that there is no alternative if the food/health/consumer interrelationship is to be tackled realistically. Towards this end we suggest the formation of a small but elite committee, at DG director or deputy director level, spanning the DsG with responsibility for the implementation of food and health policies in all of the sectoral activities of the EEC such as food production, processing, health, consumer, and toxicology areas. Such a committee with the aid of a number of experts could discuss overall strategy in the food/health/consumer areas and could open the necessary administrative and budgetary doors required in order to get meaningful coordinated activity underway. In its early stage this could take the form of a modestly sized workshop (ca 100 experts) with the theme 'Food, Health and the Consumer - what policies does Europe require'. The recommendations in this report could form a base for part of this workshop but other key areas such as preventive medicine, microbiological food poisoning, food safety and toxicology, and others, would need to be included. Arising from this, coordinated activity could be extended to four or five interdisciplinary expert groups each containing a range of expertise but all including one or two experts on the formulation/implementation of policy. These activities could all take place within one year and could be considered as phase 1. The findings would then be discussed by the elite committee who could then initiate phase 2, i.e. the implementation of some of the policies.

The alternative to the above is to maintain the status quo; although one must consider if this is possible given the pressures that are mounting on the food system. The complexity of the food system has already been referred to in the general introduction and is such that an inter DG coordinated approach is necessary to ensure that the system meets all the demands that may be placed on it. Better informed consumers will increasingly demand safer, higher quality and more varied foods with good nutritive value and this will put increased strain on agricultural production and food processing systems. The consumer lobby within the EEC is steadily gaining momentum and this in itself should facilitate the formation of the elite committee mentioned above. There is also the added incentive that food, health and consumer issues are becoming increasingly political and some politicians are already calling for action in this area.

The material noted and discussed in this report represents only a fraction of the issues which are contained within the bounds of the food system. Nevertheless many items of current importance have been highlighted and a list of recommendations/issues are outlined below. Dissemination and/or implementation of these is of paramount importance as forecasting and assessment is of little value unless it is used by administrators, policy makers and, last but not least, by politicians. The challenge to the FAST team therefore is in dissemination of the findings and in ensuring that they give rise to, and are used in, policy formulation.

The CONCLUSIONS and RECOMMENDATIONS listed below are largely self explanitory. However, some of them may need to be considered in association with the text in the report.

1. <u>Food, health and consumer issues</u> will continue to be a major challenge to all in the food production and food processing areas and also to policy makers well into the next century.

2. The <u>consumer lobby</u> in relation to food and health will grow in strength in Europe and will exert greater pressure on the food system. Consumers will increasingly demand nutritious, high quality, fresh and, in some cases, organically grown foods but also a wide range of convenience and processed foods both traditional and new - some tailored specially with health considerations in mind, e.g. low fat spreads. In order to precisely define the concerns of European consumers in relation to diet and health, a community-wide opinion poll should be conducted as soon as possible. Such a poll could provide information on the relative food concerns of Europeans or the difference in concern between population sub-groups.This should link-in with the structured debate (see 8 below) and permit an assessment of actual concern thus identifying probable limits to political action.

3.   The <u>CAP</u> has dominated the food production scene in Europe for some years and we recommend that a balancing integrated European downstream <u>policy</u> should be developed which will be concerned with the quality and safety of the food supply in human nutrition terms.

4.   Recognising the key importance of 1-3 above we propose the formation of a small but <u>elite committee</u> across Directorates General (DsG) (at Director or Deputy Director level) in the CEC with responsibility for food, health and consumer issues. The function of the committee would be to 'open administrative and budgetary doors' which would facilitate interdisciplinary coordination of some of the issues in 1-3 above and to expedite the preparation of draft policies which will be needed to deal with the challenge of the food, health and consumer issues in the next 20 years.

5.   We recognise that <u>microbiological food poisoning</u> is a major, and in many cases an increasing, public health problem in many developed countries.   This issue is not considered in this report and should be the subject of a separate study.

<u>CURRENT HUMAN NUTRITION THINKING</u> (CHNT)

6.   Health is influenced by lifestyle, environment and genetic factors. Diet is often singled out unfairly as the major cause of many health problems; however it must be put in context as it is only a component of lifestyle and an even smaller one of environment.   For example, in time research may show that <u>genetic factors</u> are the most important and we propose an EEC-wide <u>family.medical history study</u> with the express aim of obtaining greater information on the cause of morbidity and

mortality within and between families. This could be pursued via the health ministries in the different countries.

7. As a follow-on from (6) we recommend increased research into the genetic aspects of many diseases but especially in the lipoprotein, cholesterol fields in relation to atherosclerosis, thrombosis and CHD.

8. There is still disagreement, controversy, and even confusion, among experts concerning some of the key nutrition issues of today - for example recommended daily allowances for some nutrients, the cholesterol, fat and salt issues, the role of trace elements, the effects of mild overweight, the effects of dietary fibre - just to mention a few (see CHAPTERS 1 - 3). Arising from (4) above, the elite committee should expedite the formation of interdisciplinary groups where food production, food processing, medical and nutrition scientists could meet to reach greater consensus on some of these issues. Down-stream from this the CEC should encourage structured and informed public debate between scientists, industrialists, food producers and the general public using all available communications media.

9. While most of the nutrition related research being carried out by the 'primary producers' (i.e. researchers in nutrition, medicine, physiology, biochemistry) is well-founded and of a high standard, there are, however, some aspects of research procedure which are a cause for concern. These include:

a) extrapolation of results of animal experiments to humans

b) extrapolation of results from 'at risk' groups to whole populations

c) use of small numbers of human subjects in human nutrition studies

d) research often funded by vested interests

e) 'overuse'/abuse of epidemiology

Researchers therefore should be aware of these pitfalls.

10. Most statements on human nutrition issues emanate from expert groups.
However, their recommendations are not always well founded for a
number of reasons:

a) there may not be sufficient information available as an input to
allow a comprehensive output

b) an expert group may be influenced excessively by one or more of
its members who have strong views and imposing personalities

c) an expert group may be the organ of, or may be unduly influenced
by, a vested interest

11. Arising from (10) is the key issue of the number of times an expert
group meets.   In the past, major consensus statements/recommendations
have emanated from expert groups that met only once, i.e. for one or
two days with little opportunity for further dialogue and revision of
ideas.   We recommend therefore that such groups meet on a number of
occasions over a period of time.

SPECIFIC NUTRIENTS AND RELATED AREAS

12. We recommend further research on the antithrombotic effect of
fish oils and also on the effects of certain vegetables on platelet
function.

13. Recent suggestions that vitamins C and E influence CHD through their
role as free radical scavengers warrant continuing in-depth scientific
investigation.

14. <u>Regression of atherosclerosis</u> is a key issue in relation to the effect of diet on incidence of CHD. Rapid non-invasive techniques for measuring the regression of atherosclerosis are urgently needed in order to enable routine screening programmes to be established.

15. Recent evidence suggests that <u>sodium and calcium</u> may <u>interact/ synergise</u> in reducing blood pressure. Attempts to restrict sodium intake in populations and in mild hypertensives coupled with the desire to reduce fat intake (via dairy products) could reduce sodium and/or calcium levels to a level at which the interaction/synergism between them could not take place. This area needs thorough research. It is likely that dietary calcium may also influence osteoporosis; however, scientific evidence in this area is still conflicting.

16. <u>Weight control</u> for health and social reasons is a major aim for many people in developed countries. Continued research is essential on mechanisms of energy use/disposal in man via thermogenesis, exercise, so-called 'bad converting', and through other routes, with emphasis on genetic aspects.

17. Most nutrients come in fresh food in 'dilute' form. Yet man tends to extract them and use them in concentrated form. Good examples of this are the taking of macro doses of vitamin C and the drinking of fish oil in order to obtain a high dose of eicosapentaenoic acid. We suggest that these and other similar nutrients should be obtained mainly by consuming the foods that contain them.

DIETARY RECOMMENDATIONS, FOOD AND NUTRITION POLICY

18. The relative merits of promoting a <u>European consensus on dietary recommendations</u> should be explored; if such an EEC-wide approach is believed to have advantages, a carefully composed group representing all member states and bodies (producers, processors, consumers, medical etc.) should be assembled for a significant time-period before issuing any findings.

19. In the absence of such a step (18), the following broad <u>consensus statements</u> (based on expert groups) could define <u>nutrition policy</u> in member states.

   a) obesity (or overweight) is a predisposing factor in the development of many diseases and should be avoided

   b) since fat is a concentrated energy source and because a connection between fat intake and cancer and CHD appears likely total fat intake should be decreased and saturated fat should be partially replaced by polyunsaturated (PUFA, see 22 below). This in turn means produce less fat and/or find non food uses for fat.

   c) sugar (sucrose) is another concentrated source of energy which is a causative agent in the development of dental caries - its consumption should be reduced

   d) dietary fibre is deficient in many daily diets and because of its demonstrated therapeutic role in certain diseases of the gastro-intestinal tract, an increased intake would be beneficial

   e) salt has been implicated in circulatory disease development; intakes are currently in excess of biological requirements and should be restricted (see 23 below).

   f) points (a-e) are in accordance with the recommendations of expert groups in a number of countries (see CHAPTERS 1 and 2) who specify desirable intakes of protein, carbohydrate, fat and other nutrients.

   g) we have not defined intake values for nutrients in relation to (a-e) above because some of the goals for nutrient intakes are difficult to achieve in practice in a free-living population. There is also controversy as to what intake values should be; for example why choose a figure of less than 35% of calories from fat, why not 37 or 38%? Instead we propose the idea of moderation in eating and a balanced diet. A modest shift towards a greater

consumption of foods of plant (cereals, fruit, vegetables) and
marine orgin and a modest reduction in the intake of foods of
animal origin especially in the more Northern European
countries would go a long way towards satisfying (a-e) above
especially if a greater proportion of the food consumed is fresh
and unformulated.

20. Modification of national dietary habits can be assisted through exposure to preferred diets/foods during childhood. Modification of school lunch programmes in those member states in which they exist should be a priority with this in mind; in addition the subsidy/arrangements currently extant for liquid milk might also be applied to fruit/fruit juices as a means of increasing their consumption.

21. Recommendations stated above are compromised to some extent by the paucity of published information on dietary patterns in most member states. National food surveys are desirable, therefore, in most EEC countries in order to obtain concrete data on food intakes and dietary patterns; the results of these serve as an essential base from which more accurate dietary recommendations can be launched.

22. Most consumers equate PUFA with margarine. We propose that consumers should be made more aware of other foods that are unconcentrated sources of PUFA such as oats, oily fish and game meat. The use of relatively unrefined vegetable oils as salad dressings should be promoted more widely. A greater awareness of foods, other than margarine which contain PUFA can be promoted by nutritional labelling and consumer education.

23. With reference to 19e above we suggest that the practice of advocating certain dietary regimes for whole populations may be too extreme, e.g. restriction of cholesterol and salt intake on a population basis.

Evidence suggests that benefits from such restriction are only seen in those with high serum cholesterol levels and moderate/severe hypertension respectively. We propose, therefore, that comprehensive screening programmes be introduced in all member states to identify those at risk and moderation in cholesterol and salt intakes applied to them only.

24. Arising from 19 and 23, comprehensive preventive medicine programmes, containing a dietary component, should be introduced in all EEC countries and that initially at least, the programmes would be coordinated and funded in part by the EEC. It is possible that some of the costs could be recouped from the reduced cost of health care. Obviously preventive medicine programmes need to be tied closely to consumer education on nutrition matters (see 30).

INCENTIVES TO DIETARY CHANGE

25. In parallel with 19b and 19g above every effort must be made by the EEC to increase support (financial) for producers and food processors who are engaged in producing leaner meats and meat products and reduced fat dairy products (see CHAPTERS 3 and 1) (see also below). Current CAP regulations are aimed at limiting the output of milk and cereals and do not conflict with nutritional policy considerations.

26. Current EEC-funded advertising campaigns for full-fat milk, butter and cream are not in line with the consensus recommendations outlined above; modifications should be made to include reduced-fat dairy products. Advertising of butter and cream using Community funds may no longer be appropriate.

27. <u>Statutory compositional standards</u> exist for a number of sugar and fat-containing foods in most member states. Such legislation may interfere with the efficient marketing of sugar-reduced or fat-reduced analogues. An examination of this state of affairs is necessary to determine if this constraint is a serious one and, if so, to encourage the necessary changes in national law.

28. The ability to predict the response of consumers to <u>differential pricing</u> in closely-related products (e.g. full-fat vs reduced-fat milk) is poor owing to deficiencies in theoretical models and the necessary data (income, family size, dietary habits etc) on representative sub-groups of the Community population. Efforts must be made to improve both these shortcomings through research and an increase in the resources available to member states for the collection of the necessary population data.

29. <u>Consumer subsidies</u> may have a role to play in the stimulation of poultry, fish and cereal food consumption; in relation to the latter, attention needs to be paid to the practice of below-cost selling which concentrates on white bread (at least in the Republic of Ireland and the UK) and exacerbates the price-differential between it and brown breads. The application of direct subsidies to fruit and vegetables may not be possible because of the complex marketing system involved; other avenues for increasing consumption should be explored such as price reduction through freight/storage subsidy and an extension of subsidised disposal schemes to include schools. Continuing steps are required to ensure the standardisation of fruit and vegetable quality available at all retail outlets in the Community. Extension of fish-farming activities in disadvantaged areas of the Community in

combination with improvements in the marketing/retailing of fish are among possible mechanisms for the stimulation of fish consumption.

CONSUMER EDUCATION

30. Extensive and comprehensive nutrition education programmes in EEC countries are a major priority for at least two reasons. Firstly there is extensive mis-information and secondly recommendations/advice for prudent eating and preventive medicine can only be introduced successfully if the population is well educated in nutritional matters. The EEC, therefore, should attempt to co-ordinate the activities of member states in this area as a matter of urgency.

31. To ensure the dissemination of accurate nutritional information in an attractive format, greater mutual understanding is required between scientists and media personnel. The EEC should undertake to sponsor mechanisms for the development of such understanding by organising appropriate meetings/workshops throughout the Community on a regular basis. Consideration should be given to ways and means of encouraging interested scientists to develop communications skills in this area.

32. Arising from 31 above, support is necessary for the publication of popular books and educational material by the scientific community; financial support is required to defray the cost of such items and to support sabbatical or other leave arrangements. The establishment of a Media Resource Service embracing nutrition matters in each member state is an immediate priority - the financial outlay would be minimal but the potential benefits large.

33. Steps are required to be taken to reduce the major difference between

the operating budgets of <u>national health education organisations</u> and the advertising expenditure of <u>food companies</u>. Possibilities exist to capitalise on commercial advertising budgets by co-operating with appropriate commodity groups in marketing campaigns. Greater attention must be paid to the use by manufacturers and effects on, for example, children and teenagers of powerful advertising media such as television; control may be required over access to transmission times.

34. <u>Retail outlets</u> appear to be acceptable to consumers as purveyors of unbiased nutritional information and such shops, especially chain stores, may be appropriate vehicles for information dissemination. The joint activity between shop, food manufacturers and government in the Netherlands should be closely studied and consideration given to its extension in other member states.

35. Nutritional information from 16 <u>food promotional agencies</u> (mostly dairy and meat) in 10 countries was collected in this study. It was classified as scientific, popular, and 'recipe'; the information was, in general, accurate, unbiased and was presented in a form which would be easily understood by most consumers.

36. Consumers are expressing increasing concern about the <u>wholesomeness</u> of everyday foods and their attitudes towards food are undoubtedly influenced by their nutritional knowledge. They are not adequately informed as to the origins and true extent of potential risks in the food supply, and as to the relative importance of different sources of risk. It is recommended that:

   a) more responsibility be taken by the CEC for provision of
      impartial information to the consumer on potential hazards
      in foods.

b) the CEC encourage/require bodies representing both agriculture and the food industry to be involved in the informing process.

37. As far as most potential _risks_ from the use of _agro-food technologies_ is concerned, the consumer appears to be reasonably well protected. There are some important gaps, however, particularly in relation to agro-chemicals, and recommendations to deal with protecting and reassuring the consumer are outlined in 39 below.

38. Consumers are not sufficiently consulted in the processes which _regulate agro-food technologies_. It is recommended that fora be established to enable consumer opinions to be taken into account in the regulation of agro-food technologies. An example of this would be in the area of adjudicating on the technical justification for the use of some food additives. Consumers could indicate whether they felt that the more cosmetic food additives such as some artificial colours were really necessary in foods.

AGRICULTURAL PRODUCTION

39. While the legal use of _agro-chemicals_ appears to pose a relatively low risk for consumers, long-term and possible synergistic effects of permitted products require further study. In addition it is recommended that:

a) a comprehensive harmonised regulatory system be put in place to cover farm use of antibiotics including standards of manufacture, control of distribution and availability, and effective monitoring of residues.

b) the surveillance of use, and the monitoring of residues of all agro-chemicals be extended sufficiently to assure consumers that they are being used safely at farm level.

c) user education on correct use of agro-chemicals and on their potential hazards be introduced/expanded at farm level.

d) opportunities for reduced use of agro-chemicals be identified and encouraged: antibiotic use could be reduced through research on improved methods of animal husbandry and through research on alternatives to their use to promote growth; pesticide use could be reduced in some applications through research and development of integrated pest control systems.

40. Changes in breeds/cultivars used and modifications of some husbandry practices could improve the nutritional quality of foods both in the short and longer-term. It is recommended that:

a) changes in animal breeds and husbandry which lower the fat content of animal products be encouraged through the pricing policies under the CAP.

b) fundamental strategic research be funded by the Community on the biochemistry of the deposition of selected nutrients in key plant and animal species, on cellular mechanisms controlling this deposition, and on the effects of husbandry, in order to facilitate more profound changes in nutrient content through breeding and husbandry modification.

41. The significance of the risk to human health of chronic ingestion of the many natural toxicants found in plant species used as food may be substantially underrated. It is recommended that:

a) more research and regulatory attention be devoted to this area, both to quantify existing risks and to monitor changes in risks particularly resulting from the introduction of new cultivars.

b) consideration be given to the regulation of all chemicals in foods (natural, added, contaminating, formed, etc.) on an equal basis, distinguishing between large and small risks to consumers.

FOOD PROCESSING

42. Overall, the losses of nutrients due to most methods of food processing and storage do not appear to represent a nutritional problem for the majority of consumers. In general these losses are

315

either not excessive or are compensated for by the greater availability and variety of foods which result from food processing, by fortification of some foods such as breakfast cereals, etc. It is recommended that:

a) up-to-date nutritional methodology continue to be applied to the evaluation of the composition and bioavailability of important vitamins and minerals in key foods, and in foods resulting from novel food processes.

b) the effects of processing on nutrient loss in foods designed for sub-groups of the population such as infants who consume a limited range of foods, should continue to receive special attention.

43. Some processed formulated foods can contain high levels of refined ingredients, fats and sucrose, and low levels of dietary fibre, vitamins and minerals, and as a result, can contribute to nutritional imbalance. It is recommended that:

a) the CEC encourages industry to develop more 'healthier' formulations or novel products which better meet consumers' dietary needs. This could be done for example through support for specific R and D projects in this area.

b) because of the difficulty of substantially reducing the levels of some key ingredients such as fats, salt, etc, in formulated foods, the CEC should consider funding fundamental research to explore the possibilites for imitating their functional properties in food systems, through the use of other ingredients considered to constitute less nutritional hazard.

44. Although it is technically impossible to subject a food process to the same level of toxicological evaluation as is applied to, for example, food additives, the evidence from chemical analyses and from decades of human experience indicates that most food processes do not appear to pose toxicological hazards for consumers. It is recommended that:

a) research attention continue to be directed towards evaluating the limited number of chemical entities produced during processing which are considered toxic or require further safety assessment. These include products of browning and pyrolysis reactions, lysinoalanine formation due to heating of proteins and trans fatty acids produced during hydrogenation (hardening) of oils.

b) a protocol be developed for evaluation of novel food processes, focusing on important chemical changes in combination with animal testing at moderate levels of ingestion.

45. The risks to health from <u>food additives</u> appear to be exaggerated by consumers and some press comment. However, more attention should be given to the status of the limited number of food additives which cause allergy reactions or other possible acute effects such as hyperactivity in children. Secondly, the possible long-term effects of additive intake <u>per se</u> or from possible interactions between additives and other chemicals foreign to the body have not been adequately addressed. It is recommended that:

a) the use of additives known to cause acute effects be eliminated from foods regularly consumed by children, and be prominantly labelled or eliminated from other foods as well.

b) research be funded on the long term risks of additive use, including possible synergistic effects of interactions between additives and other chemicals foreign to the body.

4.2 ACKNOWLEDGEMENTS

We thank the Commission of the European Communities (FAST Programme, DG X11) and Mr. M. McCloskey of Boyne Valley Food Ltd, Drogheda, Ireland for funding (in-part) this study, and also Mr. B. Wafer and the National Board for Science and Technology for assistance and support with/for the project workshop. Special thanks are due to the very many colleagues, scientists and professionals in Ireland and in other countries who helped so willingly with information and advice, and also to Ms. Evelyn Slavin who typed the manuscript and showed considerable patience with the authors during drafting and final preparation.